The HUDSON VALLEY
and CATSKILL MOUNTAINS

The HUDSON VALLEY

and

CATSKILL MOUNTAINS

The Best

Inns, Bed & Breakfasts, Restaurants,
Country Auctions, Antiques Shops, Historic
Sites, Pick-Your-Own Farms, Museums,
State Parks, Ski Centers, Fishing, Hiking,
Walking Tours, County Fairs, Wineries,
and More

Joanne Michaels
&
Mary Barile

HARMONY BOOKS
New York

To Erik, Ralph,
Stuart and our parents

Copyright © 1988 by Joanne Michaels and Mary Barile
Maps copyright © 1988 by Anita Karl and James Kemp

Published by Harmony Books, a division of Crown Publishers, Inc., 225 Park Avenue South, New York, New York 10003 and represented in Canada by the Canadian MANDA Group
HARMONY and colophon are trademarks of Crown Publishers, Inc.

Manufactured in the United States of America

Design by Ron McCutchan

Library of Congress Cataloging-in-Publication Data

Michaels, Joanne, 1950–
    The Hudson Valley and Catskill Mountains.

    1. Hudson River Valley (N.Y. and N.J.)—Description and travel—Guidebooks.
2. Catskill Mountains (N.Y.)—Description and travel—Guidebooks.
I. Barile, Mary. II. Title.
F127.H8M53 1988   917.47'30443 87–25094
ISBN 0-517-56825-X (pbk.)

10 9 8 7 6 5 4 3 2 1
First Edition

Contents

Acknowledgments	vii
Introduction	ix
Rockland County	1
Orange County	21
Sullivan County	51
Ulster County	77
Delaware County	123
Greene County	145
City of Albany	167
Columbia County	183
Dutchess County	207
Putnam County	245
Westchester County	261
Authors' Note	295
Index	297

Acknowl-
edgments

The acknowledgments page is usually written last and almost always read first. It usually reflects a sense of gratitude. In this case, we would like to add a sense of relief that we reached the end of the book! This feeling is shared by many of those closest to us.

We are particularly grateful to our friends and families, especially Renee and Lawrence Michaels, who often babysat while we were on the road.

Many people gave generously of their time answering our questions and supplying information; we would like to thank all of them. Sheryl Woods of the New York State Department of Commerce was enormously helpful. Sue Bain at the Greene County Promotion Department and Richard Jones in the Orange County Planning Department both went beyond the call of duty in offering assistance. We are also grateful to Vicki Barnes Davis of the Culinary Institute of America; Dardis McNamee, editor-in-chief and associate publisher of *Capital Region* magazine; Virginia Callan, Mary Zander, Joe Steiniger and Margo Jones of the Sullivan County Office of Public Information; Faire Hart at Mohonk Mountain House; Nancy Gold at Sleepy Hollow Restorations; Corbin Mann in Delaware County; and Judy Matson and Abby Pelton in the Westchester Tourism Department. Special appreciation goes to Sally Savage of Piermont, and Mark Williams and Joan Moffett of the Nyack Chamber of Commerce for their suggestions.

Just about every site manager at the historic points of interest listed in this book took time out of their busy schedules to give us a tour. All were enthusiastic and conveyed to us why their site was special. We thank them all.

And then there are those "nameless" people, those we met unexpectedly in the course of our travels. Many gave us their opinions and the names of favorite spots, based on years of growing up and living in their respective towns. They probably didn't realize at the time how helpful they were. These friendly folk got us off the beaten track where we discovered restaurants, back roads and a fishing hole or two that we probably never would have found on our own.

Intro-
duction

*During the four years
we worked together as
editors of a regional
magazine covering the
Hudson Valley and
Catskills, we realized*
that there was no guidebook available for tourists or local
residents who traveled for a day, a weekend, or on an extended journey through this diverse region. (The Hudson Valley includes the eight counties—Rockland, Orange, Ulster,
Greene, Columbia, Dutchess, Putnam and Westchester—that
surround both sides of the Hudson River. The Catskills include western Ulster County, Sullivan, Delaware and part of
Greene County.) For that reason, we wanted to share the
information we have accumulated on the job and show the
region for the fascinating place it is.

When most people think of the Hudson Valley and Catskills, they imagine mysterious mountains where Rip Van Winkle slept and played his game of ninepins, and lush valleys
where bobcats roam. True, these are part of the region's rich
history, but after traveling hundreds of miles on back roads,
thruways and even dirt paths, we know the area has more to

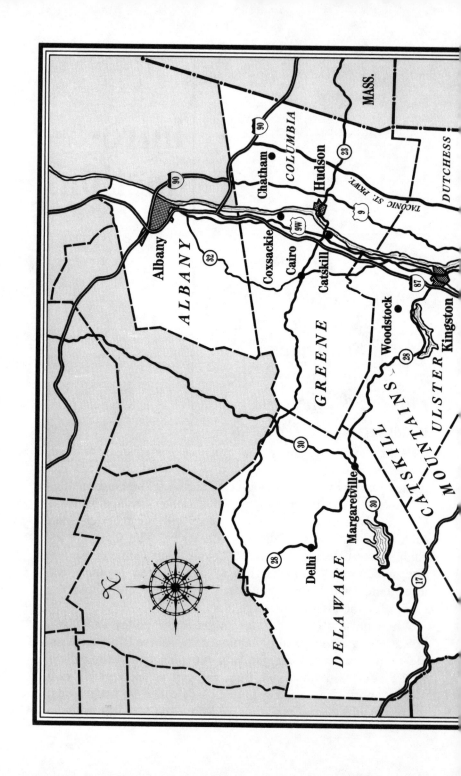

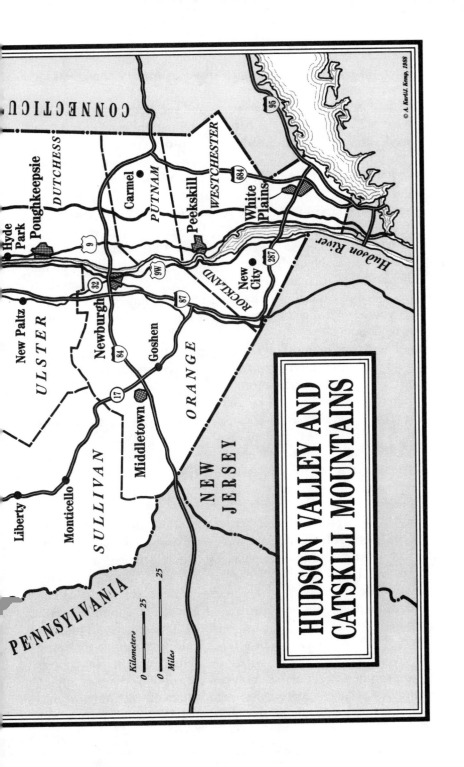

HUDSON VALLEY AND
CATSKILL MOUNTAINS

© A. Karld. Kemp, 1988

offer than that: it's a treasure trove of history, breathtaking scenery and colorful people.

Because there is so much to do and see there, we chose only what we considered "the best" of the region—whether it was food, inns, views or history. At historic sites or places of interest, we looked for unusual exhibits or tours. At hiking and fishing spots, we checked to see if they were accessible and attractive. In the case of restaurants, inns and bed and breakfast establishments, we looked for distinctiveness, quality, cleanliness and courtesy. We traveled through the area in all seasons, talked to scores of people and visited just about every site ourselves. In a few cases, we weren't able to spend the day on a particular river or at the top of a mountain, but we talked to experts who had and whose judgment we trusted. So you are getting the recommendations of "the best" people as well.

There are many different types of travelers—some with children, some elderly or handicapped, some interested in only history or outdoor recreation. The information we've included, therefore, offers a broad range of places for visiting or dining. Several of the sites listed are free of charge. We discovered that all ski areas in the region allow anyone over 70 years of age to ski free, and people between 65 and 70 pay only half price. Many of the restaurants, too, are as renowned for their less expensive lunches and snacks as they are for their gourmet dinners.

All the sights included are within 150 miles of the New York metropolitan area, and many are only a few hours by car from Boston and Philadelphia. The book is arranged in chapters by county, and each chapter contains a detailed county map. We began with the counties on the west side of the Hudson River heading north to Albany and continued with the counties south of Albany on the east side of the Hudson. You can plan a day trip or a week-long vacation, as the spirit moves you. You can be where the action is, or if you choose you can be utterly alone. You can eat some of the best apples and goat cheese anywhere, hike some of the most scenic mountains, see some of the most magnificent fall foliage and horse farms. Or you can just take a walk and discover the many other things this exciting area has to offer. The climate is temperate, the views are extraordinary, the people friendly.

Many places of interest are seasonal, as are the outdoor activities. But in most areas there are some sites open all year. The schedules included here were up-to-date at the time of publication. However, it's advisable to call ahead if you are planning an extended trip, particularly if you are going in the winter, from December through March.

You can travel the Hudson Valley and Catskills and find something to please everyone—from auctions held in dairy barns to sophisticated art galleries, from clog dancing to professional ballet companies, from barbecued chicken and watermelon to haute cuisine. There are secrets worth discovering by foot, bicycle, bus, car, train or even balloon. We hope you set aside plenty of time to explore our favorite region. And do let us know if you discover something we missed!

Mary Barile and Joanne Michaels
Woodstock, New York

Rockland County

Only 176 square miles, Rockland County packs a lot into its territory. Everywhere you look in Rockland, it seems there's a park, from the tiny vest pocket squares of green in towns and villages to the great spaces of Bear Mountain. Only 30 miles north of New York City, Rockland has defended much of its forests, wetlands, mountains and historical sites from the encroachment of urban development. Through the cooperation of wealthy patrons, civic leaders and protective citizens, areas such as Bear Mountain and High Tor were preserved from becoming, respectively, a prison site and a quarry. Today, the fruits of those early environmental battles are seen and enjoyed by all. Hundreds of miles of hiking and biking trails wind through estuarine marshes, along the Hudson River, up and over the dramatic peaks, such as High Tor. Lakes and streams teem with wildlife, and *flora* lovers will delight in the explosion of colors and scents that mark the spring wildflower season. At Stony Point Battlefield, the mountaintop meadow where American troops defeated the Redcoats is almost as it was more than

1

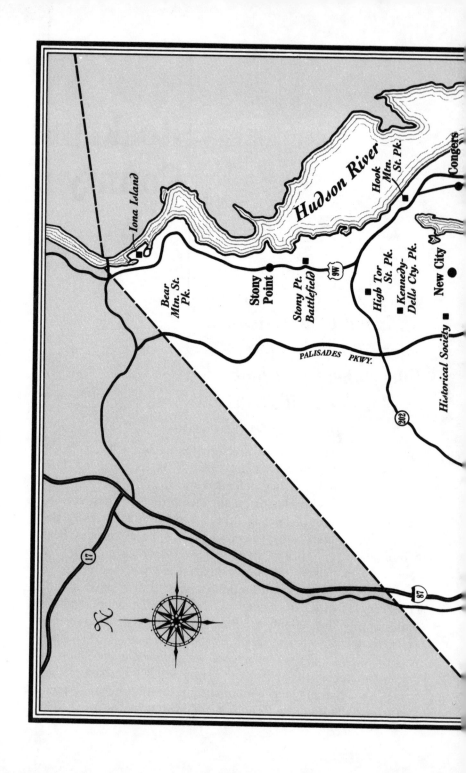

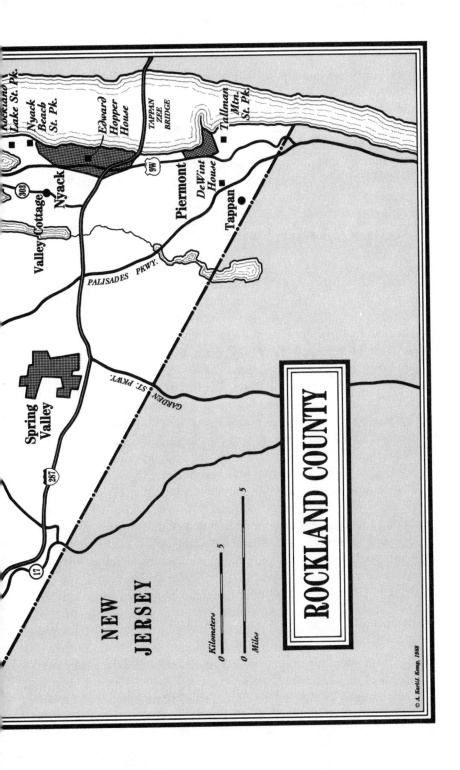

ROCKLAND COUNTY

NEW JERSEY

Spring Valley

Valley Cottage

Nyack

Piermont

Tappan

DeWint House

Tallman

Tallman Mtn. St. Pk.

Edward Hopper House

Nyack Beach St. Pk.

Rockland Lake St. Pk.

TAPPAN ZEE BRIDGE

PALISADES PKWY.

GARDEN ST. PKWY.

Kilometers
0   5

Miles
0   5

© A. Karl & Kemp, 1988

two centuries ago. In small towns and villages throughout the county, houses have been preserved with such care and a sense of history that visitors feel as if they have stepped back into another time. While touring Rockland, you will hear again and again names that made history and are still remembered in ceremonies and festivals throughout the county: Benedict Arnold, George Washington, John André, "Mad" Anthony Wayne, even Captain Kidd.

Bear Mountain

Bear Mountain State Park Part of the vast Palisades Interstate Parks system, Bear Mountain shares almost 54,000 acres with its neighbor, Harriman State Park. Noted on maps since the mid-eighteenth century, Bear Mountain has also been known as Bear Hill, Bread Tray Mountain and Bare Mountain, presumably due to its bald peak. The area that the park now covers, once the site of Forts Clinton and Montgomery, two forts of the Revolution, was slated to become the home of Sing Sing prison until public outcry and political pressure persuaded the state to change its plans in the early twentieth century. Since then, a parkway system has made the park accessible to the hundreds of thousands who visit each year, and several man-made lakes were created to add to the park's outdoor appeal. Visitors will find a four-season outdoor wonderland in Bear Mountain, featuring a wide program of activities and special events. Bear Mountain is first and foremost a park, with facilities for picnicking, swimming, hiking, fishing, roller skating and boating. At the **Trailside Museum,** the site of Fort Clinton (located near the Bear Mountain Inn; look for the path and signs), exhibits and programs describe the Native American, military and natural history of the area. Children may enjoy the zoo, with a beaver lodge (which has been cut away for easy viewing) and a reptile house. A drive, bike ride or hike along Seven Lakes Drive or Lake Welch Drive is breathtaking in fall and winter. Carl Perkins Memorial Drive, which goes to the top of Bear Mountain, is closed in bad weather. Paddleboats and rowboats can be rented at several of the lakes. If you bring your own canoe, it will have to pass an inspection before you can take it out. Special events add to the year-round fun: In January and February, professional ski-jumping competitions are held; *Festa Italiana*, star-gazing nights and special hikes highlight the spring and summer; the Country Music Festival and *Oktoberfest* are scheduled each fall. One of the most popular Bear Mountain celebrations is the annual Christmas Festival, which is held throughout December. Previous festival events included live Nativity tableaux, ginger-bread-house contests, visits from a talking bear and St. Nick. There is always ice skating, fireworks, crafts shows and lots of good food.

DIRECTIONS *Entrance is located just off the Palisades Interstate Parkway at Bear Mountain. You can also take Routes 6 and 9W to the park.*

INFORMATION *Open every day dawn to dusk, year-round. Tel. (914) 786-2701, or write Palisades Interstate Parks Commission, Bear Mountain State Park, Bear Mountain, 10911.*

Plan to spend a full day in the park anytime during the year. Pets allowed in certain areas as long as they are kept on a leash. Since this is mostly an outdoor facility, dress accordingly. It may be cool even in summer; winters can be extremely bitter. Because the Dayliner boat trip from Manhattan stops here every day, swimming areas can get very crowded, so get there early.

FACILITIES *Complete outdoor recreation facilities, rest rooms, bookshop, picnicking areas, restaurant.*

Iona Island This 118-acre island in the middle of the Hudson, now connected to the mainland by a causeway which runs over its tidal marsh, was probably used as a camping area by Woodland Indians and was later held by the British during the Revolution. When it became privately owned, Iona was used for agricultural development. The following years saw the land used as a park and a weapons depot. It is now a winter refuge for bald eagles, and only a section is open to the general public.

DIRECTIONS Cross the Bear Mountain Bridge and head south on Route 9W. Watch carefully for signs to the causeway. INFORMATION Admission is free. Closed December 1 to April 1. FACILITIES None.

Congers

Rockland Lake State Park Another jewel in the crown of the Palisades Interstate Parks system, this very popular recreation area is located at the base of Hook Mountain. The lake was once the site of an ice farm, which provided a harvest of pure, clear ice for nearly a century before the advent of modern refrigeration. The park itself is a wonderful place to explore—in addition to hiking trails, you can enjoy swimming, fishing, golf, boating, picnicking and even an exercise and jogging trail. During the winter, go ice skating on the lake or cross-country skiing and sledding on some of the challenging hills. At the **Nature Center**, you will discover live animal exhibits, special events programs throughout the summer, and guided tours. Just outside the center are the marked nature trails which run along a boardwalk, and contain Braille interpretation stops for the blind and visually impaired. The wildflowers and bird life are particularly vibrant during the spring, but there are wonders to discover here any time of the year. Children will love the Nature Center and the easy-to-walk nature trail.

DIRECTIONS Take Route 9W to the Rockland Lake exit.
INFORMATION Open year-round, although the Nature Center closes from October until May. Tel. (914) 268-3020/7598, or write Palisades Interstate Parks Commission, Administration Building, Bear Mountain, NY 10911.

Plan to make this park a daylong stop. Bring a bathing suit, walking shoes and fishing gear, but go early if planning a summer visit—this is a very popular and well-used park.
FACILITIES Picnic areas, snack stands, boat rentals, golf course, biking trails, Braille-interpreted nature walk, rest rooms.

New City

High Tor Vineyards Located near the dramatic High Tor mountain on land that was once used as an Indian burial ground, the vineyard produces quality wines with such local names as Rockland Red and Beacon White, along with the more familiar Seyval Blanc and Chancellor Noir. The winery prides itself on producing "boutique" wines—fine quality wines in limited amounts. A visit includes a tour of the production facilities, an explanation of the wine-making process and a wine tasting. The vineyards themselves are lovely, and you are free to walk around the grounds and enjoy the river views, or stop in the wine shop. A restaurant on the premises serves soups, sandwiches and excellent pastries.

DIRECTIONS *Take exit 11 off the Palisades Interstate Parkway to Route 45 north. Make a right on South Mountain Road and follow the signs.*

INFORMATION *The vineyard is open all year, weekdays from noon to 3 P.M.; weekends from noon to 4 P.M. Closed on Christmas and Thanksgiving. Call (914) 638-3204 for information.*

FACILITIES *Restaurant, wine shop.*

Historical Society of Rockland County The society has restored the Jacob Blauvelt House, an 1834 Dutch farmhouse, and added a history museum to the site. Changing exhibits offer a look at life in the lower Hudson Valley, and the museum sponsors special events like Christmas candlelight tours, a dollhouse festival and colonial cooking classes.

DIRECTIONS *Located at 20 Zukor Road in New City.*

INFORMATION *Open year-round, Wed. through Fri., noon to 4 P.M.; Sun., 2 to 5 P.M.; other times by appointment. Tel. (914) 634-9629.*

FACILITIES *Rest rooms.*

Kennedy-Dells County Park This park was once part of the estate of film producer Adolph Zukor, and is now home to a model farm. The corn grown here is harvested and sold commercially. Open year-round, Kennedy-Dells offers free use of its parcours course (a fitness trail that has marked exercise stops), tours of the farm and a trail for the handicapped.

DIRECTIONS Take Main Street from New City one mile north; watch for signs to park's entrance.

INFORMATION Admission is free. Open every day, 8 A.M. to dusk.

FACILITIES Special trail for handicapped athletes, parcours course, rest rooms.

Nyack

Driving or Walking Tour First settled by the Nyack Indians, who moved there from Brooklyn, Nyack soon became home to the Dutch who began to farm the region. When steamboats arrived, making river travel easier, Nyack became a center of shipping and boat building. The town is now known as an antiques and arts center, home to dozens of shops that offer the finest furniture, jewelry, crafts and artwork. The village sponsors many special events, such as Septemberfest and street fairs.

To see Nyack's charming architectural heritage, begin at South Broadway, near the **Nyack Public Library**, one of the libraries built with funds from the Carnegie Foundation at the turn of the century. Next to the library is a Queen Anne–style house, with a tower and fine shingle work. Heading north at 46 South Broadway, **Couch Court** is an unusual late nineteenth-century building that sports another towerlike cupola. The **Presbyterian Church** was built in 1839 in the Greek Revival style, which used columns and symmetry in an effort to capture what was considered the ancient purity of Greece. Down the street a little further, look for the **Tappan Zee Theatre**, built when movies were silent and vaudeville shows were the current rage. Across the street, the **Reformed Church** has a clock tower that dates back to 1850. On Burd Street a plaque on the bank tells a little of the history of Nyack. On North Broadway, you'll see the **Congregation of the Sons of Israel,** founded in 1870. A side trip down and around Van

Houten Road (it turns into Castle Heights), runs past riverfront homes and offers a magnificent view of the Hudson. Continue your drive up North Broadway, passing magnificent mansions and lovely eighteenth-century homes, ending at Hook Mountain State Park.

Nyack has many shops that are worth a visit, with their constantly changing displays and wares. Here are some highlights. Most shops are open Sundays, closed Mondays, but call ahead for hours. **Hand of the Craftsman**, 58 South Broadway, (914) 358-6622, offers a unique selection of handmade kaleidoscopes, as well as a huge inventory of crafts. **Gene Reed**, 75 South Broadway, (914) 358-3750, caters to those who love country decorations, including antiques and reproductions, and contemporary American folk art. **Beman Galleries**, 114 Main Street, (914) 358-3344, specializes in fine art by nineteenth- and twentieth-century American painters and offers conservation and framing services. **Sandra L. Abrams**, 85 South Broadway, (914) 354-7290, sells antique and collectible dolls. **Squash Blossom**, 49 Burd Street, (914) 353-0550, has a fine selection of Native American jewelry and silver. Furniture fans will want to stop at **Simon and Riley's**, 130 Main Street, (914) 358-0902, for eighteenth- and nineteenth-century pieces; **Patrician Antiques**, 142 Main Street, (914) 358-3104, for oak furniture; **C & D Antiques**, 142 Main Street, (914) 358-1704, for French furniture and jewelry; and **Out of the Attic**, 142 Main Street, (914) 353-2243, for Victorian oak and period pieces. **Shamrock Imports**, 2 Nyack Plaza on Main Street, (914) 358-7206, has a wide variety of clothing, jewelry, art and collectibles from Ireland. On the corner of Main and Broadway is the **Crossroads of Nyack Mall**, an antiques co-op with an impressive collection of Stieff animals. Down the street, the **Franklin Antiques Mall** has about thirty dealers. During festival days, you can expect to see many dealers set up sidewalk displays. Also artists at work, a farmer's market and entertainment.

DIRECTIONS Nyack is located north of the Tappan Zee Bridge. Take the "Nyacks" exit off the NY Thruway and follow the signs to the village.

INFORMATION Most stores in Nyack are closed only on Mondays. For detailed information about store hours and festival dates, call the Art, Craft and Antique Dealers Association at (914) 358-8443.

FACILITIES Information booth is located on Main Street.

Hook Mountain State Park

Hook Mountain State Park This park was once referred to by the Dutch as Verdrietige ("Tedious") Hook because of the winds that could change rapidly and leave a boat adrift in the river. The area was also a favored camping ground of Native Americans because of its wealth of oysters. For modern visitors, the park provides a place to picnic, hike and bike, with scenic views of the Hudson. An annual hawk watch is held each fall and spring, and you may be able to spot hundreds of hawks on a September day, so bring your binoculars. The park is also said to be haunted by the ghost of the Guardian of the Mountain, a Native American medicine man who appears during the full moon each September and chants the ancient harvest festival.

DIRECTIONS Take North Broadway east; Hook Mountain is located at the end of the road.

INFORMATION Admission is free. Open every day, dawn to dusk.

FACILITIES Hiking and biking trails.

Edward Hopper House

Edward Hopper House The American realist painter Edward Hopper was born in Nyack in 1882, and spent much of his time as a youth in the village. Several of his paintings feature local landmarks, and when he died in 1967, he was buried in the Oak Hill Cemetery. His boyhood home was rescued from demolition not long after his death, and today it is a community arts and cultural center. Exhibits have included works by Hopper, Joseph Cropsey, and Milton Avery, and the gardens of Hopper House are used for concerts and special events.

DIRECTIONS Located at 82 North Broadway in Nyack.

INFORMATION Open Fri., noon to 4 P.M.; Sat. and Sun., 1 to 5 P.M.

FACILITIES Rest rooms.

Piermont

Piermont Marsh and Tallman State Park This nature preserve covers more than 1,000 acres of tidal marsh, mountains and river, and is considered one of the most important fish breeding areas along the Hudson. Wildflowers, such as the spectacular rose mallow, abound throughout portions of the marsh, and this is a prime bird-watching area in all seasons. The area along the marsh also provides a marvelous place to view the river and a hike up the mountain offers a spectacular panorama for photographers. Tallman Park is a wonderful place to spend a summer day, since along with the natural wonders, the park has complete recreational facilities. There are even some man-made ponds that have become home to many varieties of reptiles and amphibians; ironically, the ponds were to have been part of a tank storage area for a large oil company earlier in the century. Today, especially in the spring, the ponds hum with the sound of frogs, and the woods come alive with birdcalls.

DIRECTIONS Tallman Mountain State Park is located on Route 9W in Sparkill, north of Palisades Interstate Parkway exit 4; Piermont Marsh can be reached through Tallman Park by following the bike path. An alternate entrance into the marsh is along the Erie Pier in the village of Piermont.

INFORMATION Tallman Park is open all year, 8 A.M. to dusk; in the summer, it closes at 4:30 P.M. on weekdays and 7:30 P.M. weekends and holidays. Piermont Marsh is open all year.

Tallman Park charges a small use and parking fee; Piermont Marsh is free. Tel. (914) 359-0544.

You can spend all day in both parks, especially if you make the morning hiking time and the afternoon swimming time. Arrive early, since this is a very popular park.

FACILITIES Snack stand, swimming pool, picnic areas, tennis courts, bike path, hiking paths, rest rooms.

Stony Point

Stony Point Battlefield When George Washington felt he had to demonstrate that American troops were determined to stand up to the superior British forces in the Hudson Highlands, he sent in General "Mad" Anthony Wayne to prove the point. In July of 1779, Wayne led the elite troops of the Corps of Light Infantry in an attack on the British at Stony Point. In a daring midnight raid, they routed the British from their beds and challenged their reputation as an invincible fighting force. A walking tour of the battlefield today takes visitors through a wildly beautiful park, where remnants of the British fortifications still survive. At the museum, a slide show that depicts the events that led up to the battle is accompanied by exhibits and original memorabilia that explain the tactics and strategies which brought victory to the Americans. Outside, along the walking tour path, markers explain the battle, and you will pass the Stony Point lighthouse, which was used for more than a century to aid ships on the Hudson.

DIRECTIONS Located off Route 9W in Stony Point.

INFORMATION Open mid-April through October; Wed. through Sun., 8:30 A.M. to 5 P.M. Admission is free. Tel. (914) 786-2521, or write Stony Point Battlefield State Historic Site, P.O. Box 182, Stony Point, 10980.

Plan to spend at least 1½ hours here for the museum and walking tour; allow more time if special events are planned. The museum is accessible to the handicapped.

Younger children may enjoy the special military exercises and holiday celebrations (especially Halloween) that are sometimes held at the park; otherwise, this is for older kids interested in military history.

FACILITIES Picnic area, hiking trails, rest rooms.

Tappan

DeWint House National Shrine Constructed in 1700 of Holland brick and sandstone, the DeWint House boasts the pitched roof and tile fireplace common in well-to-do Dutch homes of the period. Although the house is important for its architectural features, it is best known as the four-time headquarters of George Washington during the Revolution, and as a shrine to Washington's participation in the fraternal organization known as the Masons. It was here that Washington stayed the day the British spy, Major André, was hanged, and it is recorded that Washington asked that the shutters to his room be closed, the same shutters that cover the window today.

When the house was purchased by the Masons, the owner said family tradition held that several of the items in the house were there at the time of Washington's visits, including a hatrack, andirons and a flintlock gun. Today the house offers a look into Washington's day-to-day life during the war, along with the story of his participation in the Masons. A small carriage house museum also contains period artifacts and exhibits, and the trees around the site have been marked with identification tags. Don't miss the largest weeping willow tree in the country, 34 feet in circumference and almost 150 years old.

> DIRECTIONS *Located at 20 Livingston Avenue near Oak Road in Tappan.*
> INFORMATION *Admission is charged. Open year-round from 10 A.M. to 4 P.M., but call ahead during the winter months. Tel. (914) 359-1359.*
> FACILITIES *None.*

Tappan Walking Tour The local government here was the first in New York State to establish by ordinance a historic district, with the result that a walk down Main Street in Tappan will reveal many eighteenth- and nineteenth-century structures. **The Tappan Library**, a frame house dating from the mid-eighteenth century, boasts a restored Colonial garden in its yard. The **Yoast Mabie Tavern**, built in 1755, was used as a prison for John André, although he was, according to Washington's instructions, to be treated civilly. Just beyond the tavern, look for the **Killoran House**, an early town house built in 1835 from the bricks taken from a dismantled church. In the middle of Main Street, where it meets Old Tappan Road, the **Village Green** was the site of the public stocks and the liberty pole, depending upon the mood of the townspeople at the time. The nearby **Reformed Church of Tappan** stands on the site where André was tried and convicted of spying. Although he requested that he be shot as a soldier, the tribunal had him hanged as a spy, since to do otherwise would have been to cast doubt upon his guilt. A walk through the nearby burying grounds reveals many old tombstones. Further up the road is the **Deming-Latelle House**, best known as home of the man who manufactured the first canned baby food.

Activities

With its dozens of parks, Rockland County offers a unique chance to explore the outdoors. Each park has its own facilities and trails, and each one sets its own limits on activities. Some of the larger recreation areas have been covered in separate entries above, but the following information may make your outdoor visit even more interesting.

FARM STANDS AND PICK-YOUR-OWN FARMS

Even though Rockland County is small, you can still discover some pick-your-own places and some very well-stocked farm stands. At **Dr. Davies Farm**, off Route 9W in Congers, (914) 268-7050 (open all year) and Route 304, Congers (open from May to November), you can pick your own apples in the fall and then choose from a wide selection of berries, pumpkins, pears, plums and asparagus at the roadside stand. They also sell honey, apple cider and maple syrup in season. In Monsey, **Duryea Farms**, 101 Ackertown Road, off Saddle River Road,

(914) 356-1988 (open June, September and October), lets you choose the plumpest, reddest strawberries in summer and the sweetest apples in fall. **Smith Farms**, 291 Little Tor Road, New City, (914) 634-2856 (open from mid-July to mid-September), also has strawberries for the picking, and a large roadside stand as well. At **The Orchards at Conklin**, South Mountain Road, Pomona, (914) 354-0369 (open all year), you can pick apples, nectarines, peaches, pears, berries, pumpkin, squash and other produce. There are tours of the orchards available if you call ahead. In Suffern, **Van Ripers Farm**, 121 College Road, (914) 352-0770 (open from May to December), also has pick-your-own berries, and a roadside stand. Another Suffern Farm, **Litchult's**, 77 South Airmont Road, (914) 357-0995 (open all year), has a large selection of fruits and vegetables already picked for you, as do **Cropsey Farm**, 230 Little Tor Road, New City, (914) 634-1545 (open all year), and **Schimpf Farms**, Parrott Road, West Nyack, (914) 623-2556 (open from May to November).

FISHING

The state parks all allow fishing, but you will have to check with them for their individual regulations and restrictions. Fishing is also allowed in the Ramapo River, which has a long trout season; Route 17 has parking areas, and the waters north of Ramapo are considered good fishing spots. On Route 202 near Suffern, watch for the Mahwah River and the parking areas along its bank. The Minisceongo Creek has good fishing from the Rosman Bridge upstream to the Palisades Mountain Parkway Bridge.

HIKING

Almost every park has hiking trails that wind through the woods and sometimes over mountains. Some unusual trails, set up to commemorate the American Revolution, also provide a way to get to know local history. The 1777 Trail, the 1777 E Trail and the 1777 W Trail—known collectively as the **Bicentennial Trails**—are all under three miles in length. Located in the Bear Mountain and Harriman State Parks, you can find the trails on Route 9W, one mile north of Tomkins Cove. Just look for the diamond-shaped white blazes with red numbers. This is also the starting area for the **Timp-Torne Trail**, a ten-mile hike, which offers spectacular views down the Hudson River all the way to New York City. The trail ends at the Bear Mountain Lodge. The shorter **Anthony Wayne Trail**—a three-mile loop marked with white blazes—can be found along Seven Lakes Drive in Bear Mountain State Park near the traffic circle. Another popular trail is the **Pine Meadow Trail**, which begins at the Reeves Meadow Visitors Center on Seven Lakes Drive. If you want to climb Bear Mountain, take the **Major Welch Trail** from the Bear Mountain Inn. In Nyack, **Buttermilk Falls Park** has trails from the parking lot that end at the falls themselves, lovely in early spring. Shorter walks may be taken in **Betsy Ross Park** (Tappan), **Tackamack North** and **Tackamack South Parks** (Clausland Mountain Road, Blauvelt), and along the **Erie Trail**, which runs from Sparkill to Grandview along abandoned railroad tracks.

Where to Eat

Bully Boy Chop House (117 Route 303, Congers, (914) 268-6555) Most residents of Rockland will tell you that this is the best restaurant in the county. Specializing in steaks, chops and seafood with an English touch, they are renowned for their prime ribs, rack of lamb, English pies and Yorkshire pudding. The chef has been there for 19 years and the restaurant has had the same owner for 29 years. There are seven dining rooms. One of the less formal rooms has floor-to-ceiling windows overlooking a lovely pond with ducks. Another room is quite elegant with plush red carpeting. Homemade scones are served with butter and honey. Reservations a must. Children are welcome, but no special menu provided.

OPEN *Lunch—Mon. through Fri., noon to 2:30 P.M.; dinner— Mon. through Sat., 5 to 9:30 P.M., and Sun., 2 to 8:30 P.M.*

La Capannina Restaurant (606 South Pascack Rd., Spring Valley, (914) 735-7476) The site of this lovely French restaurant dates back to the early 1700s. Known as the Haring Homestead, after its Dutch owners in the late eighteenth century, the house is surrounded by seven acres of beautiful grounds. Nearby, the Old Pascack River roars as it goes over a dam, splashing through the glen below. The restaurant offers an extensive menu and a wine list with selections for most price ranges. Some of the house specialties are rack of lamb, duckling with cherry sauce, sweetbreads in peppercorn sauce and chateaubriand. If you've never had calf's liver, this is the place to try it. Children are welcome, but no special menu. Call for reservations and directions.

OPEN *Lunch—Mon. through Fri., noon to 2:30 P.M.; dinner— Tues. through Sat., 6 to 10 P.M.*

Cottage Cafe *(Lake Ridge Plaza, Valley Cottage, (914) 268- 3993)* This family-run restaurant is the place to head if you love seafood. The chef is a Culinary Institute graduate, and the seafood Fra Diavalo (a combination of mussels, clams, scallops and shrimp with pasta) is superb. They also serve filet mignon, chops and lamb. All desserts are made on the premises. Try the chocolate cheesecake, peanut butter pie or Swiss chocolate layer cake. Children are welcome, but no special menu.

OPEN *Lunch—Mon. through Fri., 11:30 A.M. to 4 P.M.; dinner— Mon. through Thurs., 4 to 10 P.M., Fri. and Sat. until 11 P.M., Sun., 3 to 9:30 P.M.*

Eat Your Heart Out *(64 South Broadway, Nyack, [no phone])* For breakfast or lunch, this bakery is open every day from 8 A.M. to 5 P.M.

Giulio's *(154 Washington St., Tappan, (914) 359-3657)* Fine northern Italian cuisine served in this 100-year-old Victorian house. There is a romantic candlelight setting at dinner and a strolling vocalist on Wednesday and Friday evenings. We recommend the Valdostana Vitello (veal stuffed with prosciutto and cheese in a champagne sauce) or the Scampi Giulio (jumbo shrimp sautéed with fresh mushrooms). A Tappan favorite for over 18 years. Children are welcome, but no special menu;

pasta dishes are a specialty. Jackets preferred for men; reservations suggested.

OPEN *Lunch—Mon. through Fri., 11:30 A.M. to 2:30 P.M.; dinner—Mon. through Fri., 5 to 10 P.M., Sat. until 11, and Sun., 2 to 9 P.M.*

Huckleberry's on the Hudson *(798 Beach Rd., Haverstraw Marina, West Haverstraw [1½ miles off Route 9W], (914) 429-8600)* Dine on the banks of the Hudson River in a spacious, contemporary environment where you can watch the boats pass by from the "upper" or "lower decks." The perfect spot to stop on a clear day for a hearty lunch, there is a wide selection of soups, hamburgers, salads and sandwiches. For dinner, specialties are seasoned swordfish steak and fettuccine Primavera with shrimp. Children are welcome; special menu provided.

OPEN *Every day, with continuous lunch and dinner; special Sunday brunch; reservations for five or more accepted.*

Ichi Riki *(110 Main St., Nyack, (914) 358-7977)* Excellent Japanese food; serves both lunch and dinner.

Janet Hogan's Diner Restaurant *(Route 59, West Nyack, (914) 358-1817)* If you are a devotee of diners, try this one. Open 24 hours, every day.

Raoul's *(Village Hall, 134 Main St., Nyack, (914) 353-1355)* Located in the original village hall of Nyack, the specialty here is classical French cuisine. The downstairs jail cell is the restaurant's wine cellar, while the upstairs courtroom has been converted into a private dining room. Children are welcome; but no special menu.

OPEN *Dinner—Wed. through Sun., 6 to 10 P.M.; Sunday brunch—11:30 A.M. to 3 P.M.*

The River Club *(foot of Burd St., Nyack, (914) 358-0220)* If you like sunsets and river views, stop here for a cocktail.

Romolo's *(corner of Route 303 and Tremont, Congers, (914) 268-3770/9855)* Italian cuisine, specializing in veal dishes. Try the veal Verbena (scaloppine with white asparagus, prosciutto and fresh mozzarella in wine sauce), or the filet mignon Zingara (sautéed in marsala wine with cream, ham and mushrooms.) The atmosphere is warm and homey, and this is truly a fine family restaurant. Children are welcome, but no special menu.
OPEN *Lunch—Tues. through Fri., noon to 2:30 P.M.; dinner— Tues. through Thurs., 5 to 10 P.M., Fri. and Sat., 5 to 11 P.M., and Sun., 3 to 9 P.M.*

Temptations *(80½ Main St., Nyack, (914) 353-3355)* Those with a sweet tooth, especially ice cream freaks, won't want to pass up this place. There are more than 30 dessert choices (cakes and pies) in addition to a wide selection of ice cream flavors, tofutti, cappuccino and exotic coffees. The light lunch menu features soups, quiches, pasta salads and sandwiches. Relax in the greenhouse or on the outdoor patio in season. Great for kids.
OPEN *Mon. through Thurs., 11 A.M. to 10 P.M., Fri. and Sat. until midnight; Sun., noon to 10 P.M. (later in July and August).*

The Turning Point *(468 Piermont Ave., Piermont, (914) 359-1089)* This is the place to go in Piermont—to eat lunch, brunch or dinner, to relax or to listen to live music. The restaurant was the hangout for the cast of *The Purple Rose of Cairo* when Woody Allen transformed the main street in Piermont into a movie set. For dinner, try the fettuccine with goat cheese and sliced duck or the poached salmon with tarragon and sautéed mushrooms. There are always a few nonmeat dishes on the menu, great for vegetarians. Fifteen herbal teas are listed on the menu, and nearly twenty types of beer. For Sunday brunch, try the buttermilk pancakes, vegetarian omelet, or French toast with Canadian bacon. Check the evening performance schedule, since Odetta and Tom Paxton are just two of the talents who have entertained here.
OPEN *Lunch—Mon. through Sat., 11:30 A.M. to 3 P.M.; dinner— Mon. through Thurs., 6 to 9 P.M., Fri. until 10 and Sat. until*

11 P.M. *Sunday brunch—11:30* A.M. *to 3* P.M.; *dinner—6 to 9*
P.M. *Lunch menu served after dinner hours until 1* A.M. *every night,*
2 A.M. *on Sat.*

Xaviar's at Piermont *(506 Piermont Ave., Piermont, (914)*
359-7007) An intimate spot, elegant in decor and atmosphere.
This is a perfect place for people who enjoy good food and a
little adventure at the same time. Suggested are the red snapper with mussel cream, roast pigeon with truffle sauce or
fettuccine with fennel sausage and white grapes. For dessert,
try a soufflé; maple walnut is the house specialty. Not recommended for children.

OPEN *lunch—Wed. through Sun., noon to 2:30* P.M.; *dinner—*
Wed through Sun., 6 to 9 P.M. *Closed Mon. and Tues.*

Where to Stay

Bear Mountain Inn *(Bear Mountain, 10911 [Easily accessible*
via the Palisades Interstate Pkwy. Located off Routes 9W, 9A, 9D
and 6.] (914) 786-2731). Located in the heart of Bear Mountain
State Park, the inn's rustic charm makes it a fine place to relax.
The stone and wood structure complements this panoramic
spot. All of the facilities of the park can be enjoyed. There are
60 guest rooms in the inn, all with private bathrooms, as well
as the five lodges. Prices are reasonable. Open all year, this is a
large establishment in a public park, so it is best to visit in the
off season when the crowds have disappeared.

Orange County

While traveling around Orange County, visitors are reminded in every village and in every park that this is a place that cherishes its history. Museums, restorations and historic exhibits are everywhere, from the Native American displays found in Goshen's 1841 courthouse to the West Point collection of militaria. America's early history is closely interwoven with events that occurred in Orange County. You can imagine the life of a Revolutionary soldier as he waited out the bitter winters in a wooden hut, or watch as a costumed group of interpreters re-enacts a battle that helped turn the tide of the Revolution.

Orange County is also a place where the agricultural heritage of New York is still strong, a place where vegetable farming is a way of life for families and has been for generations. Stop at a farm stand and take home some just-picked peaches, or borrow a shovel and spend a morning digging up a bushel of onions. The "Black Dirt" area is a unique farming district where some of the best of New York's produce is

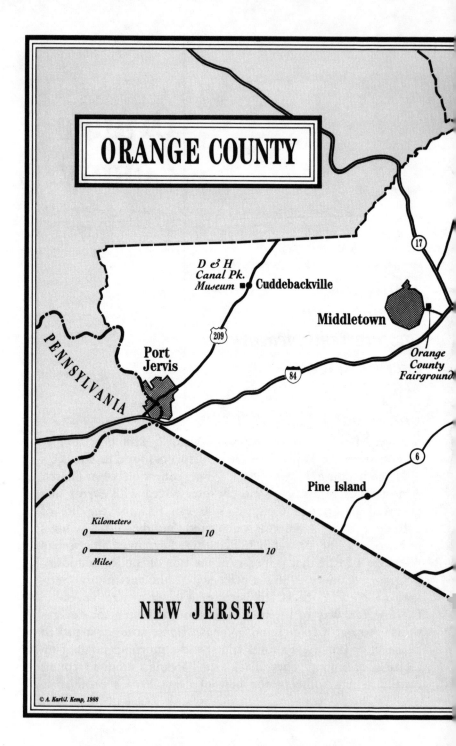

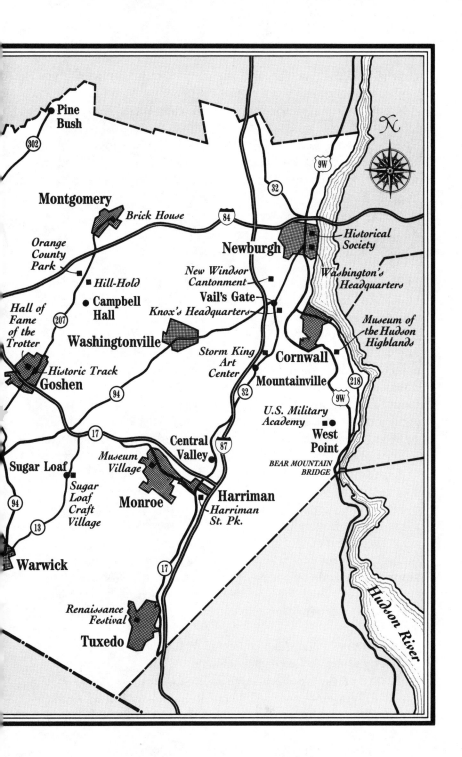

grown, and a drive through the area in early summer gives new meaning to the word bountiful.

If you are looking for more action, then spend a day at the **Historic Track** and the trotting museum in Goshen or the **Speed Skating Hall of Fame** in Newburgh. Orange County is also home to the **Renaissance Festival**, a magical blend of sorcerers, knights and fair damsels who wait to greet you at Sterling Forest.

Campbell Hall

Hill-Hold Once a section of a 300,000-acre estate, the land Hill-Hold stands on was presented to William Bull, an English stonemason, as a wedding present in the early eighteenth century. His son, Thomas Bull, built the stone house that is called Hill-Hold and is still owned by the Bull family. Fortunately for lovers of eighteenth-century architecture, the family donated the house and most of its furnishings to Orange County. The large Georgian-style mansion is graced by elegant wood- and stonework, with barrel-backed cupboards, paneling and deep-silled windows throughout the house. Rooms are furnished with many original pieces in the styles of Chippendale, Queen Anne and Empire. Two kitchens are still extant in the house: the earlier one in the basement and a newer one, added in 1800, in a separate stone wing. Like most manor houses of the era, Hill-Hold was also the center of a thriving farm. Surrounding the house are the original outbuildings, the granary, barn, summer kitchen, wagon house, smokehouse and, of course, the privy. On the working farm sheep, cows, chickens and geese are tended. Children will love seeing the farm animals, but they may find the house tour a bit dull.

DIRECTIONS Located on Route 416 in Campbell Hall; take County Route 207 north from Goshen.

INFORMATION Open late April to late October; 10 A.M. to 4:30 P.M. daily; closed Mon. and Tues. Special winter holiday hours are offered. Admission fee is charged. Tel. (914) 294-7661.

*The tour takes 30 minutes; plan on spending at least another
30 minutes on the grounds, especially if the gardens are in
bloom.*
FACILITIES *Rest rooms.*

Cornwall-on-Hudson

Museum of the Hudson Highlands Established in 1959 as a
children's educational center, the Museum of the Hudson Highlands has since expanded its natural history and environmental
programs to include such special concerns as Project SOAR,
which seeks to bring back the bald eagle and peregrine falcon
populations to the Hudson Valley, and a detailed environmental "reference collection" of animals and plants from the region. Outside, the museum offers visitors the chance to explore
well-marked nature trails that wander through forests, glens
and even an unusual tall-grass prairie. The museum itself is a
wonderful place for parents and kids to get to know the local
environment and the creatures that inhabit it. A natural history
wing houses an indoor zoo, home to local snakes, mice, moles,
turtles, owls and the beloved crow, along with a small display
depicting how the Native Americans lived before the Europe-
ans came. Two small galleries feature the work of local artists.
In the spring, a celebration called Children's Day is held;
the museum goes all out to bring kids and nature together.

DIRECTIONS *The museum is located on the Boulevard in Cornwall-
on-Hudson. Take Route 9W to Route 107, follow it to Route
218 east, make a right on Payson Road and look for the signs.*
INFORMATION *Open from September to June—Mon. through
Thurs., 2 to 5 P.M.; Sat., 12 to 5 P.M.; Sun., 1:30 to 5 P.M.;
closed Fri. July and August—Mon. through Thurs., 11 to 5 P.M.;
Sat. 12 to 5 P.M.; Sun., 1:30 to 5 P.M. Closed Fri. Donation
is suggested. Tel. (914) 534-7781.*

*Outdoor trails are marked. Plan on walking at least one
hour and dress appropriately. Inside, you will want to
spend at least 30 minutes, more if you bring the kids.*
FACILITIES *Gift shop, rest rooms.*

Cuddebackville

Delaware and Hudson Canal Park This 300-acre park, a registered National Historic Landmark, recalls an era when coal, lumber and other goods were moved from Pennsylvania to New York by a combination of water, mules and back-breaking labor. The huge barges were often run as family businesses, with the crew consisting of parents and their children. And there wasn't much room for profit: the barges moved at a leisurely three miles per hour. Although open year-round, special seasonal events are held to evoke a slice of life from mid-nineteenth-century New York State. Past demonstrations have included ice cutting, autumn nature walks, ghost story evenings and maple syrup making. The annual D. W. Griffith silent film festival seems unusual, until you watch the films and realize that many of them were produced in the Cuddebackville area. Older children will be fascinated by the special events days.

DIRECTIONS Located just off Route 209 on Hoag Road (just below where Routes 209 and 211 intersect), about ten miles south of Wurtsboro; watch carefully for signs.

INFORMATION The park is open all year, but the museum is closed January through March. During the season, the museum hours are Wed. through Sun., 10 A.M. to 4 P.M. A fee is charged. Tel. (914)754-8870, or write Neversink Valley Area Museum, Box 263, Cuddebackville, 12792.

Plan to spend an hour here, in the museum and walking the canal. Dress appropriately.

FACILITIES Gift shop, picnic area, rest rooms.

Goshen

Hall of Fame of the Trotter Messenger and Hambletonian, pacers, trotters and standardbreds—all call to mind the speed and grace to be found on a trotting track, and the history and color of their sport can be discovered at this unique theme museum in Orange County established in 1951. Trotters and pacers (trotters move their right front and left rear legs at the same time, while pacers move both legs on one side at the same time) have long been a part of American history; such notable figures as George Washington, Abraham Lincoln and Ulysses S. Grant spent time breeding and racing them. At the Hall of Fame of the Trotter, the history of the sport can be traced through dioramas, prints, exhibits and statues, displayed throughout the former Good Time Stables. Galleries contain permanent displays such as the huge collection of Currier and Ives prints, famous racing silks, and the amazing Hall of Immortals, which consists of dozens of small, lifelike statues that recall the greatest men and horses of the sport. Restored stalls have full size replicas of horses and their equipment, while upstairs you can see the sulkies and sleighs the horses pulled. There is even a room that reproduces the interior of the clubhouse from the nearby historic track. The room is so well maintained that you expect to hear the rustle of programs and voices of members as they discuss the best bet in the next race. The Hall of Fame also offers films and shows in the auditorium, as well as changing gallery exhibits throughout the year.

DIRECTIONS *Located at 240 Main Street, Goshen.*
INFORMATION *Open all year—Mon. through Sat., 10 A.M. to 5 P.M., Sun. and holidays, noon to 5 P.M. Admission fee charged.*
Plan to spend at least an hour here, much more if you are a devotee of the sport. Call ahead if handicapped accessibility is a concern; the lower floors are fairly easy to move around on. The Weathervane Gift Shop is a delight.
FACILITIES *Gift shop, rest rooms.*

Historic Track The only sports facility in the United States that is a National Historic Landmark, it has been hosting meets in the area since the 1830s. Although the Grand Circuit races only visit here once a year, the track is also used as a local training facility, so you will be able to see pacers, trotters and a local blacksmith or two no matter when you visit. The track is such a local institution that some of the private boxes have been passed down through families for generations.

DIRECTIONS Located directly behind the Hall of Fame of the Trotter.

INFORMATION Dates of races vary. Call or write for information: Box 192, Goshen, NY 10924, (914) 294-5333.

FACILITIES Snack bar, picnic area, rest rooms.

Middletown

Orange County Fair One of the oldest county fairs in New York State. Started as an agricultural display between 1818 and 1825, local interest didn't really begin to build until 1841, when the New York State Agricultural Society entered the picture. From then on, the fair was a hit. The 1841 extravaganza featured horses, cows, pigs, farm exhibits and races, and things haven't changed much over the years. A visit to the fair will turn up top-name entertainment, scores of food booths, thrill-a-minute rides and some rather unique events such as pig races, where swift-footed swine dash around a track to reach the purse: a cookie. Or visit the lumberjack exhibition, where the skills of woodsmen are displayed along with log-rolling contests. Also Native American shows, stock car racing and petting zoos. The finest local produce, livestock and home baked goods are for show and sale, and you may even get a chance to see an old-fashioned tent circus.

DIRECTIONS At the County Fairgrounds, located in Middletown at the junction of Routes 84, 17 and 6.

INFORMATION Fair dates usually run from late July to early August; gates open at noon. Admission is charged. Call Orange County Tourism for more information, (914) 294-5151.

Plan on spending the afternoon and evening at the fair, since there is so much to see and do. The weather can be very hot and humid at this time of year; dress accordingly and bring a sunhat.

FACILITIES Picnic areas, food concessions, rest rooms.

Monroe

Museum Village of Orange County The daily life of preindustrial America has been preserved and re-created at this fascinating museum. Set up like a small crossroads village, there are more than 35 buildings on a site that houses crafts, equipment and agricultural displays. At the blacksmith's shop, artisans hammer and pound hot metal into a door latch or horseshoe. The thump-thump of a foot-powered loom comes from the weaver's loft, where you may have a chance to try out the treadles yourself. In the newspaper office, the master printer and the printer's devil (apprentice) are composing the weekly paper, and at the potter's workshop, butter churns and mugs take shape on the wheel. Costumed guides answer questions and permanent exhibits trace the history of Orange County through photos, prints, and everyday tools and accessories. Previous special events have included magic shows, cheese making, tinsmithing, kite flying and square dancing. Every year there is a Civil War encampment; the largest held in the Northeast, it includes battles, camping demonstrations and drills. Don't miss the reconstructed dinosaur models of the mammoths, which once populated the Black Dirt area of the county.

DIRECTIONS Located on Museum Village Road in Monroe; from the N.Y. Thruway, take exit 16 to Route 17 west. Take exit 129 and follow signs.

INFORMATION Open May and June, and September through December—Wed. through Fri., 10 A.M. to 2 P.M.; Sat. and Sun., noon to 5 P.M. July and August—Wed. through Fri., 10 A.M. to 5 P.M.; Sat. and Sun., noon to 5 P.M. Open holiday Mondays. The museum is also open for certain seasonal events. Admission is charged. Tel. (914) 782-8247, or write Museum Village in Orange County, Monroe, 10950.

Walking tour of the village can take a leisurely afternoon; add more time for special events, such as cider pressing in autumn.

FACILITIES Snack bar, gift shop, picnic area, rest rooms.

Montgomery

Brick House A treasure trove of early American furniture and decorative arts owned by the same family since 1768. Now run by the county, the house—a red brick Georgian mansion—is considered one of the finest private homes built between New York and Albany in the eighteenth century. It was a meeting site for officers during the Revolution, and many of the original furnishings are still intact. Pieces include a very rare seventeenth-century chest from Connecticut, fine crystal, Lafayette china (produced to honor the French hero) and an Eli Terry shelf clock. Also the site of a large autumn antiques show.

> *DIRECTIONS Take the N.Y. Thruway to exit 17 (Newburgh); take Route 17K into Montgomery and follow signs.*
> *INFORMATION Open for tours on weekends only from mid-April through mid-October, 10:30 A.M. to 4:30 P.M. Admission fee charged for the tour. Tel. (914) 457-5951.*
> *FACILITIES Footpaths, rest rooms.*

Mountainville

Storm King Art Center This 350-acre park and museum has one of the world's largest displays of outdoor sculpture. The permanent collection contains more than 130 works by over 90 contemporary artists, including Isamu Noguchi, Louise Nevelson, Alexander Calder and Mark diSuvero. The surrounding landscape is beautiful, with a backdrop of Schunnemunk Mountain. Truly one of the most impressive stops in Orange County.

> *DIRECTIONS Take the N.Y. Thruway to exit 16. The art center is off Route 32 north, on Old Pleasant Hill Road; follow signs.*
> *INFORMATION The museum is open Wed. through Mon., from noon to 5:30 P.M., mid-May through October 31. The park is open Wed. through Mon., from noon to 5:30 P.M., April 1*

through Thanksgiving. Donation suggested. Tel. (914) 534-3115.

FACILITIES *Gift shop, picnic tables, rest rooms.*

Newburgh

Balmville Tree An odd treat, but worth a visit. The tree has been standing since 1699 and has a trunk circumference of more than 25 feet.

DIRECTIONS *Located just past Route 9W in Newburgh. Make a right turn onto Chestnut Lane and a left turn at the end of the street. The tree is in the middle of the road.*

Historical Society of Newburgh Bay and the Highlands

Gives regularly scheduled tours of its 1830s neoclassical-style building. There are changing gallery exhibits and an annual celebration of landscape architect Andrew Jackson Downing's birthday.

DIRECTIONS *Located at the Crawford House, 189 Montgomery Street, Newburgh.*

INFORMATION *Call for hours. Tel. (914) 561-2585.*

FACILITIES *Rest rooms.*

Washington's Headquarters If Jonathan Hasbrouck's stone mansion could speak, it would say that Martha and George slept here, as did several aides-de-camp. In fact, the end of the Revolution was announced on the grounds. Set on a bluff overlooking the Hudson River, the house was started in 1750, but not really finished until 1782, when Washington's troops added a gunpowder laboratory, a barracks, a privy and a larger kitchen. Washington remained here for almost 1½ years, waiting for the British to leave New York under the terms of surrender. The house and grounds were acquired by the U.S. government in 1849 and became the first national historic site.

Visitors can see firsthand how the Revolutionary armies lived and worked. The orientation center museum has displays of clothing, equipment and memorabilia from the War of Independence, including some of the first president's personal items. There are uniforms, field shovels, decorations and even a few links from the chain that stretched across the Hudson and was meant to deter the British. The story of the Revolution truly comes alive inside Hasbrouck House, where Washington is seen as a man who endured problems, boredom and loss of the privacy that was so dear to him. Visitors are guided through the eight rooms in which Washington and his staff lived and worked. The dining room where George and Martha ate their meals still contains the original Dutch jambless fireplace, which is open on three sides. The plain bedrooms and offices are sparsely furnished, and a field bed with its tentlike covering speaks clearly of the winter's cold, while bedrolls in the hallways show that not everyone was fortunate enough to have a room. The grounds are well kept and offer wide views of the Hudson River. Special events are held at the site throughout the year. Both George and Martha's birthdays are celebrated, along with a kite day, military musters and Christmas tours.

DIRECTIONS *Located at 84 Liberty Street in Newburgh; take Route 17 from the N.Y. Thruway or I-84 to Route 17K to downtown Newburgh. Watch carefully for the signs to the museum; parking available.*

INFORMATION *Open April through December—Wed. through Sat., 10 A.M. to 5 P.M. Also open Washington's Birthday, Memorial Day, Independence Day, Labor Day and certain winter days. Admission is free. Tel. (914) 562-1195, or write Washington's Headquarters, 84 Liberty Street, P.O. Box 1783, Newburgh, 12550.*

The tour of the house takes 20 minutes; plan on spending at least 30 minutes in the museum. Call ahead if handicapped accessibility is a concern. Across the street is the Newburgh Preservation Association (87 Liberty Street), which offers inexpensive walking and car tours of historic Newburgh on Sun. at 1 and 3 P.M. Tel. (914) 565-6880.

FACILITIES *Rest rooms.*

Sugar Loaf

Sugar Loaf Crafts Village Once a bustling stagecoach and river stop, this area lost much of its trade when the railroads bypassed it in the mid-nineteenth century. But in the last two decades, Sugar Loaf has regained its spirit; many craftspeople have moved into the area and set up their workshops. The crafts village is open all year and is a terrific place to look for a special gift or add to a collection. The shops include places that make handcrafted rag dolls, stained glass, sculpted wooden objects, handwrought pewter, photographs and portraits. As befits an arts colony, there are fine crafts fairs and art shows throughout the year, as well as a fall festival and holiday carolling. The village is lovely and an excellent place to spend the afternoon taking in the views and the talent.

DIRECTIONS *Take exit 16 from the N.Y. Thruway to Route 17 west for 8 miles to exit 127. Follow the signs.*

INFORMATION: *Open Tues. through Sun., 10 A.M. to 5 P.M. Most of the shops are open all year; but weekends are the best time to catch the artists at home. Admission is free. Tel. (914) 469-4963, or write Sugar Loaf Guild, P.O. Box 125, Sugar Loaf, 10981.*

Allow at least a morning or afternoon to explore the village. There's lots of walking—King's Highway and Wood's Road have many shops to explore—and you will be outside for much of the time, so dress accordingly. Not recommended for kids, unless they love to shop.

FACILITIES *Restaurants, rest rooms.*

Tuxedo

New York Renaissance Festival Knights and ladies, sorcerers and their apprentices, fools, varlets, bumpkins and wantons all gather on the glorious grounds of Sterling Forest Ski Area each year to re-create the lusty days of merry England. The festival runs for eight consecutive weekends in August and September, and it presents a colorful, noisy look at a misty period of time somewhere between King Arthur and Shakespeare. Falconers show off the skills of their birds, opera and Shakespeare are presented at the Globe Theatre, Maid Marian flirts with Robin Hood, ladies dance beneath a Maypole and the extensive rose gardens are open for strolling. Craftspeople display and sell their wares, and the aromas of foods such as "steak on a stake" (really turkey legs), mead and cheese pie flavor the air. The living chess game, where thirty-two people/pieces cavort on a grassy playing field is a wondrous sight. The actors play their roles throughout the entire festival, so authenticity combines with the personal touch.

DIRECTIONS On Route 17A, just west of Route 17. Take N.Y. Thruway to exit 15; follow signs to Route 17.

INFORMATION Runs weekends in August and September, 11 A.M. to 6 P.M.; call for exact dates. Admission fee charged. Tel. (914) 351-5171, or write Creative Faires, New York Renaissance Festival, P.O. Box 844, Tuxedo, 10987.

This is an all-day event, and if you visit again, chances are the entertainment will have changed. The festival is mainly outdoors, so dress accordingly and comfortably. Take the shuttle bus from the parking lots, which are large and confusing, but don't forget to note where you parked the car.

FACILITIES Food concessions, gifts and crafts, theatre, rest rooms.

Vail's Gate

Knox Headquarters For several periods during the Revolution, the Ellison family's stone house served as headquarters for the Colonial officers. Generals Henry Knox, Horatio Gates and Nathanael Greene were only a few of the men who met in the house and planned campaigns in its gracious rooms. Today it has been restored to the way it was when camp beds and folding desks displaced the fine eighteenth-century furniture of the Ellisons.

DIRECTIONS Located off Route 94 on Forge Hill Road, east of Vail's Gate.

INFORMATION Also located here is the Jane Colden Native Plant Sanctuary, dedicated to the memory of the first American woman botanist. The house and sanctuary are open all year; no admission charge. Call ahead for hours. Tel. (914) 561-5498.
FACILITIES None.

New Windsor Cantonment Washington's troops waited out the last months of the Revolutionary War here, in anticipation of an announced cessation of hostilities. More than 10,000 soldiers, officers, cooks, blacksmiths, wives and other camp followers constructed the snug log cabins, outbuildings and a meeting hall, and here's where Washington quelled a mutiny of his troops, who resented Congress's slowness with wages and pensions. After the war, the buildings were auctioned off for the lumber, and the land was unused until the state acquired 70 acres and began restoration of the site. A visit to the cantonment today offers a look into the everyday life of the Revolutionary soldiers. At the orientation center, a slide show discusses the history of the area during the war, and displays depict the difficulties faced by both the leaders and the troops. One fascinating display is of an original Badge of Military Merit, which Washington presented to several soldiers and is now known as the Purple Heart. A walkway leads from the center to the cantonment site, where the parade grounds and the buildings have been re-created. Costumed guides go about their business of blacksmithing, drilling, cooking and even entertaining (a fife player may be on hand). Although many of the buildings have been reconstructed from sketches that remain from the era, one small cabin is original. When the soldiers' huts were sold, one was carted away and became an addition to a local house. There it remained for 150 years, until its importance was realized, and it was returned to the site.

DIRECTIONS Located in Vail's Gate, on Temple Hill Road off Routes 32 and 300.
INFORMATION Open Mid-April through October—Wed. through Sat., 10 A.M. to 5 P.M.; Sun., 1 to 5 P.M. Also open Memorial Day, Independence Day and Labor Day. Admission is free. Tel.

(914) 561-1765, or write New Windsor Cantonment, P.O. Box 207, Vail's Gate, 12584.

If you watch the slide show (a bit dull), visit the center and watch the demonstrations on the grounds, you should set aside a full afternoon. The site is outdoors, so dress accordingly. Call ahead if handicapped accessibility is a concern. Children will enjoy the costumed interpreters. Special events are often scheduled here.
FACILITIES Picnic area, rest rooms.

West Point

Constitution Island and the Warner House To visit a Hudson River Island, take the boat from West Point to Constitution Island. There you will find a seventeen-room Victorian mansion that was home to the Warner family from 1836 to 1915. The daughters, Anna and Susan, grew up on the island and were best known for their writing; Anna wrote many hymns, including "Jesus Loves Me," and Susan's *Wide, Wide World* was a best seller. The sisters were Bible class instructors for West Point cadets during the late nineteenth century, and today their home is a museum, furnished with their original possessions. Also on the island are the remains of Fort Constitution, a Revolutionary era fort, and the lovely Anna B. Warner Memorial Garden. The garden is particularly lovely in late June, and the surrounding Hudson is glorious anytime.

DIRECTIONS *Take Route 9W to West Point, enter United States Military Academy gate and take first right after the Hotel Thayer. Dock and a large parking lot at end of street.*

INFORMATION *Tours are given at 1 and 2 P.M. on Wed. and Thurs., from mid-June through late September. Only forty-three people per tour; reservations required. Tel. (914) 446-8676 at least two weeks in advance. There is an admission charge. An unusual outing; will interest just about anyone.*

FACILITIES *Picnic tables, gift shop, hiking trails, rest rooms.*

United States Military Academy Situated on the bluffs overlooking the Hudson River, this is where the nation's Army officers have been trained since 1802, where Benedict Arnold attempted to bring the British to power, where such distinguished cadets as Robert E. Lee, Ulysses S. Grant and Douglas MacArthur once marched and where dropouts such as James Whistler decided that his talents lay in more artistic areas. Tradition is important at West Point, and tradition is what you will find here, from the Long Gray Lines of cadets to the quiet cemetery and imposing stone barracks. Your first stop should be the visitors center near Thayer Gate. Here you will find a small display about cadet life, maps, a gift shop and an orientation movie, which is more about the cadets than about the history of the academy. Pick up a guide to the academy grounds, drive up Thayer Road and park in the marked lots. Then head to the museum at Thayer Hall, which houses one of the foremost collections of military memorabilia and equipment in the world. Uniforms, weapons, field equipment, art and flags from the sixteenth century to the present are displayed, with material from America's wars given major exhibition space (open every day, except Christmas and New Year's, 10:15 A.M. to 4:15 P.M.). Walk up Cullum Road to Trophy Point, where a memorial, cannons and a huge piece of chain recall past wars. The 150-ton chain was used to close off the Hudson River to British ships during the Revolution, and although unsuccessful, it represents American ingenuity at its best. To the rear of the memorial is the "plain," the drilling area that was used by Baron von Steuben to train and parade the troops. It is still used on Saturdays for full-dress parades by the cadets. (If it's a football Saturday, the plain will be mobbed with parents and visitors; arrive early for parking and a view.) Next, follow the map to Washington Road and stop in at the cadet chapels. Another restored section of the point is Fort Putnam, which was used as a fortification in the Revolutionary War and now has exhibits that depict a soldier's life during the period. It also offers a panoramic view of the surrounding mountains. Throughout the tour, you will see cadets as they go to and from classes and training. Although some rules, like squaring off for meals, have been relaxed, much tradition remains, including the uniforms and military discipline.

West Point is also famous for its football games, played at Michie (pronounced My-kee) Stadium. But tickets are in short supply, so call ahead if you want to go to a game.

DIRECTIONS Located near Route 9W, just north of Bear Mountain State Park; follow the signs.

INFORMATION The USMA is open all year, except Thanksgiving, Christmas and New Year's. The Visitors Center is open every day, March to December, and Wed. through Sun. during January, February and part of March, from 8:30 A.M. to 4:30 P.M. Admission to the sites free; ticket charge for football games. Tel. (914) 938-2638/5261, or write Information Center, United States Military Academy, West Point, 10996.

A tour of the USMA takes several hours, more if you stay for a game or the dress parade. Wear comfortable walking shoes and dress appropriately for outdoor weather. Bring a camera for the parades; call ahead if handicapped accessibility is a concern. Do not park in reserved areas or you risk upsetting a general! Older kids will enjoy the colorful parades and the museums.

FACILITIES Picnic areas, gift shop, rest rooms.

Activities

BALLOONING

For spectacular views of the countryside, try a balloon trip over Orange County. Two companies will arrange trips, which can only take place under perfect conditions: little or no wind and no approaching storms. Call **Rise and Float**, Randall Airport, Middletown, (914) 343-3235 or (212) 582-4260, or **Fantasy Balloon Flights**, Port Jervis, (914) 856-7713, for information and rates.

BOAT CRUISES

One of the best ways to see the Hudson is from the river itself. **Hudson Highlands Cruises** offers daily cruises during the summer, leaving from the West Point dock. Call (914) 446-7171 for schedules and information.

FACTORY OUTLETS

Factory outlets have come a long way from the dingy shops of the past, and a stop at **Woodbury Common** (Route 32, Central Valley) will prove this. With more than fifty factory outlet stores under one roof, the setting itself is a lovely Colonial-style mall. Call (914) 928-SHOP for a list of the stores and their hours.

FARMS

Orange County is standardbred country in New York State; it is also home to a number of thriving dairy farms. Some of these establishments welcome visitors who can learn firsthand about the business and pleasures of horse breeding or dairy farming. Children are fascinated by the chance to see cows being milked and horses being groomed.

The following farms invite tourists. It is a good idea to call in advance for an appointment. (All of the farms listed are horse-breeding farms unless otherwise specified.)

Blue Chip Farm, Bates Lane, Walkill, (914) 895-3930, a horse-breeding farm, is open to the public daily from 10 A.M. to 4 P.M. **Castleton Farm,** Sarah Wells Trail, Goshen, (914) 294-6717, also specializes in horse breeding, in particular standardbreds. Call for an appointment. Also worth a visit are **Alnoff Farms,** Searsville Road, Walden, (914) 778-5421 (open 9 A.M. to 4 P.M.), **Excelsior Horse Farm,** Bullville, (914) 361-2112 and **Lana Lobell Farm,** Route 416, Montgomery, (914) 457-5572, another horse-breeding farm. **Clover Knoll Farms,** Route 207, Campbell Hall, (914) 294-6387, a dairy farm, is open every day, from 7 A.M. to 8 P.M., all year. **Blooming Hill Farm,** Blooming Grove, (914) 496-9694, is a great place for people interested in maple syrup making; tours offered in March, during the season.

FARM STANDS AND PICK-YOUR-OWN FARMS

Because so much of Orange County is used for agricultural purposes (in the Black Dirt area, more than 10,000 acres are under cultivation), you will find dozens of farm stands throughout the area. Some specialize in one particular fruit or vegetable, others offer a wide variety and there are pick-your-own farms, too.

The Pine Island area offers several top-drawer farm stands and pick-your own farms. **Apple Hill,** Glenwood Road, Route 517 south of village, (914) 258-4158 (open September and October), lets you pick the apples and peaches they raise. A unique farm is **Dattolico Organic Farm,** Mission Land Road, two miles west of Route 1, (914) 258-4762 (open late May through mid-October), which sells pick-your-own vegetables grown without chemical sprays. The selection here is wide and includes beans, onions, spinach, peas and squash (no fruits). At **Rogowski Farms,** 334 Pulaski Highway, (914) 258-4109 (open mid-July through October), you can pick onions, lettuce and pumpkins; and **Walter Kowal,** Pulaski Highway, (914) 258-4393 (open August through November), sells onions only. Two other large roadside stands in Pine Island are **J & H Farms,** Feagles Road, (914) 258-4743 (open May through November), and **Pine Island Farm Fresh Produce,** Pine Island Turnpike (open all year), which stock lots of local produce including honey, eggs and cider. In Warwick, **Applewood Orchards,** Four Corners, (914) 986-1684 (open September and October), has a roadside stand with vegetables, but they specialize in pick-your-own apples, including Delicious, MacIntosh and Macouns. Also features wagon rides, flower and herb gardens and a picnic area. Campbell Hall is home to **Halfway Acres**, Purgatory Road, three miles east of Goshen off Sarah Wells Trail, (914) 294-7869 (open late April through October), where you can pick blueberries, asparagus, peppers and tomatoes, or buy ready picked melons, beans, peas and other healthy treats. **Hodgson Farms**, Albany Post Road, Route 52, Montgomery, (914) 778-1432 (open June through October), lets berry lovers buy or pick strawberries and raspberries, and later on in the season, huge yellow pumpkins.

Bee & Thistle Herb Farm, 51 Angola Road, Cornwall, (914) 534-7436 (open Tues. through Sun., 1 to 5 P.M.), is a charming shop and farm specializing in herbs, spices and related products. Tours of the gardens by appointment. **Swissette Herb Farm,** Clove Road, Salisbury Mills, (914) 496-7841, sells herbs and herb plants, dried spices, herbal and medicinal teas, sachets, potpourri, organic honey, jams and homeopathic products. Also has lecture tours. Located off Route 94, southwest of Vail's Gate; open Tues. through Sun., May through October, 1 to 5 P.M., or by appointment.

HIKING

Hikers can indulge themselves on trails that range from easy to "experienced only." The **Appalachian Trail** weaves through the southwest section of the county; call the Palisades Interstate Parks Commission at (914) 786-2701 for maps and specific trail information. At **Black Rock Forest,** Route 9W, north of West Point, there is a good system of both marked and unmarked trails of all levels of difficulty. Two other parks have trails of varied difficulties: **Schunemunk,** Route 32 in Highland Mills, has six marked trails, the longest of which is eight miles, and **Winding Hills Park,** Route 17K, Montgomery, (914) 457-3111, with trails, a picnic area and a nature study section. **Harriman State Park,** Harriman exit, N.Y. Thruway, (914) 786-2701, has hiking trails, swimming and a variety of other outdoor activities.

ICE-SKATING

Ice-skaters can find wintry fun at the **Delano-Hitch Recreation Center,** 375 Washington Avenue, Newburgh, (914) 565-3260 (open until 11 P.M.). There's a warming hut, and admission is free. Some of the regional speed-skating finals are held here, so if you are a fan of this sport, call and ask about upcoming meets. Also at the recreation center, the **Speed Skating Hall of Fame,** a small museum, is open Mon. through Fri., 8:30 A.M. to 4 P.M. Exhibits include photos, equipment and memorabilia of the earliest speed skaters through those who participated in the last Olympics.

SCENIC DRIVES

The term "scenic drive" in Orange County is almost redundant; there are so many well-maintained roads where the pace is unhurried and the views are lovely that a drive around Orange is certain to please. Even the thruway softens up a bit as it moves through the Harriman area—drivers can see deer at twilight and apple blossoms in the spring. Route 9W is an attractive drive, but it turns spectacular along the section known as Old Storm King Highway, between West Point and Cornwall. (It is also curvy and steep, so be careful in bad weather.) For a lovely country drive past lakes and trees, start at Harriman and take Route 6 east across Bear Mountain State Park to the Bear Mountain Bridge; from there, 9W north offers vibrant Hudson River views on its way through West Point, Cornwall and into Newburgh. Once in Newburgh, look for Route 32 around Cronomer Hill Park, which is a breathtaking sight in summer and fall. Another noted scenic highway in Orange County is Hawk's Nest Drive, Route 97, near Sparrow Bush. The road runs along the Delaware River for a short distance, but you can then follow Route 209 north to the **D. & H. Canal Park** (page 26). And a different type of view is found along Route 17A, which cuts through the rich farming area around Pine Island.

SKIING

At the **Thomas Bull Memorial Park Area,** Route 416, south of Montgomery, (914) 457-3000 (open all year), you can downhill ski both day and night during the season, or enjoy a cross–country tour, spin across an icy lake on skates or slide down a hill on sleds. Skiing is also available at **Sterling Forest**, Route 17A, Tuxedo, (914) 351-2163/4788. Both day and night sessions, as well as snowmaking capabilities, rentals and a restaurant on the site. Call for daily ski reports.

WINERIES

Three wineries in Orange County are open to visitors: **Brotherhood,** Route 94, Washingtonville, (914) 496-9101, and **Baldwin Vineyards,** Hardenburgh Road, Pine Bush,

(914) 744-2226. They offer tours and tastings, but call ahead for hours. Baldwin has some excellent wines that have won awards in various competitions. **Brimstone Hill Vineyard,** Brimstone Hill Road, Pine Bush, (914) 744-2231, is open during the summer months Thursday through Sunday.

Where to Eat

The Barnsider Tavern (Kings Highway, Sugar Loaf, (914) 469-9810) This tavern has a beautiful taproom with hand-wrought beams and country decor, and a glassed-in patio room that provides a view of the Sugar Loaf crafts community. During the winter months, a crackling fire is always going. The menu of burgers, quiches, chili, onion soup and spinach salad makes this place perfect for lunch. Children are welcome.
OPEN *Daily from 11:30 A.M. to 10 P.M.*

Brewster House 1762 Restaurant (Temple Hill Rd. [Route 300], New Windsor, (914)561-1762 or 562-2018) A registered landmark, this Colonial-era fieldstone house dates from 1762 and contains the original beams, floors and doors. It was built by Samuel Brewster, who made the chains that crossed the Hudson River at West Point to stop the British. The house specialties include lobster, beef Wellington, duck à l'orange, poached salmon, veal Oscar and barbecued shrimp. There is also a seafood bar with oysters, clams, jumbo shrimp and smoked fish. Choose from a tempting variety of cakes and pastries to top off your meal. A piano player entertains on Friday and Saturday nights. Children are welcome; special menu provided.
OPEN *Lunch—Mon. through Sat., 11 A.M. to 2:30 P.M.; dinner—5 to 10 P.M. Also open Sun., 11 A.M. to 9 P.M.; closed Tuesdays.*

Bull's Head Inn (Sarah Wells Trail, Campbell Hall [between Goshen and Washingtonville], (914) 496-6758) Enjoy candlelight dining (with live classical music on Mon., Wed. and Thurs.) in this 1763 restaurant. Continental cuisine features house specialties such as Bull's Head Oysters (on the half-shell with Beluga caviar and Russian vodka), and Don's Chicken-by-the-Sea (chicken breast stuffed with crabmeat, shrimp and scallops). Children are welcome except on Saturday nights; no special menu.

OPEN *Dinner—Wed. through Mon., 5 to 10 P.M. and 3 to 10 P.M. on Sun.*

The Burlingham Inn *(Ulsterville Rd., Pine Bush, (914) 744-2717)* Country atmosphere and continental cuisine.

Commodore's *(482 Broadway, Newburgh, (914) 561-3960)* A wonderful, old-fashioned ice cream soda fountain and chocolatier in downtown Newburgh that has been in business for over 50 years. From the outside, the place looks unassuming, but a step inside will transport you back to your childhood. The family's chocolate candies are made entirely by hand with the finest ingredients. There are the usual delicious standbys— truffles, cordials, mints and marzipan—as well as more exotic delights. The Swedish fudge and almond bark are a couple of our favorites. Perfect for kids of all ages.

OPEN *Mon. through Fri., 9 A.M. to 9 P.M.; Sat., 9 A.M. to 6 P.M.; and Sun., 10 A.M. to 5 P.M.*

The Country Horseman *(Route 284, Westtown, (914) 726-3040)* Fine Continental cuisine in an informal atmosphere.

88 Charles Street Cafe *(88 Charles St., Montgomery, (914) 457-9850)* Enjoyable Italian cuisine—specialties of the house include veal piccata, shrimp scampi and calamari fra diavalo. Children welcome.

OPEN *Lunch—Mon. through Sat., 11:30 A.M. (noon on Sat.) to 3 P.M.; dinner—5 P.M. on; Sun., 1 P.M. on.*

Flo-Jean Restaurant *(Routes 6 and 209, Port Jervis (914) 856-6600)* Situated on the banks of the Delaware River, this establishment has been in business since 1929. The building was formerly used to collect tolls for the bridge. On the upper level, the main dining room offers scenic views of the river, while the intimate Toll House lounge, on the lower level, is more casual. The Continental cuisine is of good quality. Children are welcome; limited menu available.

OPEN Lunch—Wed. through Sun., noon to 3 P.M.; dinner—4:30 to 9 P.M.; Sunday brunch—noon to 4 P.M. and dinner, 4 to 8 P.M. Closed Mon. and Tues.

Gasho of Japan *(Route 32, Central Valley, (914) 928-2277)* This authentic, graceful 400-year-old Japanese farmhouse was dismantled in Japan, shipped piece-by-piece to its present site and reassembled. Gasho features hibachi-style fare. As you sit at heated steel-topped tables, Tokyo-trained chefs dazzle both eye and palate by preparing filet mignon with hibachi snowcrab, prime beef and lobster tail before your eyes. Shrimp tempura, scallops, and eel teriyaki are some of the other specialties. All dinners include soup, salad, vegetables, rice and tea. After dinner, take a leisurely stroll through the Japanese gardens. Children are welcome; special menu provided.

OPEN Lunch—Mon. through Sat., noon to 2:30 P.M.; dinner— Mon. through Fri., 5:30 to 10 P.M. and until 11 P.M. on Sat.

Hawk's Nest *(Route 97, Port Jervis, (914) 856-9909)* A wonderful place for breakfast or lunch after canoeing on the Delaware River. The views are absolutely spectacular. Great pancakes, waffles, homemade ice cream, and omelets. The restaurant sits at the peak of the river's gorge like a hawk's nest, and on a clear day a stop here should not be missed. Children are welcome.

OPEN April 1 to December 1—Mon. through Fri., 11 A.M. to 7 P.M., until 9 in July and August; Sat. and Sun., 8 A.M. to 7 P.M., until 9 in July and August.

The Jolly Onion Inn *(Pine Island Turnpike, Pine Island, (914) 258-4277)* A local tradition, serving Continental cuisine.

La Masquerade *(Route 17M, Goshen, (914) 294-6888)* The French and Continental cuisine here is first-rate. The restaurant is housed in a recently renovated 150-year-old building. Inappropriate for children.

OPEN *Lunch—Tues. through Fri., noon to 3 P.M.; dinner—Tues. through Sat., 5:30 to 10 P.M., and Sun., 4 to 8 P.M.; Sunday brunch, noon to 3 P.M. Closed Mon.*

LaMonica's *(Main St., Goshen, (914) 294-9341)* Italian cuisine is the specialty here, and it is well prepared.

National Hotel *(73 Clinton St., Montgomery, (914) 457-5048)* Located in a historic district, this restaurant is one of the oldest public houses in continuous operation anywhere. Formerly a stagecoach stop and a stopover for bootleggers running whiskey to New York City during prohibition, it is now a casual eating and drinking establishment. There is a two-story front porch where lunch is served outdoors in warm weather. Soups are excellent, especially the onion. Other specialties include the 6-ounce burgers and steak fries, chili, roast beef with French dip and salads of all kinds. Everything, including desserts, is homemade. Children are welcome, there is even an antique high chair.

OPEN *Every day, noon to midnight.*

Painter's Tavern *(Village Square, Route 218, Cornwall-on-Hudson, (914) 534-2109)* Perfect for lunch or dinner. Hamburgers, creative and unusual sandwiches and salads are available, as well as steaks, ribs, fish and nightly dinner specials. The sun-dried tomatoes, mushrooms and prosciutto in a cream sauce on angel hair pasta is especially good. More than seventy imported and domestic beers to choose from. Children are welcome; smaller portions served upon request.

OPEN *Lunch and dinner—daily, 11 A.M. to 10 P.M.; Sunday brunch—noon to 4 P.M.*

Quail Hollow Restaurant *(Route 208 and Round Hill Rd., Washingtonville, (914) 496-5495)* Housed in a renovated Southern-style mansion, the magnificent redwood bar was crafted from wood the owners brought with them from California. The specialty of the house is quail, but there is a wide selection of other dishes. An Old World menu is a unique feature of this establishment. With only a day's notice the chef will prepare roast suckling pig or turkey for parties of four or more. Visit this restaurant on weekends, as the menu may be limited on weekday nights. Children are welcome, but no special menu.

OPEN *Lunch—Wed. through Sat., 11 A.M. to 3 P.M.; dinner—5 to 9 P.M., until 10 on Fri. and Sat., and Sun. 3 to 9 P.M. Reservations necessary on weekends.*

Sugar Loaf Inn *(Kings Highway, Sugar Loaf, (914) 469-9885)* Country dining in a Victorian setting amid plants and flowers. A good place for lunch or drinks, their home-baked breads and desserts are especially good. The emphasis is on freshness and variety, and the entrées are both classic and unusual. In the summer, enjoy dining in the garden. Children are welcome.

OPEN *Lunch—Tues. through Sat., 11:30 A.M. to 3 P.M.; dinner—Tues. through Sun., 5 to 9 P.M.; Sunday brunch, 11 A.M. to 3 P.M.*

Ward's Bridge Inn *(Ward St., Montgomery, (914) 457-3488/ 9677)* A well-kept secret, this romantic restaurant filled with American country antiques is one of Orange County's finest and definitely worth a detour. They serve first-rate steaks and seafood, as well as an array of imaginative specials. Children are welcome; smaller portions served upon request.

OPEN *Lunch—Mon. through Fri., 11:30 A.M. to 2:30 P.M.; dinner—Mon. through Thurs., 5 to 10 P.M., until 11 P.M. on Fri. and Sat., and Sun., 4 to 10 P.M.*

Warwick Inn *(36 Oakland Ave., Warwick, (914) 986-3666* This 165-year-old mansion has been owned and operated by the Wilson family for the past 25 years. The original mouldings, fireplaces and antiques add to the cozy atmosphere of the inn. Roast prime ribs of beef and fresh roasted turkey are served

Friday through Sunday. Seafood specialties include baked stuffed shrimp, swordfish and broiled stuffed flounder. Reasonably priced. Children are welcome; special menu provided.
  OPEN *Wed. through Sat. at 5 P.M.; Sun. at 1 P.M. Reservations suggested.*

Yobo *(Union Ave. near N.Y. Thruway exit 17, Newburgh, (914) 564-3848)* Enjoy Pan-Asian cuisine—hibachi steaks, Korean bulgogi, Indonesian sates and all the provincial cooking of China—under one roof. Children are welcome.
  OPEN *Lunch—Mon. through Fri., 11:30 A.M. to 3 P.M.; dinner—5 to 10 P.M. Also Sat. and Sun., 12:30 to 10:30 P.M.*

Where to Stay

Bed and breakfast establishments are limited in Orange County. There are motels with good, standard accommodations in Middletown, Newburgh, and Port Jervis.

Gasho Inn *(Route 32, Central Valley, 10917, (914) 928-2387)* The history of Gasho's building began over eight centuries ago, when a defeated samurai clan fled to the mountains in Japan. There the warriors and their families developed a building style characterized by high-arched roofs and strong wooden planks that were lashed and pegged together without nails. Primarily known for its fine restaurant, Gasho also has overnight accommodations surrounded by lovely Japanese gardens, a pond and teahouses. Use the two outdoor tennis courts at no extra charge. Twenty-five rooms with private bathrooms; no breakfast is served. Open all year.

Hotel Thayer *(U.S. Military Academy, West Point, 10996, (914) 446-4731)*. The Hotel Thayer reflects a long-ago period of grandeur, with many guest rooms overlooking one of the most scenic parts of the Hudson River—the Hudson Highlands. Although not included in the room rate, the dining room serves breakfast on the terrace, which offers a breathtaking panorama of the Hudson Valley. The hotel is in need of some restoration work, but overall it's a lovely spot to stay, especially if you are going to tour West Point. Open all year. Make reservations well in advance, if possible. One-hundred-seventy rooms with private bathrooms.

Tara Farm Bed and Breakfast *(R.D. 2, Kiernan Rd., Campbell Hall, 10916, (914) 294-6482)* Fred and Megan Hughes are former English innkeepers who now welcome guests to their three-acre N.Y. farm complete with horses, chickens, ducks, dogs and cats. Guests are permitted to bring their own pets. A proper breakfast is served each morning with imported English bacon, sausages, puddings and farm fresh eggs. Children will adore this establishment. Open all year. Two rooms available; share one bathroom.

Sullivan County

Only 90 miles north-west of New York City lies Sullivan County, 1,000 square miles of outdoor paradise. Along the Delaware River, which snakes along the border and down into Pennsylvania, the untamed country is home to bald eagles, rocky glens and rugged cliffs. To the north, visitors will discover the charm of silvery lakes, lush forests and narrow valleys where tiny villages nestle alongside burbling streams. Sullivan is also home to some of the world's best trout fishing, and on opening day of the season—rain or snow—the rods and flies are taken from storage rooms across the county to become part of the annual dream of catching the big one. Only a small percentage of the county is considered agricultural, but there are dairy farms, pick-your-own fruit and vegetable markets and organic farming centers. Most of all, though, a drive through Sullivan County is a reminder that this area was the frontier not too long ago, a place where bears, bobcats and the mysterious panther haunted the sleep of woodsmen and pioneers.

51

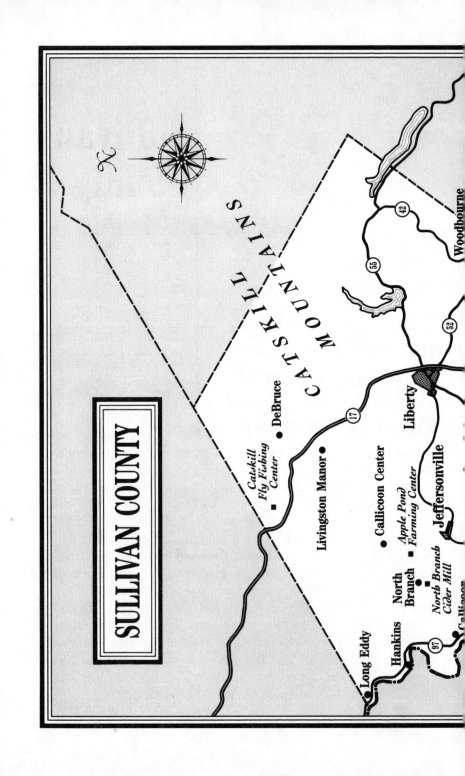

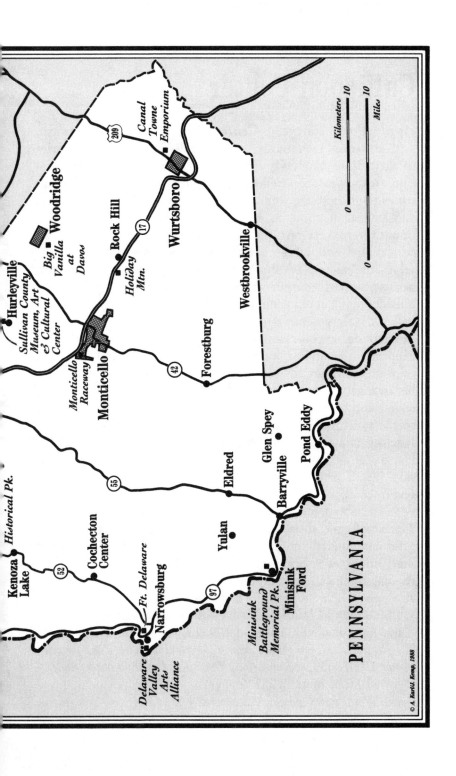

Kenoza Lake

Historical Pk.

Cochecton Center

52

Ft. Delaware

Narrowsburg

Delaware Valley Arts Alliance

Yulan

97

Minisink Battleground Memorial Pk.

Minisink Ford

PENNSYLVANIA

Hurleyville

Sullivan County Museum, Art & Cultural Center

Woodridge

Big Vanilla at Davos

Rock Hill

17

Holiday Mtn.

Monticello Raceway

Monticello

42

Forestburg

55

Eldred

Glen Spey

Barryville

Pond Eddy

Westbrookville

Canal Towne Emporium

209

Wurtsboro

Kilometers   10

0

Miles   10

0

© A. Karl/J. Kemp, 1988

Callicoon Center

Apple Pond Farming Center Today, most farms are run with advanced technology, and the older methods and theories of agriculture are slowly being lost in an avalanche of information from weather satellites, computers and genetics laboratories. But there are some farmers who cherish the older ways and believe if the land is worked well, it will still yield a bountiful harvest. At the Apple Pond Farming Center, an educational and working farm, visitors can judge for themselves the success of organic farming practices, coupled with horse-powered equipment. The farm is located on a rocky hillside, with enchanting views of meadows, mountains and valleys. Here you can enjoy one of several unique tours, which can include wagon rides, a sheep-herding demonstration, bee-keeping, haying and logging. Visitors ride around the farm on a horse-drawn wagon, and in the winter sleigh rides may be arranged. The farm is stocked with sheep, horses, goats, cows, and several incredible border collies, whose dedication to the task of sheep herding is worth the trip. Founder Dick Riseling is a fascinating host who so loves the farm and the history of agriculture that he makes visitors wish they could stay just a little longer. And since the farm offers a well-respected apprentice program, you may find yourself visiting with students from around the country and around the world. The small gift shop stocks items that are made from farm products. Special activities, like lamb roasts, foliage drives and draft horse workshops are held throughout the year, but they require advanced reservations. This is a working farm so the atmosphere here is informal—don't expect a neat little restoration.

DIRECTIONS Located on Hahn Road outside of Callicoon Center. From Route 17, take exit 100 at Liberty to 52 west, go eight miles to Youngsville, then right on Shandelee Road for one and a half miles, left on Stump Pond Road for two miles, and left on Hahn Road. Watch for signs.

INFORMATION Open all year, morning to evening, but you must call ahead for reservations. Admission fee charged. Tel. (914)

482-4764, or write Box 65, Hahn Road, Callicoon Center, 12724.

The wagon tours take at least two hours; other tours may be longer. Since this is a working farm, dress accordingly; it gets very windy on the mountainside, even when the weather is warm. Ask about handicapped accessibility; the people here are very helpful and accommodating.
FACILITIES Picnic area, gift shop, rest rooms.

Kenoza Lake

Stone Arch Bridge Historical Park This three-arched stone bridge, which spans the Callicoon Creek, is the only remaining one of its kind in this country. Built in 1872 by two German stonemasons, the bridge was constructed from hand-cut local stone and supported without an outer framework. Replacing an earlier wooden span that finally collapsed from the constant weight of wagonloads of lumber, the Stone Arch Bridge gained fame not only for its graceful design and unusual construction, but for an unusual murder which took place on or near the bridge in 1892. A local farmer, believing that his brother-in-law put a hex on him, convinced his son that only the brother-in-law's death could lift the curse. So the young man carried out the murder and dumped the body into the river. The case drew enormous publicity because of the witchcraft angle, and there were even reports of a ghost appearing on the bridge at times. Today the bridge is surrounded by a landscaped park, but the ghostly legend remains.
DIRECTIONS Located at the junction of Routes 52 and 52A in Kenoza Lake.
INFORMATION Open all year, from dawn to dusk. Admission is free. Tel. Office of Public Information at (914) 794-3000, ext. 160.
A nice place to enjoy the outdoors and a little bit of local history. There are nature trails, an interpretation site and a playground for younger children. Fishing and picnicking are allowed.
FACILITIES Snack stand located down the road at the Three Arch Inn, rest rooms.

Minisink Ford

Minisink Battleground One of the unusual and often forgotten Revolutionary War battlegrounds in the region, this site offers visitors a chance to walk along trails that tell stories of both nature and combat. In July 1779, the area's most historic battle took place when a group of American rebels were defeated by Mohawk Indians in a massacre that took almost fifty lives. In an eerie postscript, the bones of the dead were not buried until almost half a century after the battle because the area was considered a wilderness and not many people visited it. Today the 56-acre park has three walking trails from which to explore its history and woodlands. Marked trails have audio devices that tell the story of the park and written trail guides that can be picked up at the interpretive center. The **Battleground Trail** (less than one mile) depicts the tactics and strategy of a woodlands skirmish, including stops at Sentinel Rock, where the lone American defender was killed; Hospital Rock, where a rebel doctor lost his life while tending his wounded charges; and Indian Rock, which legend says was set up to commemorate the dead. The **Woodland Trail** (approximately one mile) meanders through a wetlands area, understory, second growth and fern areas. The map points out the trail's flora and describes some of the animal life you may encounter, such as the bald eagle. On the **Old Quarry/Rockshelter Trail** (2 miles), discover the logging, quarrying and Native American histories of this section through trail markers. You may also want to plan a visit to the battleground in time for the small, annual memorial service which is held each July 22 to honor those who fell in battle.

DIRECTIONS Located on County Route 168, off Route 97.
INFORMATION Open May through October, dawn to dusk. Admission is free. Tel. (914) 794-3000, ext. 160.

Plan to spend two or three hours on the walking tours and wear comfortable clothing. Detailed guidesheets provided, but you are requested to return them at the end of the tours. There is also a small interpretive area that explains the history of the battle-

field. Those who like walking through the woods on marked trails will enjoy this site. There are lots of wild blueberry bushes on the trails. Not recommended for young children.
FACILITIES *Interpretive center, picnic grove, rest rooms.*

Roebling's Suspension Bridge Built by the designer of the Brooklyn Bridge, this bridge on the Delaware River is the oldest of its kind still standing. The aqueduct was constructed because canal boats and logging rafts kept crashing into each other on the river. Roebling's solution was to build the canal above the river; the aqueduct would actually carry the canal boats over the river itself. The aqueduct was turned into a bridge crossing in the late nineteenth century, and today it still carries traffic across to Pennsylvania.
DIRECTIONS *Look for the historic marker opposite the entrance to Minisink Battleground.*

Monticello

Apollo Plaza More than two dozen factory outlets and discount shops are located here, including Bass, Jonathan Logan, Van Heusen, Campus, Arrow, Aileen and Corning. Most sell clothes, but there are outlets for perfume, jewelry and kitchenware.
DIRECTIONS *Located on lower Broadway. Watch for large sign and parking field.*
INFORMATION *Open daily.*
FACILITIES *Snack stands, rest rooms.*

Broadway Theatre This Art Deco movie theater has been restored to its days of grandeur and now features movie classics from the 1930s and 1940s. There is also a small collection of memorabilia at the Hollywood Canteen snack shop next door.
DIRECTIONS *Located at 336 Broadway.*
INFORMATION *Open daily during the summer. Tel. (914) 794-8300.*
FACILITIES *Snack bar, rest rooms.*

Monticello Raceway Recognized as one of the world's fastest half-mile tracks for harness racing, Monticello Raceway is home to many famous pacers and trotters. Because it is not as large as other harness tracks, Monticello has smaller crowds and plenty of parking. But the action at Monticello is just as heart-pounding, the crowds just as enthusiastic. The grandstand is glass enclosed and the racing goes on rain or shine. On special days you can meet the drivers with their horses. If you don't know a thing about betting, just ask your neighbor—racing fans make friends fast. Races are scheduled in the evening. You can even dine in comfort, while taking in the action from your table.

DIRECTIONS Take Route 17 to exit 104.

INFORMATION Racing year-round; post time is usually 7:30 P.M. and 1:30 P.M. on Sundays, but exact racing schedules vary so call ahead. Admission is charged. Tel. (914) 794-4100

A racing card or schedule may include a dozen races, so expect to spend about four hours for the full card. Call ahead regarding handicapped accessibility. You may also want to inquire about dress codes in the dining room and clubhouse. Children are allowed into the track, but cannot place bets.

FACILITIES Gift shop, full service restaurant, snack stands, rest rooms.

Narrowsburg

Fort Delaware Museum of Colonial History Much attention is paid to the people who settled the main cities of New York, but those who decided to take on the wilderness are often forgotten. At the Fort Delaware Museum, the daily life of the wilderness settler is explored through exhibits, crafts demonstrations and tours. The fort is a reconstruction of the original frontier settlement of Cushetunk on the Delaware River, built when stockades and stout log homes offered the only protection from hostile Indians and later English troops. The fort is made of logs and consists of a small settlement entirely surrounded by high log walls or stockades. During the tour, you will see the blockhouses—where arms and ammunition were stored—settlers' cabins, a meeting house, blacksmith shop, candle shed, loom shed and more. Outside the fort walls is a small garden, planted with crops typical of the era, as well as the stocks, which were used to discipline minor infractions of the law. Costumed guides and staff members demonstrate skills and crafts from the period, including candle making, smithing and even weaponry. Special events are scheduled throughout the season, so your visit may contain a demonstration by soldiers of the Revolution, weavers or cooks.

DIRECTIONS Located on Route 97 in Narrowsburg.

INFORMATION Open daily from the last Wednesday in June through Labor Day; weekends starting Memorial Day, from 10 A.M. to 5:30 P.M. Admission fee is charged. Tel. (914)252-6660/ 3279, or write Fort Delaware Museum, Narrowsburg, 12764.

The tour takes approximately an hour; if you have children with you, plan to spend several hours watching the craft demonstrations. Some walking and outside exhibits so dress accordingly. The museum is perfect for kids.

FACILITIES Picnic area, snack stand, gift shop, rest rooms.

North Branch

North Branch Cider Mill Still uses a turn-of-the-century cider press and is the only mill licensed in the state of New York to produce hard cider. It's a great place to watch cider being made and even sample a glass. A well-stocked roadside stand sells apples and pumpkins in the fall and stocks Christmas trees in November and December. Inside, the cider press thumps away, and there is a small snack area with homemade cakes and pies.

DIRECTIONS Located on the main street in North Branch.

INFORMATION Open daily from April through December. Tel. (914) 482-4823.

FACILITIES Snack bar, rest rooms.

Roscoe

Catskill Fly Fishing Center Fly-fishing enthusiasts will certainly find a lot to do in Sullivan County, home of some of the best trout streams in the nation; and while you're here, don't miss this small but fascinating museum. The center offers a changing exhibit of fly-fishing equipment such as rods, reels and flies, memorabilia and photographs. Special appearances by well-known anglers and craftspeople take place during the season on weekends, and the center will try to assist visitors with their questions on local fishing.

DIRECTIONS *Take Route 17 to exit 94. Located on Main Street.*
INFORMATION *Open April through September, Thurs. through Sun. Call (607) 498-5500 for information during the season, or (914) 439-4810 year-round.*
FACILITIES *Rest rooms.*

Wurtsboro

Canal Towne Emporium Originally opened in 1845 as a dry goods establishment near the Hudson and Delaware Canal, and now restored to its turn–of–the–century splendor. The fixtures, furnishings and equipment are all antiques, including the first electric coffee mill ever used in the store, advertising prints and store jars. Today the emporium sells fine furniture, handcrafted items and decorative accessories as well as books.

DIRECTIONS *Take Route 17 to exit 113 (Route 209); located at the intersection of Sullivan and Hudson streets.*
INFORMATION *Open daily except Tues. and Wed. during January and February, from 10 A.M. to 5 P.M. Tel. (914) 888-2100.*
FACILITIES *Restaurant; rest rooms next door.*

Wurtsboro Airport Established in 1927 and home to the oldest site in the United States where soaring is practiced. Soaring is done in sailplanes, motorless craft that are towed into the air and released; the pilot then sails the plane on the air currents before coming in for a landing. A 20-minute demonstration flight with a certified pilot can be arranged; if you enjoy the sport, flight instruction is available.

DIRECTIONS Located on Route 209.

INFORMATION Open daily all year, weather permitting. Tel. (914) 888-2791.

FACILITIES Rest rooms.

Activities

ANTIQUES

Searching for these treasures in Sullivan County can take you to a dusty little shop on a side road or into a full-fledged auction barn where the prices are steep and the sales are fast. Many antiques shops here are open all year, although a call before you go may save you the disappointment of discovering that the owner stepped out for the afternoon. There are dozens of shops throughout the county, but at least three areas have a large enough concentration that you can visit a few places without traveling far. But don't forget to look for the smaller shops that are often just a room in someone's house; even if the selection is limited, the dealer may be very knowledgeable about one particular antique or collectible. In Monticello, there's **Alice's Antique Supermarket**, Route 42, (914) 794-5946, which carries an always changing general line. **Gustave Antiques**, Route 42, (914) 794-1611, has lots of Art Deco items and a mixed bag from other periods, while **Caylee's Curios**, Rubin Road off Route 42, (914) 794-7493; **Cracker Barrel Jr. Antique Shoppe**, five miles south of Monticello on Route 42, (914) 794-2418; and **Dingle Daisy Antiques**, Dingle Daisy Road off Route 42, (914) 794-5939, have appealing selections of items in the general line. **Elegante**, 284 Broadway, (914) 794-2656, carries exotic jade, ivories and collector plates, while **Linnea's Antiques**, behind Miss Monticello Diner on Broadway, (914) 794-7299, specializes in dolls and doll furniture and **Yankee Barn Antique Lighting**, 199½ Broadway, behind diner, (914) 794-7299, stocks rewired antique lamps and parts. Visitors to Liberty will want to spend some time in **My Mother's Place**, 20 School Street, (914) 292-8655, or watch for the auctions run by Pamela Moore Epstein, who owns the shop (listings appear in the local newspapers). A real mix can be found at **Main Street Antiques and Collectibles**, 311 North Main Street, and **Around the Corner Antiques**, 98 North Main Street (914) 292-5080, both of which offer good general selections. Doll lovers should look for **Sunny Hills Antiques**, Corrigan Road, (914) 292-6125, where dolls, linens, collectibles and antiques tempt the buyer, as do the wares at **Treasure Box**, 342 Chestnut Street, Route 52W, (914) 292-8585, which also carries fine decorative accessories. Parksville is home to several large antiques display rooms and auctions. **Liberty Antique Warehouse**, Route 17 between exits 97 and 98 on Quickway, (914) 292-7450, announces sales in the local papers and draws dealers and buyers from all over. **Memories**, Route 17 between exits 97 and 98 (watch for signs), (914) 292-4270, is a huge shop that stocks everything from furniture to glass, as does **Quickway Antiques**, Route 17, (914) 292-3947. Three other shops to watch for if you are in those areas: **Going Hollywood**, Eldred, (914) 557-8829 (Art Deco specialties); **Malmaison**, Jeffersonville, (914) 482-5753 (French furniture and collectibles); and **Tusten Mountain Antiques**, Tusten, (914) 252-3379 (very large general line).

ARTS

An organization active in sponsoring excellent shows, exhibits and workshops, the **Delaware Valley Arts Alliance** is headquartered in the Arlington Hotel in Narrowsburg, a National Historic Register structure. Worth watching out for. Call (914) 252-7576 for information on upcoming shows. The **Sullivan County Museum Art & Cultural Center** stores and displays county memorabilia and artifacts, and also holds exhibitions of local artists' work. Tours are available; the center is located in Hurleyville and is open every day. Call (914) 434-8044 for information. A summer stock theater housed in a 120-year-old barn can only mean more fun, and that's what you'll have when you attend one of the **Forestburgh Playhouse**'s performances. Drama, comedies and musicals are all on the bill, and there is a dinner theater and cabaret format in the fall. Located in Forestburgh. Call (914) 794-1194 for schedules.

CANOEING AND RAFTING THE DELAWARE

Canoers and rafters enjoy the Delaware's rapids and eddies from spring to fall. Both the Upper Delaware (from Hancock to Port Jervis) and the main section of the river (from Port Jervis to the Chesapeake) are used for canoeing and rafting, although there are sections that are particularly good for novices and the less adventurous. As with any other water sport, a few rules and suggestions will make your trip comfortable and safe; some rental agencies have their own rules, which they will impress upon you before they hand you the equipment. Most ask that you know how to swim and that flotation gear be worn by anyone in a canoe or raft—it looks harmless, but the Delaware can reach depths of 15 feet! If you go when the weather is cooler, early spring or late fall, you must wear a wet suit or woolen clothes since even one dunking can result in hypothermia. For your own comfort take along sunscreen, lightweight sneakers, extra clothing, snacks and a hat. In general, spring canoeing is rougher, because the water is cold, fast and deep from the thawing winter snows, so you may want to wait until summer, especially if this is your first time out. Several companies rent equipment, provide a ride back to your car and a guide if necessary; trips can range from a few hours to a few days.

Hankins House, Route 97, Hankins, 12741, (914) 887-4423, arranges canoe or Jon boat (a stable, flat-bottomed boat) tours either north to Hancock or south as far as Port Jervis. The longest tours are 55 miles, the shortest about six, but you must stay at the Hankins House to rent their equipment. **Lander's Delaware River Trips**, Narrowsburg, 12764, (914) 252-3925, has excellent day trips and camping trips for canoers and rafters of all abilities. These are well-run tours, and the company also offers the fun of a Delaware River Dash and Splash race in May. **Wild and Scenic River Tours and Rentals**, Barryville, 12719, (914) 557-8783, combines river and off-river trips to make for an unforgettable weekend. They have rafts, canoes—and for the experienced, kayaks—and the tours will take you into Pennsylvania, with stops for fishing, biking and swimming. (There's even a visit to Zane Grey's Pennsylvania home.) Also in Barryville is **White Water Canoe Rentals**, River Road, (914) 557-8178, with rafts, canoes, kayaks and tubes at the ready. They offer a wide range of trips, and campsites are also available. Two canoe rental companies are in Pond Eddy: **Three River Campground**, (914) 557-6078, and **Silver Canoe Rental** (914) 856-7055, both on Route 97, Pond Eddy, 12770. Three River has campgrounds, rafts and canoes; Silver Canoe offers rafts, kayaks, canoes and guided tours.

FARMS

A once-a-year event in August sponsored by the Cooperative Extension, **Down on the Farm Day** lets you see how modern dairy farms work. The date and place vary, so call the Cooperative Extension at (914) 292-6180 for information. Located in Woodridge, **Egg University** is an egg farm that offers tours of its facilities during July and August. Call (914) 434-4519 for more information; there is a tour fee. The **Fish Hatchery**, located in DeBruce, exit 96 off Route 17 on Mongaup Road, is where more than half a million trout are spawned each year. The pools are alive with fish and there are interpretive areas. Call (914) 439-4328 for further information.

FARM STANDS AND CHRISTMAS TREE FARMS

Nothing tastes like freshly picked fruits and vegetables that still have the blush of the sun and the field on them. Harvesting begins here in late spring with asparagus and berries, and ends in the late fall with pumpkins and apples, although some stands stock local eggs, maple syrup and honey year-round.

There are also lots of small family-run farm stands that carry only one or two items and are open for only a few weeks a year. Keep an eye out for these stands, too; they often have the best of whatever it is they grow. But whether you pick the produce yourself or buy from a roadside stand, the selection and quality in Sullivan County are excellent.

Apple Pond Farming Center, Hahn Road, Callicoon Center, (914) 482-4764 (open year-round), is an organic farm that sells a variety of fruits and vegetables at its roadside stand. Since they are a little off the beaten track, you may want to combine a tour of the farm (see page 54) with a visit to the farm stand. You'll find a large, well-stocked stand at the **Gorzynski Farm**, Route 52, Cochecton Center, (914) 252-7570 (open Wed. and Sun., June through October), which offers melons, strawberries, corn, parsnips and herbs among others. At **Bridge Farm**, Fox Mountain Road, Livingston Manor, (914) 292-6299 (open June through October), you can pick your own raspberries and select from a large roadside stand that has fruits and vegetables. **Reinshagan Farms**, Hurd Road in Bethel, watch for signs, (914) 583-4558 (open May through October), lets you harvest strawberries, asparagus, cucumbers, peas, peppers and tomatoes, and the **Walter Warner Orchard**, Callicoon Center Road, Jeffersonville, (914) 482-3746 (open October and November), specializes in pick-your-own apples. For those who enjoy these showy blooms, a stop at **Regan's Iris Farm**, Fish Creek Road, Fishs Eddy, (607) 637-5399, is sure to please. There are irises, herbs and bulbs for sale in season.

Another popular harvest in Sullivan County is Christmas trees. The many "choose and cut-your-own" farms let you decide which evergreen is perfect for you, but there are some things to remember if you want to go this route. Always call ahead to make certain the farms are open for harvesting, which usually starts December 1. And since some of the farms are off the beaten track, ask for detailed directions. Unless you own a truck, you will have to tie your tree onto the roof of your car or put it in the trunk, so be sure to bring some rope and a protective blanket. Bring your own saw; while some farms provide them, they are often very dull. Dress warmly, bring a Thermos of hot chocolate and remember to pick a tree that will fit where you're planning to put it.

Theodore Nied, Jeffersonville, (914) 482-5341; **Onusz-kanycz Farm**, North Branch, (914) 482-4838; **Pine Farm Christmas Trees**, Livingston Manor, (914) 482-4149; **Jim Phillip's Country Store**, White Lake, (914) 583-4478; and **Winkle-stein Farm**, Kenoza Lake, (914) 482-4976, are open daily, usually until Christmas Eve. The following farms are open weekends only or require an appointment for weekday visits: **Weiden's Mill**, Narrowsburg (914) 252-3293; **Fred Weber Tree Farm**, Yulan, (914) 557-8440; **Robert Roberts**, Woodbourne, (914) 434-7237; and **Forever Green Christmas Tree Farm**, Westbrookville, (914) 754-8282.

FISHING

Sullivan County is a fisherman's paradise. The famed Willowemoc and Beaverkill streams produce prize-winning trout each year, in addition to being recognized as the cradle of American fly-fishing. The Delaware River offers its rich bounty to the patient angler, as do Mongaup Creek and Russell Brook. Then there are the icy lakes of the county, with such entrancing names as Kiamesha, Kenoza, Swan and Waneta. There are literally hundreds of fine fishing areas in Sullivan County, and too little space here to do them all justice. The following general information, however, will assist you in finding the perfect spot to enjoy a rocky stream, a sunny sky and just maybe a record trout.

The county's streams and rivers are famed for their trout, including brook, brown and rainbow, but bass, pickerel, walleye, muskies (muskellunge) and shad are also plentiful. All streams on state lands are open to the public; other streams often have public fishing rights through state easements, which are indicated by signs. New York State does require fishing licenses for persons over 16, as well as special reservoir permits. (Call the New York City Board of Water Supply for specific information.) There are strict fishing seasons for certain species, and you could be in for a heavy fine if you disobey the law, so be sure to check out the seasons before you fish; the brochure that you receive when you get your license should answer all your questions. Licenses may be obtained at many sites throughout the county, including village and town offices, sporting goods stores and fishing tackle shops. Specific information on fly-fishing is found at the **Catskill Fly Fishing Center** in Livingston Manor, (914) 439-4810, and Roscoe (607) 498-5500 (see page 60).

The **Beaverkill** is one of the largest known trout streams in the world, and may be reached from Roscoe, Livingston Manor, Lew Beach, Beaverkill and Rockland. Fly-fishing equipment may be purchased in Roscoe at **The Beaverkill Angler**, Broad Street, (607) 498-5194; **Country Junction Mall**, (607) 498-5194; **Jay Dreher Supply**, (607) 498-4333; and **The Little Store**, (607) 498-5553. **Walter Dette** on Cottage Street, (607) 498-4991, will tie some flies for you. The **Willowemoc Creek** is found between Roscoe and Livingston Manor along Old Route 17; **Mongaup Creek** runs from Livingston Manor to Mongaup Pond; the **Neversink River** is at Claryville on county Routes 19 and 15; and you can pick up the Delaware River at East Branch on Route 17. Among the lakes are **Kenoza** (Route 52, Kenoza Lake Village), **Swinging Bridge** (Route 17B, Mongaup Valley), **Swan Lake** (Route 55, between Liberty and Kauneonga Lake), **White Lake** (junction of Routes 17B and 55), **Waneta Lake** (county Route 151 in Deckertown), **Cable Lake** (Route 17 northwest of Roscoe, end of Russell Brook) and **Kiamesha Lake** (Route 42, Kiamesha). There are two preserves in Sullivan County that allow fishing without a license, but there are admission fees here, as well as a charge based on the number of pounds of fish caught. For information, call **Eldred Preserve** (914) 557-8316, and **Lakeside Fishing Preserve** (914) 439-9839. County and town parks also allow fishing, among them **Town of Thompson Park**, north of Monticello, (914) 796-3161; **Hanofee Park**, Route 52, Liberty, (914) 292-7690; **Lake Superior Park**, Dr. Duggan Road, between Routes 17B and 55 in Bethel, (914) 794-3000, ext. 217; and the **Stone Arch Bridge Historical Park**, Route 52 near Kenoza Lake. Those who enjoy the bracing thrills of ice fishing will want to write to the **Roscoe-Rockland Chamber of Commerce**, Box 443, Roscoe, 12766, for specific information and conditions. Spring and summer fishing conditions along the Beaverkill and Willowemoc rivers can be obtained by calling a 24-hour hotline at (607) 498-5350, from April 1 to July 1.

SCENIC DRIVES

With its more than 1,000 square miles of countryside, just about any drive through Sullivan County will reveal exquisite views that change with the seasons. The earliest blush of spring may be enjoyed by driving along any back road, or even on the "Quickway" (Route 17); summer is lush and lazy anywhere you turn; fall splashes the meadows and forests with color; and winter here can be lovely in spite of the cold.

If you want to travel the southernmost section of Sullivan County, and see some spectacular river and mountain scenery, start your tour in Monticello. From there head south on Route 42 to Sackett Lake Road (you will go through a town called Squirrel Corners), keep south to Forestburgh Road where you will make a right. This is the reservoir area of Mongaup Falls, a good spot to sight bald eagles. At Route 97, head west along the river drive known as Hawk's Nest; you will pass Minisink Park and Roebling Aqueduct (see pages 56–57). At Narrowsburg (home of Fort Delaware; see pages 58–59) head north on Route 52 to Liberty, where you can pick up Route 17 back to Monticello if you desire.

Here's a second drive which will take you past some of the few remaining covered bridges in the county. Begin at Livingston Manor (exit 96 on Route 17) and turn onto Old Route 17 for the Vantran covered bridge, one of the few existing bridges constructed in the lattice-truss and Queen-post styles, built in 1860. Go back to Livingston Manor, and follow the signs east from town along DeBruce Road to Willowemoc, which has a covered bridge that was built in 1860 in Livingston Manor, then cut in half and moved to its present site in 1913. From Willowemoc take Pole Road to West Branch Road, which leads into Claryville. The Halls Mills Covered Bridge, built in 1912, is on Claryville Road over the Neversink River.

Head south from Claryville to Route 55, then west back to Liberty.

Another sight worth making time to see is **Tomsco Falls**, often called the "Niagara of Sullivan County." These spectacular waterworks are lots of fun to see, especially on a hot day. Located off Route 209 in Mountaindale, there are daily tours of the area, in July and August, Sunday tours in May, June, September and October. Call (914) 434-6065/7774 for more information.

Other roads that offer scenic views include Route 209, Routes 55 and 55A. Route 17, also called the Quickway, is the main north-south road through Sullivan County and provides access to most of the region's scenic areas.

SKIING

While downhill skiing in Sullivan does not revolve around huge resorts like Hunter or Gore, it does have a few centers that offer lots of fun for all ages. **Big Vanilla at Davos**, Route 17 exit 109, Woodridge, (914) 434-5321, has twenty-three trails and slopes that are serviced by nine lifts. Snow-making capabilities keep the action going all season, and if you don't know how to ski or you don't have equipment, the school and ski shop will take good care of you. There is also a snack center with a view of the surrounding mountains, and a lodge where you can relax after a day on the slopes. **Holiday Mountain**, Route 17 exit 107 at Bridgeville, (914) 796-3161, has both day and night skiing, on weekdays and weekends, and the slopes can be covered with man-made snow if nature doesn't live up to her promises. The longest run here is 3,500 feet, and the vertical drop of the area is 400 feet, so this is a good place for both beginners and experts to try out their skills. A ski shop, snack stand and trailer parking are all available, although a call ahead is recommended if you plan to stay the night.

There are so many places to ski cross-country in Sullivan County that you would have to spend several winters here in order to try all the trails. Many local parks allow skiing for free, but often the trails are not groomed, nor are there nearby rentals available. At the large area resorts, some trails are open for a fee to day visitors, but if you are uncertain of a hotel's policy, it is recommended that you call ahead; policies may also change from year to year. **Big Vanilla at Davos** and **Holiday Mountain** offer cross-country skiing, as does the 160-acre **Town of Thompson Park**, Old Liberty Road, 4½ miles past Monticello Post Office, (914) 796-3161 (open dawn to dusk, no rentals); 110-acre **Hanofee Park**, off Route 52 east on Infirmary Road in Liberty, (914) 292-7690 (open 10 A.M. to 4 P.M., rentals and fee, heated trail hut on weekends); and 260-acre **Walnut Mountain Park**, Walnut Mountain, Liberty, (914) 292-7690 (rentals, fee, heated trail hut on weekends).

Where to Eat

Bernie's Holiday Restaurant (off *Route 17, Rock Hill, (914) 796-3333)* The largest restaurant in Sullivan County and also one of the best. Try visiting on "gourmet Friday" for a truly sumptuous meal. The specialty here is Chinese and American cuisine and the Cajun dishes are also first-rate. Children are welcome; special menu provided.

OPEN *Sun. through Thurs., 5 to 10 P.M. and Fri. until 11 P.M.; Sat. open 2 to 11 P.M. Closed Mondays, October through May.*

Eldred Preserve (P.O. *Box 111, Route 55, Eldred, (914) 557-8316)* The dining rooms here overlook three stream-fed ponds stocked with rainbow, brown, brook, tiger and golden trout, as well as 2,000 acres of unspoiled forest. Needless to say, the specialty here is trout caught from the preserve's ponds. The fish is served many ways including smoked. All baking is done on the premises. There is also a twenty-one-room motel (all rooms have private bathrooms) and two private lakes, which are open for bass fishing and boat rentals. Guests may enjoy the tennis courts and outdoor pool in the warm weather, and cross-country skiing and ice fishing in the winter. Children are welcome; special menu available.

OPEN *Daily for dinner from 6 P.M.*

Fort Westbrook Inn *(Route 209, Westbrookville, (914) 754-8381)* A New York State landmark building constructed in 1750, now the only fort and oldest house in Sullivan County. The walls are three feet thick and the original planking survives in the dining room. The building served as a trading post and tavern during the Revolutionary War, and it is said that many of the era's notables, including Benjamin Franklin, stopped here. Specialties include roast duckling, stuffed trout, chicken Kiev, roast loin of pork and sauerbraten. The kitchen is run by European-trained chef-owner Fred Kelly. All entrées accompanied by an assorted appetizer platter, soup, spinach salad, a country-style vegetable casserole and potato. Not recommended for children.

OPEN *Wed. through Sun. from 5 P.M. Closed Mon. & Tues. Reservations suggested.*

Ginger's Country Restaurant *(Route 97, Long Eddy, (914) 887-4528)* The building that houses this charming, old-fashioned restaurant was once a blacksmith shop and part of the forge is still there. Specialties include roast duckling, New York strip steak, homemade lasagna and a hot and cold buffet, available at every meal. Nearby Santa's Workshop and Lollipopland will enchant the kids. Children are welcome; meals half-price.

OPEN *Daily from May 1 to January 1, from 8 A.M. to midnight.*

La Mingotiere *(Route 17 [exit 112], Wurtsboro Hills, (914) 888-9912)* An excellent Italian restaurant serving dinner only.

The Oak Table *(DeBruce Rd. [off Route 17], Livingston Manor, (914) 439-3999)* Tasty Continental cuisine is served here. Open from April 1 through November 30.

Old Homestead Restaurant *(Bridgeville Rd., Monticello, (914) 794-8973)* Enjoy country dining at an old stagecoach stop on the Cochecton-Newburgh Turnpike. This 35-year-old restaurant specializes in steak and lobster, and all baked goods are made on the premises. There is an old covered bridge over the Neversink just outside. Children are welcome; special menu provided.

OPEN *Dinner—Mon. through Fri., 4:30 to 9:30 P.M. and Sat. until 10:30 P.M.; Sun., 4 to 9:30 P.M.*

The Orchard Inn *(Glen Spey Rd., Glen Spey [off Route 9], (914) 856-8300)* Decorated with brass chandeliers and American art and antiques. Specialties of the house include game pie, veal Orchard Inn and riverhouse shrimp. A pleasant place to enjoy dinner in the country. Children are welcome; special menu provided.

OPEN *Dinner—Mon., Wed. through Sat., 5 to 10 P.M.; Sun., 1 to 9 P.M. Closed Tues.*

The Repast *(Sullivan St., Wurtsboro, (914) 888-4448)* This small, elegantly appointed Victorian-decor restaurant features fine country fare. Lunch specialties offered are crepes, quiches, chef's salad, baked Brie and croissant sandwiches; for dinner, veal saltimbocca with pesto, chicken with almonds and banana liqueur, stuffed trout, duck à l'orange, prime ribs and a host of daily specials. All breads and desserts are baked on the premises. Children are welcome at lunch when a special menu is provided; discouraged at dinner.

OPEN *lunch—daily, 11 A.M. to 3 P.M.; dinner—Thurs. through Sun., 5 to 9 P.M.*

Where to Stay

Beaverkill Valley Inn *(Beaverkill Rd., Lew Beach, 12753, (914) 439-4844)* This national historic site, built in 1893 and restored in recent years by Laurance Rockefeller, offers a perfect retreat for those who love the outdoors. Located within the Catskill Forest Preserve, near hiking trails and some of the best fishing anywhere, the inn also has tennis courts and an indoor pool. During the summer you can bike, hike or fish and in the winter, cross-country ski. Open all year. Twelve rooms with private bath; eight with shared facilities.

Chez Reaux (229C Budd Rd., Woodbourne, 12788, (914) 434-1780) This newly renovated house on 12½ acres with views of the Shawangunks, is surrounded by pine forest. In warmer weather there's tennis and volleyball. Continental breakfast consisting of fresh breads, muffins, cheeses, cereals, fruits, tea and a special house coffee. Open all year. Five rooms with private baths; fifteen with shared bathrooms. Children must be 12 or over.

Dai Bosatsu Zendo (Beecher Lake, Lew Beach, 12753, (914) 439-4566) This 10-year-old Zen Buddhist monastery on 1,400 wooded acres overlooking Beecher Lake, which at 2,700 feet above sea level is the highest lake in the Catskills, is open to visitors. Harriet Beecher Stowe lived here for a time and is said to have written parts of *Uncle Tom's Cabin* here. There are no TVs, phones or recreational facilities, but the rooms in the guest house are carpeted and comfortable. Some have fireplaces. The cost per night is exceedingly reasonable and includes three vegetarian meals (breakfast, lunch and dinner). Open during July and August only. There are eight rooms; one with private bath, four more share two baths and three share one bathroom.

DeBruce Country Inn (286A DeBruce Rd. [off Route 17], DeBruce, 12758, (914) 439-3900) This inn, constructed at the turn of the century, is located within the Catskill Forest Preserve and on the banks of the Willowemoc Stream known for its great fishing. A restaurant serves three meals a day. The Pilgrim pumpkin soup, stuffed trout, quail and veal with artichokes and potatoes are some of the specialties. The Dry Fly piano lounge is the perfect place to unwind at the end of the day. Open all year. Two suites have private bathrooms; ten rooms share five bathrooms.

The Inn at Lake Joseph *(County Rd. 108 [off Route 42], P.O. Box 81, Forestburgh, 12777, (914) 791-9506)* A nineteenth-century Victorian mountain retreat nestled in the Catskills and surrounded by acres of forest. Built by a prosperous business-man, he then sold the house and it became the summer retreat of Cardinals Hayes and Spellman. A private, spring-fed lake offers boating and fishing. There are two tennis courts as well. This is a secluded spot where every detail is attended to, making it one of the country's best inns. The dining room is open to the public by advance reservation only. Open all year. The mansion has six fireplaces and each guest room has a canopied bed, Persian rugs, lacy linens and fine antiques. Six rooms with private bath; three share a bathroom. The carriage house is perfect for families, with its own library, TV and stereo.

Lanza's Country Inn *(Shandelee Rd., R.D. 2, Box 446, Livingston Manor, 12758, (914) 439-5070)* A 75-year-old building with a tap room and restaurant downstairs houses this family-owned and -operated inn. Guest rooms—each is different—are furnished with period pieces and some have canopied beds. The Continental breakfast includes homemade breads, jams, juice and coffee. A lake nearby for swimming, fishing and boating, and five miles of cross-country ski trails. An optional modified American plan is available for those staying two or more nights; it includes a full breakfast as well as dinner. Open all year. Seven rooms, all with private baths. Children over 12 only.

New Age Health Farm *(Route 55, Neversink, 12765, (914) 985-2221)* A great place to stay, especially for those on special diets.

Tennanah Lakeshore Lodge (*on Tennanah Lake, Roscoe, 12776, (607) 498-4900*) A beautiful, full-accommodation spa.

The Vegetarian Hotel (*Box 457, Woodridge, 12789, (914) 434-4455*) Open from May through September.

Ulster County

Settled in the seven-teenth century, Ulster County is a lesson in the successful inter-weaving of two cultures. As in New York City, first the Dutch and later the English found their way upriver to the lush farmlands along the Hudson. Snug, well-built homes were constructed of stone, brick and wood, many of which still stand today and are open to the public. Ulster was not always blessed with peace and wealth, however; it was the scene of conflict during the American Revolution, when the city of Kingston was burned by the advancing British, and spies were hanged in outlying apple trees. But the area was rebuilt through the years, and the outer regions of the country grew so that today Ulster is a study in contrasts. Businesses have settled alongside farms and artists' colonies thrive among boutiques. A visit here will lead you through the stockade area of Kingston, where the names of the streets sound suspiciously like those in seventeenth-century New Amsterdam, and the strong Dutch influence remains.

The outdoors here offer the sportsperson a chance to fish,

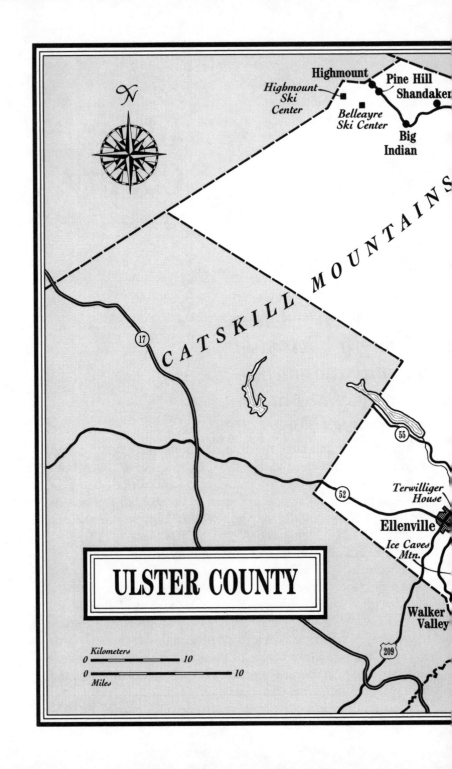

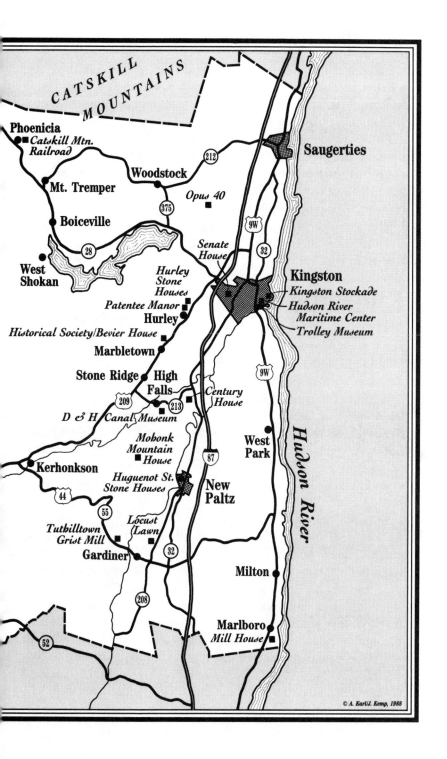

CATSKILL MOUNTAINS

Phoenicia
■ Catskill Mtn.
Railroad

Woodstock
212

Mt. Tremper
Opus 40

375

Saugerties

9W

Boiceville

28

32

West
Shokan

Senate
House

Hurley
Stone
Houses

Kingston
Kingston Stockade
Hudson River
Maritime Center
Trolley Museum

Patentee Manor

Hurley

Historical Society/Bevier House

Marbletown

Stone Ridge ● High
Falls

209

213

9W

Century
House

D & H Canal Museum

Mohonk
Mountain
■ House

West
Park

Kerhonkson

87

Huguenot St.
Stone Houses

New
Paltz

44

55

Tuthilltown
Grist Mill

Locust
Lawn

Gardiner

32

Milton

208

Marlboro
Mill House

52

Hudson River

© A. Karl/J. Kemp, 1988

ski and hike in mountains that it's said are still haunted by the witches and goblins of centuries past. Or stop at a farm stand to sample an apple fresh off the tree or spend some time in a field picking ripe, juicy raspberries. Ulster County is mountainous, flat, river-lined and forested by turns; there's enough here to keep visitors busy for another century or so. The county is easy to travel, with several major roads and enough off-the-beaten-track byways to please even the most-seasoned traveler. Bring a camera when you visit, because the seasons in Ulster are dramatic and changing, with spring giving way to summer overnight, and winter making guest appearances as late as April.

Ellenville

Ice Caves Mountain and Sam's Point These are Registered Natural Landmarks, areas that have been set aside as exceptional examples of American natural history. The park and lookout point are circled by a driving road that offers unparalleled views of Ulster and the surrounding counties, but it is at Sam's Point that you will want to get out your camera and binoculars. Formed by glaciers, the point is a little less than half a mile above sea level and offers a flat viewing area where you can spot five states on a clear day. There are safety walls here, but you'll feel suspended over the valleys and roads that stretch out below; if you are afraid of heights, this stop should be avoided. Sam's Point supposedly got its name from a trapper who, fleeing an Indian war party, jumped over the edge and landed safely in some trees. Take the nature trails that lead to such natural formations as Cupid's Rock, Moss Pool and the Fabulous Snow Springs. The trails are well-marked and equipped with handrails. Tours are self-guided through the use of well-placed signs and brochures. A walk will take you past chasms and tunnels, around incredible balanced rocks and into lighted caves with remarkable mineral formations. Explore at your own pace while choosing the number of stops you want to make.

DIRECTIONS *Located on Route 52 in Ellenville.*
INFORMATION *Open April 1 to November 1, 9 A.M. till dark.
Admission fee charged.*
   *The walking and driving tour will take at least 1½ hours. Wear
comfortable shoes and bring a sweater if the day isn't very hot.
Great for children.*
FACILITIES *Picnic areas, gift shop, rest rooms.*

Gardiner

**Locust Lawn, Terwilliger House, Little Wings Wildlife
Sanctuary** These three sites are within minutes of each other,
and all are administered by the Huguenot Historical Society of
New Paltz. Locust Lawn, a mansion in the Federal style, was
built in 1814 by Colonel Josiah Hasbrouck, a Revolutionary
War veteran. The elegant white mansion still houses a fine
collection of eighteenth- and nineteenth-century furniture and
decorative arts, as well as several portraits by the American
itinerant painter, Ammi Phillips. Since Locust Lawn remained
in the Hasbrouck family until the 1950s when it was donated
to the Historical Society, many of the original furnishings
remain. Also on the site are outbuildings typical of a farm of
that era, and visitors can see the carriage house, smokehouse
and slaughterhouse. One rare artifact found here is the great
ox cart that was used to transport supplies to the beleaguered
army at Valley Forge.
   Down the road from Locust Lawn stands the Terwilliger
House, built in 1738 and left almost untouched over the last
two and a half centuries. This is a fine example of the architectural style used by the area's Dutch and French Huguenot
settlers. Built of stone, with a center hall and great fireplace,
the house has been furnished in the style of the era. Outside,
visitors may follow a cleared path over the Plattekill Brook to
a small graveyard where members of the Terwilliger family
and their slaves are buried. In the Little Wings Wildlife Sanctuary, several nature trails are ready to be explored, and more
than thirty species of birds have been sighted on and near the

refuge's pond. The magnificent wildflower garden is especially lovely in the spring, when lady's slippers, Dutchman's-breeches and wake-robin bloom.

> DIRECTIONS *Locust Lawn and the Terwilliger House are located on Route 32, outside of Gardiner. The Little Wings Wildlife Sanctuary is located just west of Locust Lawn on Jenkinstown Road, off Route 32.*
>
> INFORMATION *Locust Lawn and the Terwilliger House are open Memorial Day through September; tours available. Little Wings Wildlife Sanctuary gives tours by reservation only. Call (914) 255-1889, or write Huguenot Historical Society, P.O. Box 339, New Paltz, 12561.*
>
> FACILITIES *Picnic tables, rest rooms.*

Tuthilltown Grist Mill The mill was built in 1788 by Selah Tuthill, who used the power of the Shawangunk River to grind wheat and corn into flour. Today the mill is still in use and has changed little over the last two centuries. The owners grow much of their own grains on a 400-acre farm, but what makes the mill unique is that it is the only one in the United States allowed to grind the flour used by Orthodox Jews at Passover. Visitors can enjoy a guided tour and will want to take home some of the mill's flours, which are sold in the shop under the name "Falling Waters."

> DIRECTIONS *Located 500 feet south of the intersection of Route 44/55 and the Albany Post Road.*
>
> INFORMATION *Call (914) 255-5695 for tour information; hours may vary.*
>
> FACILITIES *Gift shop, rest rooms.*

Widmark Honey Farm They offer bears and honey, but here the bears have been raised as family pets and will entertain you with wrestling, climbing and bicycling antics. A perfect outing for anyone with small children to amuse; adults will also enjoy the displays of beehives and apiary equipment. A retail shop sells lots of varieties of honey and local farm goods.

DIRECTIONS Located on Route 44/55 in Gardiner.
INFORMATION Bear shows given throughout the summer and fall; tours of the apiary all year. Call for hours. Admission fee charged. Tel. (914) 255-6400
   Plan to spend at least an hour here when the bears are entertaining or if you take a honey tour.
FACILITIES Rest rooms.

High Falls

Delaware and Hudson Historical Society Museum This museum is dedicated to the history and lore of the great Delaware and Hudson Canal. Built in the early nineteenth century, the canal was used to ship coal from the mines in Pennsylvania to the factories of New York; later, cement was shipped south to be used in bridges and skyscrapers. The designer of the D&H Canal was also responsible for the Erie Canal, and the locks, basins and dams were engineering wonders of the era. In the museum, visitors will be able to see a bird's-eye view of the canal and its original workings, as well as a look at what life was like on the canal boats during the six-day trip. While you are in the museum, ask for a copy of the self-guided tour of Locks 16 to 20, then head across the road for the 45-minute walk. Along the tour you will see excellent examples of stonework, snubbing posts, weirs, locks and loading slips.
   DIRECTIONS Take Route 213 to High Falls, turn right on Mohonk Road; the museum is on the left and the locks are across the road.
   INFORMATION Open May through October; hours vary. Admission is free. Write to Delaware and Hudson Historical Society Museum, Mohonk Road, High Falls, 12440, or call (914) 687-9311.
   Allow at least an hour for the museum and the walking tour.
FACILITIES Rest rooms.

High Falls Grist Mill Privately owned and opened only by appointment, but if you are particularly interested in American mills, it's worth trying to arrange a tour. This 1765 mill was carefully restored by the present owners, who worked with European craftsmen in order to maintain the integrity of the restoration.

INFORMATION *Write to Clarence Hansen, High Falls, 12440, or call (914) 687-7385.*

Highmount

Belleayre Mountain October Festival Held each Columbus Day Weekend at Belleayre Ski Center in Highmount. The fun goes on all day and includes fall foliage sky rides, German bands, authentic German food and beer, crafts and demonstrations, and a ski swap and sale. The festival is well-run and keeps growing in popularity every year; so get there early and bring an appetite.

DIRECTIONS *Take Route 28 west to Highmount. Follow signs.*
INFORMATION *There is ample parking and courtesy buses from the parking lots to the gates. Admission fee charged.*
FACILITIES *Food, rest rooms.*

Hurley

Hurley Patentee Manor This National Historic Landmark is a combination of a Dutch cottage built in 1696 and a 1745 Georgian manor house. The manor was the center of the Hurley Patent, a 96,000-acre land grant that included the land between Woodstock and New Paltz and that today has been reduced to the 5 acres surrounding the house. On a visit to Hurley Patentee, the seventeenth-century Hudson Valley really comes alive. The rooms boast walls 45 inches thick! Although the house is privately owned and maintained, the owners have restored most of it to its original condition, and have furnished the rooms with antiques of the period, including a chair once owned by Sir William Johnston and an eighteenth-century desk with a secret drawer. The basement of the manor has one of the few indoor animal pens still in existence, and is also the display area for Hurley Patentee Lighting, a company that specializes in handwrought reproduction lighting pieces. The owners of the Manor are friendly, enthusiastic and well versed in local history, so don't miss out on this tour. Children will find the attic museum to be especially interesting.

DIRECTIONS Take Route 209 south to Hurley; follow old Route 209 to the manor.

INFORMATION Open July 15 to Labor Day; call ahead for tour schedule. Admission fee charged.

The tour takes about 30 minutes, and there are several flights of stairs to be climbed.

FACILITIES Rest rooms.

Hurley Stone Houses The village of Hurley was established in 1651 by Dutch and Huguenot settlers, who built wooden homes along the Esopus Creek. After a short war with the Esopus Indians resulted in the burning of much of the settlement, the homes were replaced with stone structures, twenty-five of which are still standing. Hurley was a hotbed of activity during the Revolution, serving as the state capital when Kingston was burned and offering a resting place for troops and a meeting place for spies. Later a stop on the Underground Railroad which helped slaves flee north to Canada, Hurley was also the childhood home of the activist and abolitionist Sojourner Truth. Visitors can still walk around the town and see the largest group of stone houses remaining in the country. Although the homes are open only one day a year (the second Saturday in July), Hurley is still worth a walk in any season; many of the houses have historic plaques outside that tell something of their history and lore. Along Main Street, look for the **Polly Crispell Cottage**, which was once used as a blacksmith shop; it was built in 1735. This house was also equipped with a "witch catcher," a set of iron spikes set into the chimney, presumably to discourage witches (or birds) from flying in. The **Jan Van Deusen House** became the temporary seat of New York's government in 1777, and a secret room was used to store important documents. The outer door is set off by the work of an early Hurley black-smith and a date stone is visible. Stop in at the Van Deusen Antiques Shop, which is now located in back of the house, and chat with the owners while you look over their fine stock of furniture and decorative pieces. Also on Main Street: the **Dumond House**, which was used to confine a convicted British spy before he was hanged across the road on an apple tree, the **Parsonage,** built in 1790, and the **Elmendorf House** (once the Half Moon Tavern), built in the late 1600s. A burial ground can be found between Crispell and Elmendorf build-ings. If you drive west on Main Street, follow the Hurley Avenue Extension to the left, and you will see several more stone buildings.

On the second Saturday in July, Hurley opens its privately owned stone houses for tours. The houses have all been re-stored, and the owners provide historical commentary and sometimes practical advice on living in an old house. The Reformed Church hosts a country fair the same day, and there are shuttle buses to some of the outlying homes.

A corn festival is held in mid-August and celebrates the local sweet corn industry. Held on the grounds of the Reformed Church, the festival offers lots of crafts and lots of corn. Fresh ears with butter are cooked by the thousands, and the cafeteria serves everything from corn chowder to corn bread.

DIRECTIONS Take exit 19 off the N.Y. Thruway to Route 209 south; Hurley is the first exit on the right.

INFORMATION Walking tour map of Hurley may be obtained by writing to the Hurley Heritage Society, Box 1661, Hurley, 12443. Old Stone Day tours begin at 11 A.M. Call (914) 331-7374 for further information.

Kingston

Hudson River Maritime Center and Rondout Landing For almost two centuries, the Hudson River was a major water highway between New York and Albany. One of the ports of call along the way was the Rondout Landing in Kingston, once a bustling area of boat yards and rigging lofts that echoed with steam whistles and brass ship's bells. But when shipping on the Hudson fell into decline, so did the fortunes of the Rondout; then, in 1980, the Hudson River Maritime Center was opened with the goal of preserving the heritage of the river. The center has since restored several riverside buildings as well as some historic vessels, and visitors can now see a working part of the Hudson's legacy. There is also an exhibit hall which displays changing shows of marine art, and a huge boat shop and rigging loft. Here is where ships are built or restored, and watching a ship being rigged is like stepping back in history. The craftspeople are fascinating and will answer just about any question regarding Hudson River boating and sailing. Outside is an always-changing display of river vessels. The site is also the home of the Hudson River Antique and Classic Boat Society; the 1899 steam tug, *Mathilda*, is docked here, as is the cruise boat, *Marion T. Budd*. Visitors to the landing have also included the presidential yacht, *Sequoia*, and the sailing ships *Clearwater* and *Woody Guthrie*. Special weekend festivals are held throughout the year, including the Clearwater's Pumpkin Festival, sailing regattas and tours of the Kingston Lighthouse. A shad bake was once a popular way to celebrate the coming of spring to the region, and the Hudson River Maritime Center has revived this May tradition. The fish are grilled outdoors, and there is plenty to eat, drink and see. Call for date.

DIRECTIONS Located at the foot of Broadway in Kingston; N.Y. Thruway exit 19.

INFORMATION Open from May to October—Wed. through Sun., noon to 5 P.M. Admission fee is charged. Tel. (914) 338-0071, or write Hudson River Maritime Center, Rondout Landing, Kingston, 12401

Plan to spend at least 1 hour touring museum and viewing boats.
FACILITIES Gift shop, rest rooms.

Kingston Urban Cultural Park Visitors' Center

Kingston Urban Cultural Park Visitors' Center Urban cultural parks were designated by New York State as a way of preserving and developing urban settings with special historic and cultural interest. The center offers orientation displays which cover the entire Kingston area. Directions for self-guided walking tours are available at the center, and guided tours may be arranged by appointment.

DIRECTIONS Located at 308 Clinton Avenue, Kingston, with a satellite office at the Maritime Museum.

INFORMATION If you are spending time in Kingston, set aside several hours for a tour, the city is full of lovely architectural styles. Call (914) 331-9506 to arrange a guided tour.

FACILITIES Rest rooms.

Old Dutch Church Organized in 1659, the Reformed Protestant Dutch Church of Kingston has served the people of the area continuously since then. The present building was built in 1852; its bluestone exterior is in the Renaissance Revival style, and the windows are Tiffany. Local tradition has it that the bell was cast from silver and copper items donated by the congregation and that one of the church's earlier steeples may have been haunted by a goblin. Inside you will see several bronze statues, as well as memorabilia from the 1600s onward. Outside take time to walk through the churchyard, and view the fine examples of early gravestone art. In spring, thousands of yellow and red tulips planted in honor of the Netherlands line the church walks.

DIRECTIONS Located at 272 Wall Street in the uptown area of Kingston.

INFORMATION Tours may be arranged by calling (914) 338-6759, or writing P.O. Box 3006, Kingston, 12401.

FACILITIES None.

Senate House When the New York State government was forced to leave New York City during the Revolution, they sought safety upstate. The house in which the men met was built in the seventeenth century by a Dutch settler, Wessel Ten Broeck, and was partially burned by the British in 1777. Today, after numerous nineteenth- and twentieth-century additions and changes, the house has been restored to reflect its part in history. Visitors can see several rooms, including the kitchen, with its huge fireplace and dozens of tools for preparing meals, and the meeting room where the state constitution was hammered out. Outside there is a lovely rose garden, worth a special trip in June. A second building on the site, the **Loughran House**, was added in 1927; displays there explain the part New York played in the Revolution through the use of artifacts, maps and illustrations. One room of the museum is given over to the works of Kingston native John Vanderlyn, an artist who was considered one of the finest painters in nineteenth-century America. Upstairs there are portraits by the nineteenth-century folk artist, Ammi Phillips, as well as local memorabilia. The Senate House and Loughran House celebrate the Christmas holidays in traditional style.

DIRECTIONS *The museums are located at 312 Fair Street, Kingston.*

INFORMATION *Open April through December—Wed. through Sat., 10 A.M. to 5 P.M. and Sun., 1 to 5 P.M. Admission is free. Tel. (914) 338-2786.*

Guided tour of the Senate House takes 20 minutes; plan on spending at least 30 minutes in the Loughran House. Call ahead if wheelchair accessibility is a concern; the staff will make special arrangements.

FACILITIES *Information desk, rest rooms.*

Trolley Museum For anyone who remembers the ring of a trolley bell or the rolling ride of self-propelled car, this is the place to stop. Housed in an old trolley shed along the Rondout, the museum has several antique trolley cars as well as displays that chronicle their history.

DIRECTIONS *Take Broadway south to the Rondout; follow the signs to the museum at 89 East Strand.*

INFORMATION *Trolley rides available along the Hudson River from Memorial Day to Columbus Day. Call (914) 331-3399 for the schedule.*

FACILITIES *None.*

Marbletown

Bevier House Built in the late 1680s, this stone house now serves as the headquarters of the Ulster County Historical Society, and it's a treasure trove of odd collections and memorabilia. Once a single-story Dutch farmhouse, much of the present structure was added during the last three centuries. Throughout the house you will see fine Hudson Valley Dutch and Victorian furniture in addition to the tool and kitchenware collections, ceramic pottery from an early factory in Poughkeepsie, portraits and decorative accessories. The Bevier House has avoided becoming a very formal museum so things are not always well identified, but the house is fun to explore and the tour guides are willing to spend time with visitors.

DIRECTIONS *Located six miles south of Kingston on Route 209.*
INFORMATION *Open June through September—Wed. through Sun., 1 to 5 P.M.*
FACILITIES *Rest rooms.*

Marlboro

Mill House Built in the early eighteenth century by a Sephardic immigrant and fur trader, Luis Moses Gomez, Mill House is the oldest Jewish residence on the American continent. Gomez traded with the Esopus Indians for furs and farmed land in the area; as his grain production increased over the years, he added a grist mill beside the stream that would become known as Jew's Creek. The large, handsome house boasts walls that are almost three feet thick, as well as a second-story addition that was built by an officer in Washington's army. The interior of the house still retains the original fireplaces Gomez built, along with some antique furnishings and Judaica.

DIRECTIONS *Located off Route 9W on Mill House Road in Marlboro.*
INFORMATION *Restoration is in progress, but tours of the site can be arranged by writing to The Mill House, Mill House Road,*

Marlboro, 12542, or by calling (914) 236-3126. Tours must be arranged at least three weeks in advance, so plan ahead if you want to stop here.
FACILITIES Rest rooms.

New Paltz

Snyder House Sits directly across from the old Delaware and Hudson Canal, which was used to transport shipments of cement. There are ruins of the old kilns on the Snyder property, and the house is open for tours, although the gracious interior is furnished with reproduction antiques. It is the carriage house that is worth the stop, because the original owner was a collector of old sleighs and carriages; there are more than twenty, dating from the 1820s to the 1940s. Phaetons, wagons, cutters and sleighs are all here and in beautiful condition, something rarely seen outside of larger museums.

DIRECTIONS Take Route 32 north from New Paltz to Route 213; watch for the signs.
INFORMATION Tours by appointment only, from June through September. Admission charged; no children allowed. Call (914) 658-9900 or (914) 255-1660 for more information.
FACILITIES Rest rooms.

Huguenot Street's Stone Houses In 1677, a group of twelve Huguenot men purchased almost 40,000 acres of land from the Esopus Indians and began the settlement which was referred to as "die Pfalz," after an area in the Rhineland Palatinate of Europe. By 1692 the original log huts were being replaced by stone houses, several of which still stand today as a result of the efforts of the Huguenot Historical Society. A trip to New Paltz offers a unique chance to see what life was like three centuries ago in upper middle-class homes. The walking tour begins with **Deyo Hall** and **Grimm Gallery**, which were, respectively, a glass factory and private home before they were combined into the orientation center. Visitors here will see a large collection of local artifacts, including furniture, costumes and portraits from the area. All the buildings are owned by the historical society, and many still have the original furnishings. At the **Abraham Hasbrouck House** (1692), the dark rooms include a cellar-kitchen, which was the heart of village social life, and a built-in Dutch bed. Other houses of the period include the **Bevier-Elting House**, which is distinguished by a long well-sweep and covered walk for the convenience of the ladies; the **Freer House**, with its mow door to make moving provisions into the attic easier; and the **Dubois Fort**, which now houses a lovely, home-style restaurant and—it is said—a ghost. Possibly the most interesting house is the **Jean Hasbrouck House**, which once served as a store and tavern. Downstairs there is a bar and grill, as well as a jambless fireplace with its curtainlike decorations; upstairs there's a massive brick chimney, the only kind of its type in the United States. A collection of spinning equipment is on display, as well as hundreds of household items. Several other area buildings are open to the public, including the reconstructed **French Church**, the Federal-style **LeFevre House**, and the **Deyo House**, which is a seventeenth-century home that was later remodeled. This tour should not be missed by anyone who loves history; it is really one of the best anywhere. Older children may like the tours, but they are generally lengthy and too historically detailed to interest younger visitors.

DIRECTIONS *Located on Stone House Street, off Route 32 in New Paltz.*

INFORMATION *Open late May through September—Wed. through Sun., 10 A.M. to 4 P.M. Admission is charged for tour; gallery and museum free. Tel. (914) 255-1889, or write Huguenot Historical Society, P.O. Box 339, New Paltz, 12561.*

Plan to spend at least 30 minutes in the museum and shop; the short tour takes approximately 1½ hours, the long tour about 3 hours. There is a lot of walking and stair climbing involved; dress for outdoor weather.

FACILITIES *Gift shop, rest rooms.*

Mohonk Mountain House When Alfred and Albert Smiley built this resort in 1869, they were determined to preserve the surrounding environment as well as offer gracious accommodations to visitors from the city. Guests here could hike the nearby Shawangunks, take a carriage ride around the manicured grounds or enjoy the carefully tended flower beds. There was a lake for ice skating as well as croquet lawns; while indoors, the hotel itself was furnished in the best of the Victorian era: acres of polished oak paneling and floors, hidden conversation nooks and overstuffed, homey furniture. Mohonk has endured the last century with timeless grace, and visitors today will find many things unchanged. The resort is still dedicated to preserving the natural world, and the gardens have won awards for their beauty. Mohonk sits on a trout-stocked lake which also becomes the focus of special winter carnival weekends. There is a stone tower atop the mountain which offers a six-state view on a sunny day. Hikers, birders, horseback riders, and cross-country skiers will find Mohonk unequaled in its offerings. Day visitors are welcomed here, but it takes more than a day to even sample all of the surprises at Mohonk; plan at least a long weekend here if possible.

DIRECTIONS *Located 6 miles west of New Paltz; take Route 299 west over the Walkill River, turn right at the Mohonk sign, then bear left and follow the road to the gate.*

INFORMATION *Open all year; call ahead for skiing and hiking information. Tel. (914) 225-1000, or write Mohonk Mountain House, New Paltz, 12561.*

Day visitors should plan to spend at least an afternoon on the Mohonk site, exploring the grounds or hiking up to the observation tower. Note that there are some limits placed on day visitors' use of facilities.

FACILITIES *Dining room, gift shop, ice cream parlor, rest rooms.*

Saugerties

Mum Festival For the entire month of October, Seamon Park is one big chrysanthemum celebration. Thousands of mums bloom throughout this 17-acre park, and the display of yellow, lavender and rust flowers in variously shaped beds is breathtaking.

DIRECTIONS Located on Route 9W, south of town.
INFORMATION Open from 9 A.M. until dark, with walking paths, decorative pools and fountains, craft shows and live entertainment on weekends.
FACILITIES Small playground.

Opus 40 and The Quarryman's Museum

In 1938, artist Harvey Fite's bluestone quarry outside of Saugerties was merely the source of material for his sculptures. But as work on the individual pieces progressed, Fite realized that the terraces and steps he had created as a backdrop for the sculptures had themselves become the focus of his work. Naming the site Opus 40 because he believed it would take 40 years to complete, Fite set about creating a vast environmental work, which would eventually contain six acres of steps, levels, fountains, pools and paths. Each of the hundreds of thousands of bluestone pieces were hand cut and fitted, and the 9-ton central monolith was lifted into place with a boom and winches. Today Opus 40 is open to the public as an environmental sculpture and a concert site. Fite, who had studied theology and law and worked as an actor and teacher, also built a museum to house his collection of quarrymen's tools and artifacts. The museum offers a rare glimpse into an almost lost way of life.

DIRECTIONS Located on Fite Road, off Glasco Turnpike; take N.Y. Thruway to exit 20.
INFORMATION Open May through October—weekdays, 10 A.M. to 4 P.M.; Sun., noon to 5 P.M. Closed Tuesdays. Saturdays are reserved for special events. Admission fee charged. Tel. (914) 246-3400, or write Opus 40, High Woods, Saugerties, 12477.
    Tour guides available to answer questions; plan to spend at least an hour here. This is a walking tour; appropriate shoes are recommended.
FACILITIES Rest rooms.

Overlook Observatory

Both home and scientific workshop to astronomer Bob Berman, visitors to the observatory can get a guided tour of the night sky with all its mysteries and quirks, planets, stars and constellations. The observatory has the latest equipment for viewing the heavens, and Bob is a knowledgeable and enthusiastic guide.

DIRECTIONS Located on West Saugerties Road, between Saugerties and Woodstock.

INFORMATION Call Bob Berman at (914) 246-4294 to arrange an appointment, or write to him at 2573 West Saugerties Road, Saugerties, 12477.

Woodstock

The 200-year-old town of Woodstock has a long tradition of attracting creative people. In the spring of 1902, Ralph Radcliffe Whitehead, an Englishman schooled under John Ruskin, was searching for a place where an arts colony could be organized. With two friends, Whitehead bought seven lush farms, and formed a community called Byrdcliffe (named by combining Whitehead's middle name with that of his wife, Jane Byrd McCall). Workshops for metalworkers, potters and weavers were soon built, and over the years the colony has attracted a variety of artists and craftspeople. During the 1930s, jazz singers came here, as did Pete Seeger in the late 1940s. The 1960s brought Bob Dylan, Joan Baez and Peter, Paul and Mary, and the town became a haven for what were then called beatniks. In 1969, a concert actually held nearly fifty miles away on a farm in Bethel (Sullivan County), made Woodstock a rock music legend.

Today the town is still a gathering place for talent of all types. This fact is easily proven by taking a walk through the bustling, sometimes eccentric but never dull village. The surrounding mountains create a dramatic backdrop for the local galleries and shops, and a few hours will pass very easily in a leisurely walk. Woodstock's main thoroughfare is Mill Hill Road, which eventually becomes Tinker Street (according to legend, a tinker's wagon sank into the spring mud here, and the horse's bells can still be heard on quiet days). Just about everything in town can be reached by an easy walk, although parking can be a problem. Try the lots on Rock City Road or

Tannery Brook Road; the town offers limited parking on weekends. In the center of town is the **Kleinert Arts Center** and the **Crafts Shop**, both of which are housed in an eighteenth-century building. The center is a showcase for the visual and performing arts, with gallery shows and concerts presented throughout the year. Across the street is the **Laughing Bear Batik**, a unique store that stocks locally made batik and hand-dyed clothing, as well as imported goods. An unusual shop called **Three Geese in Flight**, located on the Village Green, sells books of Celtic lore, poetry, history and magic to enchant readers of all ages. Books with a local theme can be found at **The Golden Notebook** on Tinker Street, while fine photography can be viewed at **The Catskill Center for Photography.** Don't miss some of the tiny side streets, where shops are tucked away in corners. And if you get tired, sit awhile on the Village Green and watch the colorful parade of people go by.

ART Tours The creation of Woodstock resident Abigail Robin, these fun and educational tours are organized to help visitors discover the hidden corners of Woodstock and the Hudson Valley that are often overlooked. Under the guidance of Ms. Robin, you can explore the Woodstock arts colony from behind the scenes, visit the nearby Zen and Buddhist monasteries or walk along the trails that surround the lovely Byrdcliffe Art Colony, to name a few.

> INFORMATION *Will arrange overnight visits, group tours and day trips designed to suit specific interests. Tel. (914) 679-7969, or write to Abigail Robin, P.O. Box 553, Woodstock, 12498.*

Byrdcliffe Arts Colony Built in the early twentieth century in reaction to the artistically poor industrial revolution, this cluster of buildings has remained as a refuge for both local and visiting artists. Today you can attend concerts, shows and barn dances at the colony, as well as hike the surrounding 600-acre preserve.

> DIRECTIONS *Take Rock City Road to Glasco Turnpike, go approximately one mile; Byrdcliffe Road is on the right.*

INFORMATION Performance schedules can be obtained by calling the box office at (914) 679-2079, or writing the Woodstock Guild, 34 Tinker Street, Woodstock, 12498.
FACILITIES Rest rooms.

Maverick Concerts Founded in 1916 by author Hervey White, the Maverick Concerts were to be a blend of the best that chamber music and the natural world had to offer. White wanted to encourage other "maverick" artists, and he was able to attract some of the best string and wind players to the glass and wood concert hall. The small building seats only 400, but many people still enjoy hearing the concerts from the surrounding hillside, a setting that was White's idea of perfection. The concerts are now honored as the oldest chamber series in the country, and they are still attracting the best chamber groups in the world, among them the Tokyo, Mendelssohn, and Manhattan String Quartets and the Dorian Wind Quintet.

DIRECTIONS Located on Maverick Road, just off Route 375.
INFORMATION Concerts held on Sunday afternoons in July and August at 3 P.M. For schedules call (914) 679-7558/7969, or write P.O. Box 102, Woodstock, 12498.
FACILITIES None.

Weed Walks To experience the outdoors, schedule a walking tour with herbalist Susun Weed. With her guidance the woods and fields become a fascinating living book of natural science, folklore, history and botany. She will teach you to recognize plants and their uses, and you can even select the site.

INFORMATION Available May through November. Tours tailored to any age group. Tel. (914) 246-8081, or write to Susun Weed, P.O. Box 64, Woodstock, 12498.

Activities

ANTIQUES

Ever since the Dutch and English came to Ulster County more than three centuries ago, the people here have been accumulating enough household and farm goods to make this area an antiquer's delight. Today there are scores of antique shops, flea markets and auctions throughout the county. Hudson Valley furniture, American cut glass, kitchenware and oriental pieces are available here in great abundance and in all price ranges. Many shops keep regular hours during the summer months, and limited hours in the winter; others are open by chance or appointment only. Auctions are listed in the local newspapers, along with flea markets and house sales. Because there are too many good shops to list them here, the following is meant only as a very general guide.

In **Saugerties** (exit 20 off the N.Y. Thruway), browsers will find more than 40 antiques dealers in and near town. The major streets for shopping include Main Street—where you'll find **Saugerties Antiques Center**, a cooperative of 25 dealers—as well as Partition Street and Livingston Street. You can spend the entire day going through the shops here, which carry everything from antique clothing to souvenir bric-a-brac.

In **Kingston**, there are at least two co-ops that are worth a visit. The first, **Skillypot Antique Company**, 41 Broadway, (914) 338-6779 (open daily, 11 A.M. to 5 P.M.), houses 25 dealers who display coins, furniture, decorative accessories and jewelry among other items. The shop is located near the historic maritime district, so you can combine antique hunting with ship watching. On Route 28, west of Kingston, there's the **Catskill Mountain Antique Center**, (914) 331-0880 (open daily, except Wed., all year, 10 A.M. to 5 P.M.), a group of 30 dealers together in a new barn. The displays are varied and attractive, and it's a fun place to browse in during a winter afternoon. In High Falls, on Route 213, you'll find **Towpath House Antiques**, (914) 687-0615 (open all year, 10 A.M. to 5 P.M.), a 10-dealer co-op with a good selection of collectibles, from eighteenth-century pieces to Art Deco. The cluster of shops along Route 209 in Stone Ridge makes for a good combination of leisurely afternoon drive and shopping. At **The Banker's Daughter**, (914) 687-9088 (open daily, 11 A.M. to 5 P.M.), 60 dealers show their wares in three buildings; there are also several outdoor shows on the property during the summer months. Stone Ridge has many shops along the main roads, most of which are clearly marked to let you know they are there. For further information, write to the Antiques Dealers Association of Ulster County, Box 246, Hurley, 12443.

BOAT CRUISES

The Hudson runs through the full length of Ulster County, and visitors can easily arrange to spend a day seeing the sights from the river. Even if you don't know port from starboard, there are tours that take all of the work but none of the fun out of a river trip. **Myles Gordon Sailing Center**, Rondout Landing, Kingston, (914) 338-7313, is open from mid-May through October, and offers sunset wine and cheese sailing trips. **Hudson River Cruises on the *Rip Van Winkle***, Rondout Landing, Kingston, (914) 255-6515, offers cruises on a roomy ship that features plenty of seating, rest rooms and a snack bar. Because the river tends to be less choppy than the ocean, the ride is always pleasant and smooth. Cruise season is from May to October, and music is provided on evening trips. Day cruises to West Point and back depart daily. This is probably the best way to see the Hudson without the crowds of larger cruise lines. One warning: bring a heavy sweater and a hat; the wind can be quite cool. **Hudson Rondout Cruises** Rondout Landing, (914) 338-6280, is the perfect choice if you're in the mood for a short trip (1½ hours). The boat goes to the Rondout II Lighthouse, where passengers disembark for a tour, and then continues south to the Esopus Meadows Lighthouse. Cruises run every day from June through October. Buffet dinner cruises run Thursday through Saturday evenings, from 7:30 to 9:30 P.M.; there's also a Sunday brunch excursion from noon to 2 P.M. On Fridays, a two-hour sunset sail departs at 5:30 P.M. All boats leave from the Maritime Center.

FARM STANDS AND
PICK-YOUR-OWN FARMS

Many Ulster County farms are still owned by the families that founded them, and the harvest season here stretches from early June's strawberries to November's great orange pumpkins. Some farm stands offer freshly baked pies and cakes, while others have recipes for you to take home along with the food; still others stock regional goodies like jams and jellies. For the adventurous, pick-your-own farms and stands let you do the work as well as giving you the choice of what you want in the basket. Most of these provide baskets, boxes or bags, but if you bring your own, the price is usually lower. But whatever method you decide on to gather in the harvest, the following is only a sampling of places to try.

The two **Gill Corn Farms**, Hurley Mountain Road or Route 209, both outside of Kingston, (914) 331-8225 (open May through November), are in sweet corn country, and that's what they specialize in, although a variety of other fruits and vegetables are offered, including pick-your-own beans and peas. **Davenport Farms Market**, Route 209, Stone Ridge, (914) 687-7446 (open April through November), has an extensive selection of local fruits and vegetables, including raspberries, grapes, corn, apples, pumpkins and melons. Also on Route 209, in Ellenville, is **Barthels Farm Market**, (914) 647-6941 (open May through November), where you can pick your own strawberries, as well as selecting from a huge local harvest. **Frankie's Farm Market**, Route 9W, Milton (open from April to December), does cider pressing on site; down the road, the **Three Brothers Egg Farm**, (914) 338-6689 (open all year), offers a different type of local "harvest." Eggs, honey, maple syrup and organically grown poultry are available, and many people stop here to buy enough to load up their freezers for the winter. Some local fruit farms specialize in pick-your-own apples, peaches and cherries. **Nemeth Orchards**, Route 9W, Ulster Park, (914) 331-3776; **Mr. Apples**, Route 213, High Falls, (914) 687-9498; **Moriellos Apple Hill Farm**, Route 32, New Paltz, (914) 255-0917; and **Wright's Farm**,

Route 208, Gardiner, (914) 255–5300, are all open during the season and welcome do-it-yourselfers. **Rogers Fruit Stand**, Route 28, Mount Tremper, (914) 688–5615, is a treat at Halloween, when hundreds of jack-o'-lanterns are lighted and set along the road to grimace at passing motorists. The stand stocks many local products, including jams and jellies, along with a dazzling array of fruits and vegetables.

FISHING

Ulster County offers the fishing enthusiast a chance to try his or her hand in scores of streams, a reservoir and the great Hudson River. The waters are well stocked with a variety of fish; trout, bass, pike, pickerel and perch are some of the more popular catches. Areas are well marked. New York State fishing licenses are required, as are reservoir permits; call the Department of the Environment and Conservation in New Paltz at (914) 254-5453 for information. Some of the better known fishing streams in Ulster County include the **Esopus Creek** (access points along Route 28, west of Kingston), **Rondout Creek** (access point on Route 209, south of Kingston), **Plattekill Creek** (access near Route 32, in Saugerties), and the **Sawkill** (access along Route 375). Most of the main access points are indicated by brown and yellow state signs; many also have parking areas. If you are not certain about the stream, ask; otherwise you may find yourself in trouble for trespassing. The **Ashokan Reservoir** is one of the more overlooked fishing areas in Ulster County, which is hard to understand when you realize that there are 40 miles of shoreline here. Trout, walleye and bass lurk beneath the waters, and there are two access points along Route 28A west of Kingston. Another site, the **Kingston City Reservoir**, requires a city permit for fishing, but it's beautiful enough to be worth the extra effort. One outstanding sports shop where you may want to stop, for both information, and equipment, is the **Esopus Fly Fisher**, Main Street, Phoenicia, (914) 688-5305. Licenses are issued here, flies are tied and equipment is sold and repaired.

HIKING

Ulster County has some of the best hiking in the Hudson Valley, but trails can be somewhat difficult to locate without a map or explicit directions. The following suggestions for afternoon or day hikes provide magnificent vistas, and they're relatively easy to find and walk.

For a variety of walks in the woods on nicely graded trails, don't overlook the **Mohonk Mountain House** and the **Minnewaska**, which are both open to day visitors (admission charged). These Shawangunk trails are excellent, although crowded in the summer, especially on weekends. You might want to go in the early spring or late fall. The Mohonk has 128 miles of paths and carriage roads to hike, and there are some first-rate spots for rock climbing as well. **Vernooy Kill Falls** can be reached by taking Route 209 to Lower Cherrytown Road in the town of Kerhonkson. Bear right and continue on for 5 miles before turning onto Upper Cherrytown Road. In another 3 miles, you'll see the parking lot on the right and the trail on the left. The trail is 3.6 miles up and back. **Overlook Mountain** is a relatively easy walk up a graded roadbed. Take Rock City Road, from the center of Woodstock to Meads Mountain Road, which leads to the trailhead (across from the Tibetan monastery). The summit takes about 1 to 1½ hours to reach, depending on how fast you travel the 2-mile ascent. You will pass the ruins of the Overlook Mountain house on the way up, and there is a lookout tower and picnic tables at the top. The easiest place to pick up the **Mount Tremper** trail is on county Route 40, about 1 mile outside of Phoenicia. The trail, which is about 4 miles up and back, has some rather steep rocky sections as it zigzags upward, but it's worth the effort. Try climbing **Wittenberg Mountain** (elev.: 3,780 feet), one of the area's most interesting and dramatic hikes. The trailhead is at the Woodland Valley State Campground, which is on Woodland Valley Road (off Route 28, west of Phoenicia). Cross the Esopus Creek and make a right, then continue for 5 miles. Identified by red trail markers, the distance on this trail to the summit is about 3½ miles. It is only a short additional hike to **Cornell Mountain** from Wittenberg, and that trail is also marked. It will take about 20 minutes to travel along the ridge that connects the two mountains. **Giant Ledge** and **Panther Mountain** are both relatively easy hikes and provide fantastic views. To get to the beginning of the trail, take Route 28 west to county Route 47 (between Shandaken and Pine Hill). Go approximately 7 miles, until you come to the Slide Mountain trailhead. Park on the right—the trail is across the road on the left. The hike to Giant Ledge is about a mile and to Panther it's another 1¾ miles. **Slide Mountain**, the highest peak in the Catskills (elev.: 4,180 feet), is one of the most well-traveled trails in the county. The round-trip hike is about 5½ miles; go in the off season (late fall or early spring), if possible, to avoid the crowds. On a clear day, the summit view includes many Catskill peaks, the Ashokan Reservoir, a grand view of the Hudson Valley and even the Berkshires. To get there, take county Route 47 from Big Indian for about 8½ miles, until you pass Winnisook Lake on the left. Park at the trailhead lot about 1 mile further.

RAPPELING

If you have ever had any desire to learn the correct way to rappel, there is a school in Phoenicia that teaches this mountaineering skill. The instructors have taught professional groups, including the Green Berets, as well as individuals. A class fee and lodgings package is available, and when you make it down the 60-foot tower you receive a certificate of completion. **The Sundance Academy of Survival** is located on Route 214 in Phoenicia. Tel. (914) 688-5640.

SCENIC DRIVES

Ulster County offers hundreds of miles of well-maintained roads coupled with some of the most spectacular scenery in the entire Hudson Valley region. It doesn't make a difference whether you travel in the autumn, with all the riotous color, or through the winter's icy beauty; Ulster will always surprise.

For a drive that offers history as well as scenery, start at Kingston (exit 19 on the N.Y. Thruway) and head south along Route 209. This is one of the oldest roads in America, the Old

Mine Road, which was a trading route between upstate New York and Pennsylvania in the seventeenth century. As you pass by Hurley, Marbletown and Stone Ridge, you will see acres of fields planted with sweet corn, the area's largest agricultural industry. The architectural style of the homes range from Dutch stone to late Victorian, and you'll see many farm stands during the summer and autumn seasons. At Route 213, head east through High Falls, along the old Delaware and Hudson Canal. Stop in at the High Falls Co-op if you like natural foods, or just continue down the road, which follows the canal. At Route 32, you can head south into New Paltz and explore the old stone houses or head north back to Kingston. The drive should take approximately 2 hours.

A second scenic route from Kingston starts by taking Route 9W south along the Hudson River. At West Park, you may want to follow the signs to **Slabsides**, once the writing retreat of naturalist John Burroughs (on your right and down across the railroad tracks; park at the bottom of the hill). It is a half mile walk through the sanctuary. Continue south almost to Highland and take Route 299 west through New Paltz, then follow Routes 44/55 for some spectacular overlook sites. At Route 209, head back north past old Dutch farms and stone houses to Kingston.

From Kingston you could also follow Route 28 to Route 28A and then back to 28. This is a circular drive that goes around the Ashokan Reservoir and is a special treat in autumn. Follow the signs to the old pump station at the reservoir and walk around the fountain or have a picnic—it's an uncrowded, undiscovered area.

SKIING

Downhill skiing in Ulster County offers the best of all worlds: country surroundings, challenging slopes and convenience to cities like Albany or New York. The largest downhill ski area in Ulster is **Belleayre Mountain**—follow Route 28 west from Kingston to Highmount, (914) 254-5600—located at the western edge of the county. Belleayre is state-run. It has a top elevation of 3,365 feet; however, it is not a tame slope: snowfall here averages 110″ a winter, and temperatures can drop to well below zero. At the upper mountain, sixteen trails are serviced by snowmaking equipment, triple and double chairlifts and a T-bar. Runs range from intermediate to extreme expert. For those who want even more challenge, there is a complete racing program, including coin-operated starting gates, clinics and competitions. The ski school at Belleayre is excellent, with patient and capable instructors who can teach beginners or help experts polish their skills. The Upper Lodge is a huge, welcoming log building with a fieldstone fireplace, bar, ski shop, cafeteria and a deck that overlooks the mountains. The lower lodge with two double chair lifts offers novice and intermediate skiers a chance to practice at their own pace. The lower lodge also has a cafeteria, nursery and ski shop. Ski season at Belleayre runs from Thanksgiving through March, seven days a week, from 9 A.M. to 4 P.M.; also 6 to 10 P.M. Sat. nights beginning the last weekend in December. There are several special events weekends during the season; for information call 1-(800)-257-7017 in New York State and 1-(800)-431-4555 outside of the state. **Highmount Ski Center** is smaller than Belleayre, but it is also considerably less crowded. Since the snowmaking capability here is limited, the best time to ski is fairly soon after a snowstorm. Highmount offers intermediate skiers a great deal of variety for a small ski center. There is a cafeteria and nursey. Call (914) 254-5265 for more information.

A smaller, family-run ski operation located just outside of Kingston, the **Sawkill Family Ski Center**, offers 100 percent snowmaking capability, three slopes and four trails, with its longest run at 1,000 feet. There's a cafeteria, and the center is open Sat., Sun. and holidays during the season. Rentals and lessons are available, and the cost is less than the larger slopes. A good place to take kids on a weekend afternoon.

Ulster County is also a perfect place for cross-country skiing. When local valleys, meadows and fields receive their annual cover of snow, new trails are broken and old ones are rediscovered. Although there are dozens of spots that offer cross-country skiing in Ulster, the following places were selected for their services and scenic offerings. **Belleayre Moun-**

tain, Route 28, Highmount, (914) 254-5601, has four cross-country trails that cover 4 miles. The trails lead through meadows, over the old Ulster and Delaware Turnpike and even past an old family cemetery. They are well marked, and range in difficulty from beginner to expert; best of all, there is no fee. Lessons and rentals are available (there is a ski rental shop just across the road from the area), and there is ample parking. Skiers can also use the lower lodge for warming up, although it is a bit of a walk from the trails. At the **Frost Valley YMCA Camp** in Oliverea—off Route 28 at Big Indian, turn left on Route 47 for 15 miles, (914) 985-2291—there are 20 miles of groomed trails that wind in and out of lovely forests and alongside streams. The trails are well marked with color codes, and there is a warming hut where you can thaw out your feet. Lessons, rentals, snacks and guided tours are all right there, and the fee for trail use is very low. At the **Mohonk Mountain House** in New Paltz, (914) 225-1000 (see pages 92–93 for directions), ski touring is raised to an art. The views from the 35 miles of carriage-road trails are breathtaking, with mountain ridges, glens and distant ranges adding to the tranquil beauty of the Hudson Valley winter. The trails are color coded and mapped; lessons, equipment and food are available, and day visitors are welcome. Trail fees vary from weekdays to weekends, but the price is a bargain considering the surroundings. Cross-country skiers will also want to pay a visit to **Lake Minnewaska**, Route 44/55, near New Paltz, with its unmatched 150 miles of novice to advanced trails that pass meadows, waterfalls and mountain views along the way. **Williams Lake Hotel**, Rosendale, (914) 658-3101, is excellent for the beginner, and especially cross-country skiers with young children. One advanced trail is particularly challenging. Great lake views.

TUBING

Very popular in the area, tubing isn't so much a sport as it is a leisurely pursuit. It doesn't take any special skills and can be done by all ages. Just rent a huge, black inner tube, put it in the water and hop on for rides that last anywhere from 1 to more than 3 hours. Maneuvering can be done with the hands, and proper tubing attire consists of old sneakers, shorts, T-shirts or bathing suits. A life jacket is recommended for those who are not strong swimmers; although the waters aren't very deep, they are cold and the currents can be swift. The tubing season lasts from May to September, and some of the rental sites will also arrange to truck you back to your car for an extra charge. You will have to leave a security deposit on the tubes, and rental does not include extras like life jackets or special "tube seats," which make it easier to stay on the tube. Tubes may be rented at **Town Tinker Tube Rental**, Bridge Street, Phoenicia, (914) 688-5553. The granddaddy of tubing services and a complete tubing headquarters, they offer transportation and life jackets. **Four Seasons Sports Shop**, Main Street, Phoenicia, (914) 688-7633, has tubes, seats, jackets and even helmets. The **Railhead Tube Company**, Route 28, Mt. Pleasant, (914) 688-7400, offers a unique chance to ride observation railroad cars along the river, then tube back down.

WINERIES

There are more than a dozen wineries in Ulster County, and the public is welcome to stop at any of them and taste a glass. Some of the wineries offer formal, guided tours of their cellars, while others just have a showroom. All of them are interesting, however, and the people who work there are often very well versed in the mysteries of enology (the science of wine making).

Benmarl Wine Company, Ltd., Route 9W, Marlboro, (914) 236-4265, calls itself "America's oldest continuously producing vineyard," since the first grapes were planted in the early 1800s. The entrance fee here covers a tour, tasting, a souvenir wineglass and the use of the picnic area, which has a marvelous view of the Hudson River. Benmarl is open from May through December and is closed on Mondays and certain holidays. Another small winery in the area is **Cottage Vineyards**, Old Post Road, Marlboro, (914) 236-4870, which produces a limited amount of premium wines. Tours and tastings are offered Saturdays, Sundays and holidays, from 1 to 5 P.M.;

other times by appointment. **Walker Valley Estate Vineyards**, Route 52, Walker Valley, (914) 744-3449, is open from May to December, with changing hours. Tours and tastings at this award-winning winery can be arranged. **The El Paso Winery**, Route 9W, Ulster Park, (914) 331-8642, is a small, unusual sort of place which produces wines sold only in their shop. The tour and tastings are free, and they're open from April to December. **West Park Cellars**, Route 9W, West Park, (914) 384-6709, offers a self-guided tour, a wine shop and a lovely, small restaurant, The Vintage Cafe. In warmer weather you can purchase a pinic basket to take outside, where you can eat overlooking the Hudson. One of the most unique of the region's wineries is the **Royal Kedem Winery**—off Route 9W, Milton, (914) 795-2240—which produces a fine line of kosher wines. Founded by the Herzog family, which has been in wine production since 1848, Kedem features award-winning examples of New York State Johannisberg reisling, Chablis, seyval blanc, honey and plum wines. The winery has an excellent guided tour, a short movie and a marvelous tasting room located in an old railroad station. The children can try Kedem grape juice, and there are picnic tables on the site. The winery is open from May to January with changing seasonal hours; closed Saturdays and Jewish holidays. The only charge is a small parking fee, which is only in effect on Sunday. **Woodstock Winery**, 62-1 Brodhead Road, West Shokan, (914) 657-2018, is open on weekends only, and you must make an appointment in advance. Adjacent to the Ashokan Reservoir, this winery produces apple wine, seyval blanc, chardonnay and ravat (a dessert wine). They buy their grapes, however, rather than growing them on the premises. **Gardiner Vineyard and Farms,** 714 Albany Post Road, Gardiner, (914) 255-0892, has a rustic winery building and tasting rooms on a 450-acre farm. The views of the vineyard and surrounding Shawangunk Mountains are spectacular. Open every day, from May through October, from 11 A.M. to 5 P.M.; Sundays from noon to 6.

Where to Eat

Armadillo Bar & Grill *(97 Abeel St., Kingston, (914) 339-1550)* Southwestern cuisine featuring Tex-Mex specialties, fresh grilled seafood, fajita steaks and barbeque. The frozen margaritas are excellent. Outdoor dining in warm weather.

La Bella Pasta *(Route 28, Kingston, (914) 331-9130)* Fine homemade pasta in an informal atmosphere, where children are welcome. Fresh soups and salads.

Bread Alone Bakery *(Route 28, Boiceville, (914) 657-3328)* Do not miss this bakery renowned for its fantastic breads—Norwegian farm bread, mixed grain, swiss peasant, Finnish sour rye and others baked in a wood-fired oven. Owner Daniel Leader regularly goes to North Dakota to get organically grown grain. Craig Claiborne rated this bread his number one choice in the metropolitan area.

Café Tamayo *(89 Partition St., Saugerties, (914) 246-9371)* This establishment, which opened in 1987, has become tremendously popular. A casual American bistro housed in a renovated 1864 landmark building, the home-style American and international cuisines feature such specialties as country pâté with spicy red cabbage, garlic and green chili, braised duck legs with mole sauce and cassoulet. Children are welcome.
OPEN *Wed. through Sun., 6 A.M. to 10 P.M.*

Christy's *(85 Mill Hill Rd., Woodstock, (914) 679-5300)* An authentic English gate house with a two-sided fireplace, beamed ceilings and cozy taproom. Fine artwork by local talent often hangs on the walls. House specialties are baked smoked chicken with honey and mustard glaze, roast duck with orange sauce and fresh fish of the day. The hearty portions and exceedingly reasonable prices attract local residents and visitors alike. Children are welcome; special menu available.
OPEN *Tues. through Sat., 5 to 11 P.M.*

Deanie's Town Tavern *(Route 212, Woodstock, (914) 679-6508)* The best place in town to go for cocktails or a nightcap. Open every day except Tues., from 4 P.M. on.

Deming Street Restaurant and Cafe *(4 Deming St., Woodstock, (914) 679-7858)* An eclectic mix of Continental cuisine, sandwiches, salads, omelets and vegetarian dishes. Special children's menu.
   OPEN *Wed. and Thurs., 7 A.M. to 10 P.M.; Fri. and Sat. until 11 P.M.; Sun. 8 A.M. to 10 P.M. Closed Mon. and Tues.*

DePuy Canal House *(Route 213, High Falls, (914) 687-7700/ 7777)* If you want to have one spectacular meal in Ulster, we highly recommend this establishment housed in an eighteenth-century stone house that was once a tavern. Try the rabbit pâté with pine nuts, poached lemon sole with salmon red pepper mousse or the chocolate date truffle in Sabra mole. Dinner is a fixed price. Children are welcome if they can sit through a leisurely meal; no special menu provided.
   OPEN *Dinner—Thurs. through Sat., 5:30 to 9 P.M. and Sun., 4 to 8:30 P.M.; Sunday brunch, 11:30 A.M. to 2 P.M.*

The Egg's Nest Saloon *(Route 213, High Falls, (914) 687-7255)* Located in a renovated building that dates back to the nineteenth century and was once a parsonage, this cozy restaurant with its unique blend of funky and traditional decor specializes in homemade soups, super-sandwiches and praeseaux (a light, crispy-crusted pizza-type dish). A great stop for lunch or drinks. Children are welcome.
   OPEN *Year-round every day from 11 A.M. to 2 A.M. During July and August breakfast served from 8 A.M. on.*

First Wok Chinese Restaurant *(Bradley Meadows Shopping Center, Woodstock, (914) 679-5680)* Offers a wide variety of Cantonese Szechuan specialties. Open every day for lunch and dinner.

The Golden Duck Chinese Restaurant *(11 Broadway, Kingston, (914) 331-3221)* Serves lunch and dinner every day by the Rondout Creek. The luncheon special is a real bargain.

Hasbrouck House Inn Restaurant *(Route 209, Stone Ridge, (914) 687-0055)* Enjoy a leisurely repast in this twenty-five-room, eighteenth-century stone mansion listed on the National Register of Historic Places. Although the menu is small (six appetizers and ten entrées), the choices change daily. All dishes are imaginatively prepared and presented, and the atmosphere is romantic. Children are discouraged.
   OPEN *Dinner—Sun. through Thurs., 5 to 9 P.M., Fri. and Sat. until 10:30 P.M.; Sunday brunch, noon to 3 P.M.*

Hillside Manor *(240 Boulevard [Route 32], South Kingston, (914) 331-4386)* This is the best restaurant in Kingston and well worth a stop for dinner. The cuisine is northern Italian and all pasta is made on the premises. Some of the specialties are the red snapper sautéed with white wine, mussels, shrimp and clams; veal saltimbocca; roast leg of lamb or Paglia and Fieno (green and white noodles sautéed with smoked ham, heavy cream and Parmesan cheese). Children are welcome, but no special menu is provided.
   OPEN *Lunch—Mon. through Fri., 11:30 A.M. to 2 P.M.; dinner—every night until 10 P.M. Reservations required on Sat. nights.*

Jane's Homemade *(305 Wall St., Kingston, (914) 338-8315)* Rich, homemade ice cream is the specialty here, along with cakes, cookies and other gourmet dessert treats. Closed Sun.

The Little Bear *(295B Tinker St., Bearsville, (914) 679-9497)* Enjoy Chinese food along the banks of the Sawkill Stream. Many vegetarian dishes are featured on the extensive menu.

Locust Tree Inn *(215 Huguenot St., New Paltz, (914) 255-7888)* Located in an old stone house built in 1759, this casual country restaurant has fireplaces in every dining room. The specialties are duck, Coquilles St. Jacques and fresh fish, among others. In the summer, outdoor dining is available. Children are welcome.

OPEN *Lunch—Tues. through Fri., 11:30 A.M. to 2:30 P.M.; dinner—Tues. through Sat., 5:30 to 10 P.M.; Sunday brunch, 11 A.M. to 2 P.M. and dinner, 3 to 8 P.M.*

Marcel's *(Route 9W, West Park, (914) 384-6700)* This cozy, romantic spot has a fireplace, dim lights and excellent French food. The specialties are rack of lamb, pasta with seafood and chicken Provençale. Children discouraged.

OPEN *Daily for dinner, 5 to 10 P.M. No reservations.*

The Montauk House Restaurant *(Albany Ave., Kingston, (914) 331-3474)* This restaurant specializes in all types of seafood, brought up daily from Long Island. Also meat and fowl dishes. Children are welcome.

OPEN *Daily for dinner, 5 to 10 P.M.*

The North Light *(46 Main St., New Paltz, (914) 255-9819)* In spite of the rickety, charmingly old building, circa 1850, there's dancing every Monday night at this reasonably priced restaurant. For lunch, try the Mexican cheese crisp salad or chicken and sour cream enchiladas. For dinner, their crispy roast duckling with orange sauce and almonds is especially good. Not recommended for children.

OPEN *Daily for lunch and dinner, from noon to 9 P.M.*

La Parmigiana *(604 Ulster Ave., Kingston, (914) 338-1026)* If you want some of the best pizza and calzones to be found anywhere, stop here. Baking is done in an old-style, wood-fired brick oven. Each gourmet pizza and calzone is made to order, and all cheeses are made on the premises. Menu choices include fresh pesto pizza or pizza with veal on a bed of broccoli sauce topped with fresh sautéed vegetables. The dough is yeast free, and desserts—cannoli, ices, Sicilian layer cake—are all homemade. Children are welcome.

OPEN *Lunch—Tues. through Fri., 11 A.M. to 2 P.M.; dinner—4 to 10 P.M.; Sat., 1 to 10 P.M.; Sun., 1 to 9 P.M.*

Port of Call *(812 Ulster Ave., Kingston, (914) 331-8850)* The place to go for large portions of seafood at reasonable prices. Children are welcome.

OPEN *Daily for lunch and dinner.*

Rudi's Big Indian *(Route 28, Big Indian, (914) 254-4005)* Nestled in a valley surrounded by mountains, the setting here is as exceptional as the cuisine. Only the freshest ingredients are used, and all breads and desserts are made on the premises. Pasta dishes, goat cheese salad, coffee toffee pie and Russian cheesecake are a few specialties. If you can't make it here for a meal, try to stop for a drink and dessert. You can dine outdoors on the deck in warm weather. This a lovely spot to relax, especially after hiking, tubing or skiing. Children are welcome; hamburgers and spaghetti available on the dinner menu.

OPEN *Thurs., Fri. and Mon., from 4:30 P.M.; Sat. and Sun., from noon.*

Schneller's *(61 John St., Kingston, (914) 331-9800)* Authentic German cuisine in the historic uptown area of Kingston. The menu features seven types of schnitzel as well as goulash, sauerbraten and fresh fish. Dessert specialties include excellent homemade strudels, tortes and cheesecake. The upstairs dining room has a European flavor, and the outdoor garden café is a delightful place to enjoy one of the restaurant's several brands of beer. The gourmet store and meat market downstairs specialize in fresh game, nitrite-free sausage, pâtés and cheeses. A perfect stop if you are planning a picnic. Children are welcome.

OPEN *Daily for lunch; dinner—Thurs. through Sun., from 6 P.M.*

Sebastian's *(Intersection of Zena and Sawkill Roads, Woodstock, (914) 679-5956)* Serving a wide variety of soups, sandwiches, salads and full dinners. The seafood and chicken entrées are the specialties here. One of our favorites is the garlic shrimp. All desserts are homemade. Children are welcome.

OPEN *Every day for lunch—11 A.M. to 3 P.M., Memorial Day weekend through October; Wed., Thurs. and Sun. the rest of the year. Dinner—Sun. through Thurs., 5 to 10 P.M.; Fri. and Sat., until 11 P.M.*

Ship Lantern Inn *(Route 9W, Milton (914) 795-5400)* This charming old restaurant is done in a nautical decor and serves Continental cuisine. The food and service are consistently excellent. House specialties include fresh fish daily, mignonette of beef Bordelaise and Saltimbocca Romana. Children are welcome, but no special menu provided.

OPEN *Lunch—daily except Sat., from noon to 2:30 P.M.; dinner— Tues. through Sat., starting at 6 P.M. Sun., open from 1 to 8 P.M.*

The Student Prince Tavern *(Route 213, Stone Ridge, (914) 687-9911)* German cuisine served in a casual astmosphere. Veal dishes are the house specialty.

OPEN *Daily, lunch and dinner.*

Sweet Sue's *(Main Street, Phoenicia, (914) 688-7852)* There are over a dozen different types of pancakes and French toast here. Our favorites are the fruited oatmeal pancakes and the walnut-crunch French toast. Breakfast and lunch served daily; everything is homemade, from soups and salads to daily specials and desserts.

OPEN *Every day from Memorial Day weekend through October, 7 A.M. to 3 P.M. Closed Wed. the rest of the year.*

Val D'Isere *(Route 28, Big Indian (914) 254-4646)* This casual French country restaurant is owned by chef Bertrand, who began his appenticeship in Bordeaux at the age of 13 and ended up cooking for the French president. Some specialties of the house are the crabmeat mode du chef, country pâté with green peppercorns and baby rack of lamb. For dessert, the chocolate mousse with hazelnuts is a treat. Children are welcome, but no special menu provided.

OPEN *Daily except Tues., starting at 5 P.M.*

Winchell's Pizza *(Reservoir Rd. and Route 28, Shokan, (914) 657-3352)* Serves unusually tempting varieties of pizza, as well as homemade ice cream for dessert.

Woodstock Pizza *(the Village Green, Woodstock, (914) 679-7416)* The perfect place to go with the kids for a snack. Try their whole wheat pizza if you've never had it before.

Yvonne's Drive-In *(Route 28, Phoenicia, (914) 688-7340)* One of the most unique restaurants in Ulster County. Owner Yvonne is a self-taught chef who offers an eclectic menu of French country cuisine. Rabbit, duck and goose are the specialties; desserts are superb. Children are welcome.
OPEN *Dinner—Fri. through Sun., April through November only.*

Where to Stay

The Alpine Inn *(Alpine Rd., Oliverea, 12462, (914) 254-5026/ 9806)* A pristine mountain lodge nestled on a hillside near the base of one of the tallest peaks in the Catskills, this inn will appeal particularly to those who love the outdoors. For 50 years the Griessen family has operated this lodge, which has an Olympic-size pool. Breakfast, lunch and dinner are served if you desire. Open all year, except during April. Twenty-two rooms with private bath and air conditioning. Children are welcome.

Baker's Bed and Breakfast *(R.D. 2, Box 80, Stone Ridge, 12484, (914) 687-9795)* Surrounded by mountains, fields and woods, this 1780 stone farmhouse is furnished with antiques, and there is a greenhouse with a hot tub. Breakfast is served in the solarium, overlooking the mountains, and includes juice, homemade breads, pastries and special dishes made with eggs and local meats, as well as their own blend of freshly ground coffee. Open all year. One suite with a sitting room has a private bathroom; five other rooms share two bathrooms. Children are permitted on weekdays only.

Buena Vista Manor *(P.O. Box 144, Route 9W, West Camp, 12490, (914) 246-6462)* California natives Bob Adams and Bill Alvarez run this bed and breakfast, which has magnificent views of the mountains. The house is filled with unusual pieces such as a unique doll collection and Mexican masks. A traditional breakfast is served and includes fresh sausage, bacon and eggs. One of the specialties of the house is French toast stuffed with cream cheese and marmalade. Open all year, except January and February. Three rooms share one bathroom. Children not permitted.

Canal Bed and Breakfast *(24 Bruceville Rd., High Falls, 12440, (914) 687-7154)* This 1830s Colonial house has been restored to its original country charm, and has a renovated cottage on the grounds that was once a loom shop. The full country breakfast includes fresh baked muffins, fruit, quiche, soufflé and vegetable cheesecake. Open all year. One room with private bath; two others share a bath. Children are welcome.

Candlewood Cottage *(Route 212, Lake Hill, 12448, (914) 679-9653)* Experience the charm of an authentic 1800s Woodstock farmhouse, located just 10 minutes away from the center of the village. The full breakfast includes fresh fruit, homemade biscuits, eggs and coffee. Enjoy afternoon tea in the garden with views of the surrounding mountains in the summer, or around the fireplace during the winter months. No smoking or animals permitted; a dog and a cat are on the premises. Children welcome. Open all year. Four rooms share two bathrooms.

Captain Schoonmaker's Bed and Breakfast *(Box 37, High Falls, 12440, (914) 687-7946)* A truly fantastic find that will be of particular interest to antiques buffs. Built in the eighteenth century, the house is furnished with beautiful antiques and country quilts that will make you feel as though you are stepping back in time. Featured in many national house and garden magazines. The hostess serves a seven-course breakfast with home-baked breads, cheese and dill soufflé, apricot strudel and blueberry walnut cobbler. Open all year. Eight rooms share six bathrooms. Children not permitted.

Glen Atty Farm *(Moonhaw Rd., P.O. Box 578, West Shokan, 12494, (914) 657-8110)* Susan and Tom Kizis own this 1840s farmhouse and working farm that includes cows, sheep, pigs, chickens and ducks. It's a great place for families with young children. The two guest rooms are furnished with antiques; one has a fireplace and one is ideal for kids with sleeping accommodations for four. A hearty breakfast of eggs, sausage and homemade baked goods is served. Open all year. Two rooms share one bathroom; two-night minimum stay on weekends. Children are welcome.

Hasbrouck House Inn *(P.O. Box 76, Route 209, Stone Ridge, 12484, (914) 687-0055)* An eighteenth-century stone mansion listed in the historic register, this inn is set on a forty-acre estate and has rooms furnished with antiques, an Olympic-sized outdoor pool, a lake and fine restaurant. Host Nick Paras serves a full gourmet breakfast to his guests. Open all year. Eight rooms share three bathrooms. Children are not permitted.

House on the Hill *(Box 86, High Falls, 12440, (914) 687-9627)* This 1825 Colonial sits on five acres of grounds and woods, with a gracious stone and hand-forged iron fence that spans the front lawn. Secluded yet within walking distance of fine restaurants, antiques shops and town, the property once furnished water to the residents of High Falls and the Delaware and Hudson locks can be seen on one side. Shelley's fresh fruit tarts and pumpkin bread are specialties of the breakfast meal here. Open Thurs. through Sun, all year. Three suites share one bathroom; one suite has a private bathroom. Children must be over the age of six.

Mohonk Mountain House *(Mohonk Lake, New Paltz, 12561, (914) 255-1000)* A National Historic Landmark, this Victorian castle hotel stands atop a mountain in the heart of 22,000 unspoiled acres in the Shawangunk Mountains. Dazzling views are everywhere and serene Mohonk Lake adds to the dramatic setting. Although the hotel offers a museum, stable, modern sports facilities, and cross-country skiing and hiking, the place is still very much the way it was in 1869 when it was purchased by the Smiley family, who still own and manage the hotel. Midweek packages are available, and some of the special weekend events—from tennis and cooking to computer immersion—are sure to interest many. Children's activities are offered for ages 2 to 13. Open all year. Of the 293 rooms, 140 have working fireplaces and 200 have balconies. All have private bathrooms except for a few, which are available at reduced rates. All guests must take the three meals per day (MAP) included in the room rate. Men must wear jackets for the evening meal. Children are welcome.

Mt. Tremper Inn *(P.O. Box 51, Mt. Tremper, 12457, (914) 688-9938/5329)* This twenty-three-room mansion, built in 1850, has always been a guest house. One of the largest bed and breakfasts in the Catskills, the inn's Victorian charm—including a parlor with a huge bluestone fireplace, a game room, library and wrap-around porch—will relax the weariest traveler. Breakfast features homemade breads, a granola-type house cereal and delicious baked egg dishes. Open all year. One suite and one room with private bath, and ten rooms share bathrooms. (All rooms have sinks.) Children not permitted.

Nana's *(54 Old Forge Rd., New Paltz, 12561, (914) 255-5678)* On twenty acres of lawn and woods, this farmhouse is a secluded country retreat with deer, raccoon, red fox and birds. Run by Kathleen Maloney, there is a full breakfast which includes home-baked bread and muffins as well as fresh fruit. Guests are invited to join the owner for stretch exercises and aerobics every morning. Open all year. One room with private bath. Children are welcome.

Nieuw Country Lloft *(41 Allhusen Rd., New Paltz, 12561, (914) 255-6533)* On a quiet road just south of New Paltz this

1740 gambrel-roofed Dutch stone house with period antiques, beamed ceilings and wideboard floors is like an escape into the eighteenth century. A claw-footed copper tub graces the bathroom, and there are six fireplaces. Country quilts cover the antique beds and the six-course breakfast features home-baked goods, freshly squeezed juices and a variety of egg dishes served in front of the fireplace or on the patio. Complimentary Hudson Valley wine is served in the evening. Open daily in July and August; weekends and holidays only September through June. Three rooms share one bathroom. Children not permitted.

Pine Hill Arms *(Main St., Pine Hill, 12465, (914) 254-9811)* Opened in 1882, the Pine Hill Arms now caters to skiers from Belleayre and Highmount. The cozy bar, known to insiders as "Claus's," is where skiers meet after the lifts close to enjoy their famous cheese fondue, gluh wine and dancing. There are two dining rooms, a hot tub and sauna, an outdoor swimming pool and four acres of grounds. Open all year, except during April and May. All thirty rooms have private baths. Children are welcome.

Rondout II Lighthouse Bed and Breakfast *(c/o Department of Public Works, 25 East O'Reilly St., Kingston, 12401, (914) 331-0682 or 338-2114)* The largest—and last—lighthouse built on the upper Hudson River, it was originally constructed in 1867 and was rebuilt in 1913. Guests here are in for a unique experience—the lighthouse is still in use today, although it has been fully automated. Access only by boat from Rondout Landing at the Hudson River Maritime Museum. Children are welcome, and will enjoy the walk to the top of the tower. The views from every room are wonderful. Open from May 1 through October 31. Three rooms share the bath.

Twin Gables *(73 Tinker St., Woodstock, 12498 (914) 679-9479)* Woodstock's oldest guest house has been managed for over 45 years by the Hoffman family. Guests will love the homey rooms, as cozy and inviting as Grandma's house. Although no meals are served at Twin Gables, it is located in the center of Woodstock, only a short walk away from several restaurants, art galleries, and shops. Open all year; two-night minimum during July, August and over holiday weekends. Two rooms have private bath; six share two baths. Children permitted at the owners' discretion.

Ujjala's Bed and Breakfast (2 Forest Glen Rd., New Paltz, 12561, (914) 255-6360) Innkeeper Ujjala ("spirit of the light" in Sanskrit) Schwartz, a former model and dancer, recently renovated this charming Victorian frame cottage on 3½ acres surrounded by apple, pear and quince trees, adding stained glass, skylights and lots of plants. She's also a fine cook, whose specialty is gourmet vegetarian cuisine. A full breakfast includes homemade whole grain breads, fresh fruit and eggs. Wine is served to guests upon arrival. Open all year. Three rooms share one bathroom; one private room with fireplace and bath. Children are welcome.

Val D'Isere Inn (Route 28, Big Indian, 12410, (914) 254-4646) In addition to their restaurant of the same name, Marguerite and Serge Bertrand operate an inn with beautiful mountain views. The Adirondack Trailways bus from New York City stops just out front, so it is a perfect choice for travelers without a car who want to be near great fishing and hiking. Continental breakfast is served. Open all year. Six rooms share two bathrooms. Children are welcome.

White House Farm Bed and Breakfast (211 Phillies Bridge Rd., New Paltz, 12561, (914) 255-8089) White House Farm, an eighteenth-century homestead, was built by Philip Hasbrouck, one of the descendants of New Paltz's twelve founding families. Nestled in the foothills of the Shawangunk Mountains, this intriguing house has a hidden room where slaves escaping on the Underground Railroad once stayed. There is also a pool and 55 acres of secluded land for guests to explore. A Continental breakfast of fresh fruit, cheese, baked goods and coffee or tea is served between 9 and 10 A.M. Open all year. Two of the rooms have working fireplaces and share one bathroom; one has a private bath. Children are welcome.

Woodland Inn Bed and Breakfast, *(8 Route 212, Lake Hill, 12448, (914) 679-8152)* Stone fences and sugar maples frame the mountain views from this nineteenth-century farmhouse only minutes from the center of Woodstock. Their full country breakfast includes home-baked pastries. Try walking to nearby Cooper Lake after your morning repast; it's truly lovely! Open all year. Three rooms share one bathroom. Children are welcome.

Delaware County

Delaware County prides itself on being "down to earth." In fact, that's how the local Chamber of Commerce advertises the charms of this breathtaking area, one of the largest counties in New York State. Sixty-four thousand acres of Delaware County land are state owned and will remain forever wild, open all year for recreational use by natives and visitors alike.

Part of the charm of the county lies also in its wealth of nineteenth-century architecture, which greets the eye in nearly every town. The lovely homes and buildings of Roxbury, Delhi, Walton, Franklin and Deposit are as graceful as the village names, and many of the homes have been turned into bed and breakfast lodgings, a lure for any traveler weary of boxlike motels. The region offers the best kind of community get-togethers, where everyone will feel at home. Visit an auction in an old dairy barn and watch Col. Eddie Roberts sell anything from fresh eggs to fine antiques. Or stop at a sap house in the spring and sample some lockjaw candy. Watch for pancake suppers and chicken and biscuit dinners, where

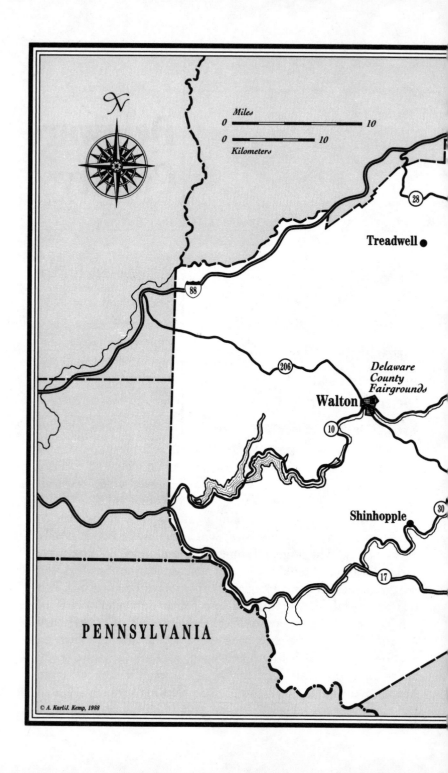

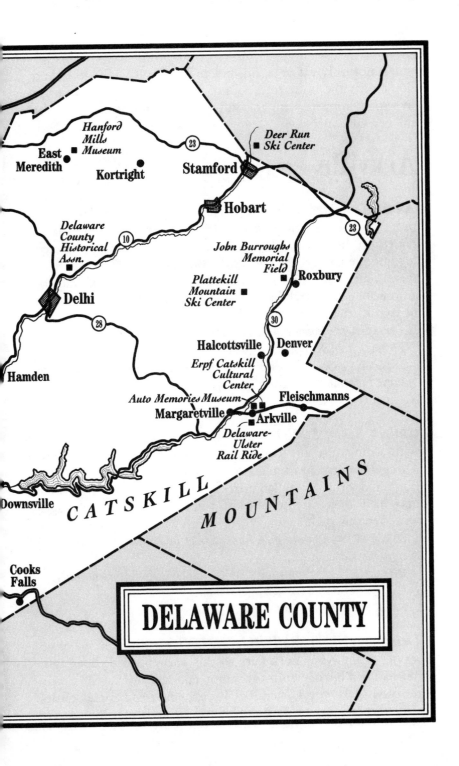

Hanford
Mills
Museum
East
Meredith
Kortright
Stamford
Deer Run
Ski Center
23
Hobart
Delaware
County
Historical
Assn.
10
John Burroughs
Memorial
Field
Roxbury
Plattekill
Mountain
Ski Center
23
Delhi
28
30
Hamden
Halcottsville
Denver
Erpf Catskill
Cultural
Center
Auto Memories Museum
Fleischmanns
Margaretville
Arkville
Delaware-
Ulster
Rail Ride
Downsville
CATSKILL
MOUNTAINS
Cooks
Falls

DELAWARE COUNTY

you'll not only eat your fill, but make new friends, too. And don't miss the boisterous county fair in Walton, where prize livestock compete with colorful quilts and homemade pies for the crowds' attention.

Arkville

Auto Memories Museum A constantly changing display of more than forty vintage cars, all lovingly restored and maintained. In the past the displays have included a steam-powered locomobile and a 1939 Packard Roadster, one of only three of this model that still survives. There are small exhibits of automobile memorabilia and visitors will often find a car buff or two to chat with.

> DIRECTIONS *Located on county Route 29 in Arkville. Take Route 28 west from Kingston.*
> INFORMATION *Admission free; donation suggested. Open late June until November.*
> FACILITIES *None.*

Church Street Station This mini–amusement park is packed with a miniature golf course, a trout pond and a batting area. The golf course has replicas of covered bridges, railroad stations and other local landmarks. Successful trout fishermen may have their catch cooked at a nearby restaurant. All ages will love this park.

> DIRECTIONS *Located on Church Street in Arkville; watch for signs from Route 28.*
> INFORMATION *Admission charged. Open according to weather. Call (914) 586-2425 for information.*
> FACILITIES *Equipment rental.*

Delaware-Ulster Rail Ride (DURR) Although the train service from New York City to this area ended decades ago, railroad and history buffs will enjoy taking a ride on the newly restored Delaware-Ulster Rail Ride, which chugs and rattles over the original trestles and track, through meadows, over streams and up mountains. Riders can choose between open-air observation cars (great for picture taking), and enclosed, restored coaches. But the real treat here is a trip in the Red Heifer, a self-propelled passenger, mail and freight car from the 1920s. All trains leave from the original Arkville Depot, a restored freight station that now houses a gift shop, snack stand and orientation center. Select rides of varying lengths to places such as Highmount, Halcottsville and Roxbury. The engineers and conductors will point out local sights and discuss the history of the trains. Special events days are also a big part of the DURR schedule, and may include the Fiddlers' Picnic, Hobo Day and the popular reenactments of old-time train robberies.

DIRECTIONS *Located on Route 28, 45 miles west of Kingston.*
INFORMATION *Open from May through October; times vary so call ahead, at (914) 586-DURR (3877). Entrance to the depot is free, and prices for the rides begin at $5 for an adult, $2.50 for a child. Easy wheelchair access.*
FACILITIES *Gift shop, picnic tables, rest rooms.*

Erpf Catskill Cultural Center A regional organization dedicated to preserving and promoting the arts and folklore of the Catskills. In an eighteenth-century mansion, the center maintains a gallery, which focuses on the works of Catskill artists and craftspeople, and also sponsors an annual Hall of Fame jazz concert that features the greats of the Big Band era.

DIRECTIONS *Located on Route 28 in Arkville.*
INFORMATION *Admission is free. Gallery open weekdays, year-round, from 9 A.M. to 5 P.M.; weekends, from Memorial Day to Labor Day, 10 A.M. to 4 P.M. Call (914) 586-3326 for exhibit schedules.*
FACILITIES *Gift shop.*

Delhi

Delaware County Historical Association A collection of historic buildings many of which have been moved to this

60-acre site, where visitors can get a taste of life in rural America during the nineteenth century. In the main building there's a special collections library and a gallery. Of particular note is the Gideon Frisbee House, a 1797 example of Federal-style architecture that served as a tavern, a private house and a meeting place of the county supervisors. The interior has been restored to reflect differing tastes from pioneer to high Victorian; the furniture and decorative arts collections include chairs from the Belter workshops, rope beds, finely woven strip carpeting, and hair and feather wreaths. The Frisbee barn houses a collection of early farming implements, as well as a permanent exhibit called "It's a Fine Growing Time," which guides the viewer through the hardships and joys of a farming year. Other buildings include a gun shop, a one-room schoolhouse, a toll house that is now a lovely gift shop, and even a small family cemetery. Recently added is a small nature walk, which follows an old farm path and ends beside a creek. The plants and flowers are well marked, bird life is abundant and the walk is short enough for young nature lovers.

The DCHA sponsors a Heritage Garden Day each year, featuring speakers and demonstrations centered around Delaware County gardening and farming traditions. Home and Hearth Day offers a look at the crafts and skills that went into running a nineteenth-century house, and the combined Tavern Day and Children's Fair offers something for everyone.

DIRECTIONS *Located 2 miles north of Delhi on Route 10.*
INFORMATION *Admission fee charged; the nature walk is free. Open May through October—weekdays, 10 A.M. to 4:30 P.M., and weekends, 1 to 4:30 P.M. Guided tours available; call ahead for special events schedules. Tel. (607) 746-3849.*
FACILITIES *Picnic tables, gift shop, rest rooms.*

East Meredith

Hanford Mills Museum A working nineteenth-century saw-mill and gristmill, the present-day museum was once the industrial center of a farming hamlet. The mill produced lumber, flour, wooden goods like butter tubs and porch posts, and even electricity, through a system of generators. Located along the Kortright Creek, the water-powered mill was owned and operated by David Josiah Hanford and his descendants. The unique site is one of only a handful of American industrial mills that worked well into this century, touched by only a few modern changes.

Visitors here will see working exhibits such as lathes and jigsaws being used to produce wooden items. In the mill itself, an elaborate system of catwalks and walkways runs through workshops, generator rooms and offices into the pully room, where ropes and leather straps work gears that turn water-power into horsepower. Downstairs the 10 foot by 12 foot waterwheel, a metal reconstruction of the original wooden one, is turned by the waters of the mill pond, making the entire building rumble and vibrate with its power.

Outside the museum is the Gray Barn, which contains agricultural and farm equipment displays, a shingle mill, the placid mill pond and the Mill Museum store. Several special events are held at Hanford Mills each year. The spring Fly-Fishing Clinic lets would-be Izaak Waltons try their hands on the mill pond. On Independence Day, an old-style fourth of July is reenacted with speeches, debates, music, games and rides, while the Children's Fair caters to the younger set. And in autumn, the Antique Engine Jamboree lets visitors see a demonstration of power sources from a time when lights didn't always come at the flick of a switch.

DIRECTIONS *Take Route 28 to the intersections of county Routes 10 and 12 in East Meredith; follow the signs.*

INFORMATION *Open May 1 through October 31—daily, 10 A.M. to 5 P.M. Admission fee charged. There is a guided tour of the mill and the grounds. Call (607) 278-5744 for information.*

FACILITIES *Picnic area, gift shop, rest rooms.*

Roxbury

John Burroughs Memorial Field Just outside of Roxbury is the studio and grave site of nature writer John Burroughs. A friend of Teddy Roosevelt, Thomas Edison and Henry Ford, Burroughs was respected as a man who swept away Victorian sentimentality and made nature study a science. Burroughs's books recalled nineteenth-century life in the Hudson Valley and the Catskills, and his writing nook, Woodchuck Lodge, is maintained at the Memorial Field. The area also contains Boyhood Rock, where Burroughs spent many hours, and Burroughs' grave site. The view from the field is breathtaking in any season, and special open house days are held throughout the summer.

DIRECTIONS *Take Route 30 north through Roxbury; watch for signs.*

INFORMATION *Open all year, weather permitting. Admission is free.*

FACILITIES *None.*

The Roxbury Arts Group (RAG) While not a historic or recreational site, RAG is still so active in sponsoring the arts in Delaware County that travelers to the region should be aware of what they offer. In July, a two-day art show is held in Roxbury, and it attracts fine artists and craftspeople from throughout the region. During the summer months, watch for events such as the Music in Historic Places chamber concerts, a series of performances held in magnificent churches and public spaces, or performances by the Metawee River Theatre Company, a performance group that uses masks, giant puppets and costumes to retell stories based on myth and folklore. If you prefer a country-style good time, make plans to attend the Roxbury County Fair, where crafts, good food and entertainment provide old-fashioned fun. Join in with the clog dancers, bid on a prize-winning apple pie or be entranced by the sounds of a hammered dulcimer.

DIRECTIONS *Concert sites vary, but the Roxbury Arts Group is located on Route 30 in Roxbury; the fair is held across the street on the grounds of the Reformed Church.*

INFORMATION *Varies with specific activities. Tel. (607) 326-7908 for information, or write Roxbury Arts Group, Roxbury, 12474.*

FACILITIES *Gallery, rest rooms.*

Walton

Delaware County Fair Part of the agricultural and social life of the region for more than a century, the county fair doesn't seem to be slowing down at all. Held for one week each August, the fair highlights the best of what farm life was—and is—all about. Livestock such as cows, pigs, chickens, rabbits and sheep are paraded before judges by proud 4-H members. The finest in local produce is carefully displayed for all to see, with new varieties competing against old standbys for ribbons. Quilts are there to admire, and dozens of craftspeople show off their talents and wares. The celebration starts off on Main Street with a parade that often includes livestock, antique cars, fire department bands and local organizations. Visitors will spend hours walking through the fair's huge display tents, seeing the latest in farm equipment, examining the newest type of corn, learning the best way to heat a house with wood, even sipping milk punch served by the Delaware County Dairy Princess and her court. Later, try your hand at the games or let the kids have fun on the carousel and Ferris wheel. You probably won't want to bid on the livestock, but the auction is popular with future farmers, who sometimes can't hide the tears when a prize-winning calf is led away. At night, the tempo picks up, with fireworks shows and the popular demolition derby and tractor pulls. And you won't go hungry here; there are plenty of home-cooked pies, sausages, and lemonade. The popcorn is served from a restored popcorn wagon that has been placed on the National Historic Register.

DIRECTIONS *Located on Route 10 in Walton; follow the signs to the fairgrounds.*

INFORMATION *Admission fee charged; parking is free. The fair usually runs the second week of August, open daily, 9 A.M. to 10 P.M. Call (607) 746-2281 for information.*

FACILITIES *Picnic areas, food stands, farmers' market, rest rooms.*

West Kortright

West Kortright Centre A former church built in the 1850s, this white clapboard building has been restored by volunteers to its former glory, replete with spire, graceful Gothic arches and stained glass windows that glow in a summer's twilight. Inside unique, rounded pews face the stage, where musicians and actors often take advantage of the building's excellent acoustics. Each performing season, which lasts from July to September, artists such as Meredith Monk, John Cage, Virgil Thomson and Teddy Wilson take advantage of the intimate space, bringing one-of-a-kind entertainment to summer visitors and area residents. The concerts and programs offer something for every musical taste, from classical chamber groups to jazz, modern to bluegrass. The annual folk musical festival fits perfectly into the setting of green fields and dusty roads, while the Candlelight Concerts achieve their own brand of magic when the original kerosene chandeliers are lighted at dusk. The intimate setting makes any West Kortright Centre concert a delight for music lovers, and you may just bump into the evening's featured performer as he or she warms up in the churchyard.

DIRECTIONS Take Route 28 to East Meredith, then follow signs.
INFORMATION Open July through September; afternoon and evening concerts. Tickets usually under $6.00. Tel. (607) 746-6325, or write West Kortright Centre, Box 100, East Meredith, 13757.
FACILITIES Picnic tables, rest rooms.

Activities

AUCTIONS

Anything can be auctioned off in Delaware County, from cows to quilts, chairs to coffins, and the nice thing is that each auction is absolutely unique. Auction lovers don't need to plan ahead, either; just pick up a local newspaper and look through the listings. You'll find some are weekly institutions, while others are one-time-only house sales or fund-raisers. If you've never been to an auction, this is a marvelous area to begin since the prices are usually reasonable and the atmosphere is relaxed; you just sign up, get an identification number and grab a chair. Get to the auction early for the inspection period, where you can check out the merchandise before you bid on it. Remember, too, that most auction items are sold as they are, where they are. You should know what you are bidding on and how you'll get it home. For your own comfort, bring a chair or two, some newspaper for wrapping all your buys, and a length of rope in case you have to tie something into the trunk of your car.

Every Saturday night at 7 P.M., those in the know head for **Robert's Auction Service**, Main Street, Fleischmanns, (914) 254-4490. Open all year, they offer everything from produce to cars, fine antiques to a better grade of junk. Eddie, the proprietor, and his son keep the stuff moving, and you'll never be bored here. The crowd is a good mix of visitors and local people, the old former hotel is warmed in the winter by a woodstove, and there are rest rooms and a snack bar. Get there early; if you don't, you may end up standing. Although **Lettis Auction Service**, (607) 432-3935, is based in Ostego County, Jim Lettis does many auctions in Delaware. His house sales are well organized and fast moving, but dress appropriately (even in July, it can be cool) and bring a chair. On Thursday nights, all year, watch for the action at the **Robinson Brothers Auction Barn**, Route 10, Hamden, (607) 865-5253. You'll find country sales chockful of interesting finds—once a magnificent slate billiard table was sold for a quarter to anyone who would haul it away! In Bovina Center, auctions are held every Saturday night by **McIntosh Auction Service** at 7 P.M., at the old creamery, Route 6, Bovina Center, (607) 832-4829. There is plenty of parking, as well as rest rooms and a snack stand. The pace here is slower than most, so a beginner may feel safer making a bid. If you like fine furniture, antique glassware, railroad lamps and fishing lures, among other things, stop at **Cable's Auction Barn**, Route 30, Downsville, (607) 363-7260. Usually held during the day these sales are a little more formal, no children or pets allowed, and there is a buyer's premium, which means you pay a certain percentage over and above the purchase price. This auction attracts serious buyers, and the stock is well worth a stop.

CANOEING

The best canoeing in Delaware County is on the western part of the county, near the Pennsylvania border. Many of the waterways are navigable even by beginners, but never attempt to canoe before checking the local conditions; especially in the spring when the Susquehanna and Delaware rivers are particularly treacherous. The easiest way to enjoy the river is to rent a canoe from an outfitter who knows the area and can provide you with the correct equipment. Deposit is home to **DeNys Canoe Sales** (they also rent), Big Hollow Road, Box 363, R.D. 1, (607) 467-2698. In Shinhopple, try **Al's Sport Store**, (607) 363-7135, a clearinghouse of canoeing (and fishing) information; also in Shinhopple is **Peaceful Valley Campsite**, (607) 363-2211, a good place to stop if you are planning to camp in the area. Peaceful Valley will rent you equipment and then make arrangements to pick you up downstream at the end of the day.

FISHING

Good fishing spots are plentiful in Delaware County because the region is crisscrossed by the East Branch and the West Branch of the Delaware River, the Susquehanna, the Beaver Kill and the Cannonsville, Schoharie and Pepacton reservoirs. New York State fishing licenses are required, and may be purchased in most sporting goods shops or at village and town offices. For reservoir fishing, special permits are required; call the Environmental Protection Office in Downsville, (607) 363-7501, for information.

Sportsmen who are after rock bass, walleye, carp or trout may want to head for one of the area reservoirs. The Schoharie (off Route 23, near the village of Grand Gorge), the Pepacton (Route 30, near Margaretville) and the Cannonsville (Route 10, near Deposit) may be fished from the banks or from a boat under certain conditions; check the rulebooks before you go out. Ice fishing is also allowed, but again there are limitations.

River and stream fishing are popular here in all seasons. At Hancock, where the Delaware River is formed from the East and West Branches, excellent brown and brook trout fishing can be found. An unusual fishing experience can be enjoyed at Hancock in the spring, when shad run upriver from Delaware Bay and Maryland. Watch for the brown and yellow fishermen access signs that indicate public access to the river and parking. On the northern border of the county is the Susquehanna River, where bass and walleye abound; here, too, access sites are at 5-mile intervals.

HIKING

There are hundreds of miles of hiking trails throughout Delaware County. Many of the larger trails are blazed with colored markers and offer lean-tos and springs for your comfort; the smaller trails, however, generally require some knowledge of the region or a very specific map. Although we've hiked many of the county's trails, we know that landscape can change from year to year, so it's a good idea to get a detailed map or one of several excellent small guidebooks to take along. Also, Delaware County is prime country for hunting white-tailed deer, and the month of November sees the woods filled with hunters. Most are careful and conscientious, but there are enough of the other kind out there to make it a good idea to avoid hiking during this period.

The **Dry Brook Ridge Trail** starts in Margaretville and 15 miles later ends in Quaker Clearing, in the town of Hardenburgh. The hike begins at a trailhead that can be reached by turning left at the Agway Store on Route 28, then making another left when the road splits. The trail includes some marvelous views at the top of Pakatakan Mountain, as well as a slight detour around a high-elevation bog. If you plan to have someone meet you in Hardenburgh at the end of the hike, call ahead; the village is small and you may be unable to find a telephone.

The **Delaware Ridge Trail** begins at Trout Pond near

Cook's Falls (exit 92 off Route 17), and connects with several smaller trails south of the Pepacton Reservoir area. The hike is long but not especially difficult, and the scenery here in the fall is gorgeous. A bonus with this trail is that it ends up at the state campground at Little Pond, where complete camping facilities are available.

SCENIC DRIVES

Since very little of Delaware County is developed, it's a perfect area to see by just driving around. Traffic is not a problem here, and the roads are generally well maintained all year, so plan a visit for any season. Deer can be a problem when driving in Delaware County, causing costly and frightening accidents; watch for them at dusk particularly in the fall and spring. And if one deer runs into the road, another will probably follow, so be alert. Also, the weather in Delaware County can be extremely variable, with unexpected springlike days in January and then snowstorms in April. Watch the road conditions carefully if you are not used to driving in snow or ice. Dirt roads may seem charming, but if they are muddy or unplowed they may also stop a car in its tracks. Unless you know exactly where you're going, it's better to stay on the paved state and county roads.

If you want to see dairy farms, cornfields, the county seat, and the Pepacton Reservoir, start in Margaretville and follow Route 28 to Delhi. Then take Route 10 to Walton, Route 206 to Downsville and get on Route 30 back to Margaretville. It's a leisurely 3-hour drive, and the views are enchanting all year. You will pass two of the remaining covered bridges in the county. (They are thought to have been built in order to make it less frightening for horses to cross over water.) One is near Hamden just off Route 10, and the second, which still allows traffic, just outside of Downsville. This drive also passes many small farm stands. One of the more interesting ones is **Octagon Farms,** which takes its name from the eight-sided house that is now a bed and breakfast. Local legend holds that the road near the farm is haunted by the ghost of a young woman killed in a carriage accident.

A second drive follows part of the old turnpike, which was once a main stagecoach route through the area, and offers open views of fields and farms, with their hand-built stone walls. From Margaretville, take Route 28 to Delhi, then Route 10 to Stamford, Route 23 to Grand Gorge and return on Route 30 south back to Margaretville. On Route 10 outside of Delhi, watch for Fitches Bridge on your right. It was built in 1869 and moved to its present location in 1885. (To drive over the bridge, take the steep drive just before the white church.) In Hobart, stop at **Breezy Acres**, a working dairy farm, and bed and breakfast establishment that has fresh maple syrup for sale. Farther on is Stamford, which was once called the "Queen of the Catskills" for its resorts and fine homes, many of which are being restored. Three miles east of Stamford take Blackberry Road to **Graig's Log Cabin Cider Mill**, (607) 652-3384, and try some fresh cider. At Grand Gorge turn south onto Route 30 toward Margaretville; the winding road passes through Long Woods, a swamplike area that gives birth to the East Branch of the Delaware River.

SKIING

Downhill skiing in Delaware County isn't the thrill-a-minute sport found at some resorts, but for the type of skier who likes uncrowded slopes, easy access and family-oriented skiing, it's perfect. At **Deer Run**, Route 10, Stamford, (607) 652-7332, weekenders and day visitors alike will find a smaller, more relaxed resort with all the amenities of the larger areas. The skiing area offers a vertical drop of 750 feet and a base elevation of 2,150 feet. Guests can stay right at the base of the slopes in the Trophy Lodge Motel, and walk or ski to the lifts each day. Three chair lifts keep the lines moving, and ticket sales are limited in order to reduce crowding. Night skiing is available and children's classes—complete with hot chocolate breaks—can be arranged. For the adult beginner, ask about the guaranteed learn-to-ski packages. Complete snowmaking capability, a lodge with a full service restaurant, bowling lanes and sport shop.

Plattekill Ski Center, Route 30, Roxbury, (607) 326-7547, is situated in a mountain "bowl," with breathtaking views of the surrounding Catskills. The summit elevation here is 3,350 feet, and the trails range in difficulty from easy to extreme expert. Plattekill offers snowmaking capabilities along with a triple chair lift, a T-bar and a pony lift for beginners. Even though the slopes can become very crowded, the feeling here is always easygoing. Plattekill is a family-run operation, and personal touches are their specialty. A nursery is available, and there are interfaith worship services each Sunday; there's even a bed and breakfast ski package available. Other amenities include seven-day-a-week skiing during the season, a lodge with an enormous outdoor deck overlooking the mountains, a rental and gift shop, lessons and lots of parking. The instructors here are especially good with younger skiers.

For cross-country skiers, Delaware County is a delight. Rolling meadows, pine forests and lots of public land combine to make the area attractive to serious skiers and novices alike. In Downsville, two sites are extra special. **Bear Spring Mountain Wildlife Management Center** (no phone) off Route 30 outside of Walton, has ungroomed trails that follow old logging roads. Skiers can find more than 25 miles of novice to intermediate trails there; be aware, however, that this area is also open to snowmobilers. Rentals are not available in the area, so be sure to bring everything you'll need for the day; the views here are absolutely magnificent, especially right after a heavy snowfall. **Round Up Ranch**, Route 206, Downsville, (607) 363-7300, is a western-style resort with 5 miles of trails. Use of the trails is free; equipment rental and lessons are available. Call ahead here to check conditions, and note that resort facilities are open to guests only. But the place is so friendly and well run that you'll want to stay the weekend. **Deer Run**, listed above, also offers an extensive system of trails for cross-country skiers. Full facilities—including rental, lessons, rest rooms, and snack bar—are available, but there is a small trail-use fee. Also in Stamford is the **Utsayantha Trail System**, which is maintained by the town and covers over 28 miles. Snowmobiles use the trails as well, but the terrain is excellent and a free trail map is available from the Stamford

Chamber of Commerce (Stamford, 12167). Rentals are available in the village. In Delhi, the **SUNY College Golf Course**, off Route 28, outside of the village, is a lovely novice-intermediate course near the Little Delaware River. There is no use fee and no rentals are available, but you're only 5 minutes from the village so snack and warm-up breaks are no problem. Many other areas in Delaware County allow cross-country skiing, especially golf courses, schools and village parks; even so, it's best to ask before you kick and glide on unmarked property.

Where to Eat

Delaware County is not renowned for an abundance of gourmet restaurants. The following, however, are some casual spots where travelers might want to stop for a light meal or snack.

The Binnekill Square Restaurant *(Binnekill Square, Main St., Margaretville, (914) 586-4884)* Open for both lunch and dinner, this establishment looks out on the Binnekill stream and has an outdoor deck and piano bar. Continental menu, with veal dishes the specialty. Children are welcome.
 OPEN *Lunch—Wed. through Sat., 11:30 A.M. to 4 P.M.; dinner—Tues. through Sun., from 5 P.M. on. Closed Mon.*

The Cheese Barrel *(Main St., Margaretville, (914) 586-4666)* An excellent selection of snacks and cheeses, great for takeout and picnics. There's a small dining area, and they carry lots of local produce. Children are welcome.
 OPEN *Daily from 10 A.M. to 5:30 P.M., from July 4 to Labor Day. All other times, closed on Sun. and Tues.*

Roxbury Run *(Denver-Vega Rd., Denver, (607) 326-7577)* Veal and Swiss dishes are the specialty here. Set beside a lovely pond, this is a popular place with skiers. Absolutely devastating chocolate fondue. Children are welcome; will prepare special items.

OPEN *Dinner—Thurs. through Sat., 5:30* P.M. *on; Sunday brunch—noon to 3:30* P.M.

The Village Inn *(Main St., Delhi, (607) 746-3200)* A diner-style breakfast and lunch place with a counter and some table seating. The food is hearty American—meat loaf, chicken and biscuits, turnovers, muffins. Everything is homemade, and it's a great place to take the children.

OPEN *Mon. through Fri., 5* A.M. *to 7:30* P.M.*; Sat., 6* A.M *to noon. Closed Sun.*

Where to Stay

Breezy Acres Farm *(R.D. 1, Box 191, Hobart, 13788, (607) 538-9338)* A working dairy farm with 120 holsteins on 300 acres. The rambling seventeen-room farmhouse with pillared porches is also a bed and breakfast, and breakfast here includes maple syrup products made on the farm; the French toast, served with maple cream, is a specialty of the house, and March visitors can see how the syrup is made. Other features: a relaxing whirlpool tub and a game room with a piano. Open all year. Four bedrooms share two and a half baths. Children are welcome.

Carriage House *(Main St., Halcottsville, 12438 (607) 326-7992)* This 100-year-old Victorian house still has the original woodwork and is furnished with period pieces. A bed and breakfast now, it has been in the same family for three generations. Homemade whole wheat bread and fresh cinnamon rolls are a specialty here, part of the hearty breakfast served to guests each morning. Sherry and herbal tea are served in the late afternoon. Open all year. Four rooms share two bathrooms. Children are welcome.

Churchside Bed & Breakfast *(P.O. Box 76, Main St., Bovina Center, 13740 (607) 832-4231)* This Greek-Revival farmhouse has been owned by the same family since the mid-nineteenth century. Antiques fill the rooms, and a full breakfast greets guests. The house is located in a charming hamlet that was once a dairy center; a popular Saturday night auction is within walking distance at the Old Creamery. Two rooms, two baths. No smoking or pets allowed. Discount for more than one night's stay; by reservation only. Open all year.

Country Studio Bed and Breakfast *(Old River Rd., Roxbury, 12474, (607) 326-7847)* This charming contemporary home has a dollhouse shop and museum on the premises. The owner, Rosemarie Torre, custom designs miniature furniture and room settings. A full country breakfast features homemade jams and baked goods. Open all year. Three rooms share one bath. Children are welcome.

Greystone Lodge *(36 Lake St., Stamford, 12167, (607) 652-7936)* Built in 1902, this historic cottage is warm and comfortable and filled with old-world charm. English and French antiques fill the rooms, and the Continental breakfast features homemade jams. Open all year. One room has a private bath; four other rooms share one bathroom. Children are welcome.

Highland Fling Inn *(Main St., Fleischmanns, 12430, (914) 254-5650)* Scotland-native Matt Farrell and his German-born wife, Iris, run this charming inn, made up of two beautiful turn-of-the century Victorian homes and six summer cottages. The full Scottish breakfast features home-style European cooking. Tennis courts and a heated pool are within walking distance. Open all year. Three rooms share one bath; nine have private bathrooms. Children are welcome.

Hilltop House *(Huckleberry Brook Rd., Box 51, Margaretville, 12455, (914) 586-4293)* This 1809 farmhouse has plenty of old-fashioned charm, as well as all the modern conveniences. Breakfast features homemade baked goods and jams, as well as fresh produce from the garden in season. Open all year. Three rooms share one bath; one has a private bathroom. A suite can be arranged. Children are welcome.

Kass Inn *(Route 30, Margaretville, 12455, (914) 586-9844/ 4841)* This family-owned inn is filled with beautiful antiques and has been passed down through three generations. Golf, fishing and cross-country skiing, as well as a restaurant on the premises. Motel, efficiencies and apartments available. Open year-round. Seventy rooms, all with private bathrooms. Children are welcome.

Lake Wawaka Guest House Bed and Breakfast *(Old River Rd., Halcottsville, 12438 (607) 326-4694)* Located on the East Branch of the Delaware River, this quiet, spacious farmhouse offers a wide variety of recreational activities nearby. Full breakfast is served. Halcottsville is a small hamlet between Roxbury and Margaretville on Route 30. Open all year. Six rooms (all doubles) share two full bathrooms. No pets or children under 10 allowed.

The Lanigan Farm *(R.D. 1, Box 399, Stamford, 12167 (607) 652-7455/6263)* A country farm with an informal atmosphere and lots of old-fashioned charm. The hearty breakfast features fresh fruits and vegetables as well as homemade muffins, breads and jams. Wine and cheese are served in the late afternoon. This is the perfect place for a large family or group of friends to stay together. Open all year. Three rooms share one bathroom. Well behaved children only.

Margaretville Mountain Inn *(Margaretville Mountain Road, Margaretville, 12455 (914) 586-3933)* This restored eleven-bedroom Victorian home was built as a boarding house and functioned as a working farm. It has a spectacular view of the New Kingston Valley from the old-fashioned veranda. Breakfast only. Open April through February. Five rooms, three with private baths. Children are welcome; no pets.

Octagon Farm Bed and Breakfast *(R.D. 1, Box 70, Walton, 13856, (607) 865-7416)* This bed and breakfast, in a historic, octagonal house built in 1855, is also a farm market. The famous farmer's breakfast here consists of pancakes or waffles with pure creamery butter and maple syrup, as well as bacon or sausage. Open all year. Four rooms share one and a half baths. Children are welcome.

Rainbow Chalet *(R.D. 2, Box 87B, Feak Hollow Rd., Walton, 13856, (607) 865-4703)* A secluded home on 20 acres of land. Overlooks a 4½-acre pond with a paddle boat, canoe and rowboat available to guests. Breakfast features their own maple syrup, home-baked breads, cinnamon rolls and muffins, as well as a tasty quiche. Open all year. Two large rooms with televisions share one bathroom. Children are welcome; baby-sitting and crib available.

Roundup Ranch *(Wilson Hollow Rd., Downsville, 13755, (607) 363-7300)* A stay at this 2,000-acre ranch is a great way for an entire family to enjoy a vacation together. A wide range of activities is available—horseback riding, golf, fishing, tennis and swimming, as well as hayrides, square dancing, volleyball and rodeos. Three meals served daily. Open all year. Forty rooms; seven share bathrooms. Children are welcome.

Scudder Hill House Bed and Breakfast *(Scudder Hill Rd., Roxbury, 12474, (607) 326-4364/4215)* This 130-year-old Federal-style farmhouse is a quiet retreat with country charm and comforts. Gourmet breakfasts include seafood soufflés and homegrown vegetables in season. All baking is done on the premises. Open all year. Four rooms share one bath; one room has a private bathroom. Children must be well behaved.

Greene County

Greene County offers the perfect outdoor experience any time of the year. In winter dramatic, snow-filled gorges yield to delicate, misty waterfalls, and skiers are just as likely to run across bear tracks as they are to discover the delights of a ski lodge fireplace. The spring reveals bright wildflowers clinging to wind-scraped rocks, and visitors to the county can watch in awe as people enthusiastically join in the Spring Rush, a grueling bike, ski and foot race. Summer celebrates its warmth with the gift of icy brooks for tired feet, and a flood of cultural festivals. The fall is a time to stop and wonder at the colors that transform the hills and towns into paint pots full of orange and red. Or take a day or two to search for the lost treasure of Rip Van Winkle. Greene County is thought to have been Rip's home, and the magic that he discovered here still lures travelers from near and far. And other ghosts haunt Greene County as well; in Leeds, if you walk along a dark country road, you might run into the spirit of the servant girl who was dragged to her

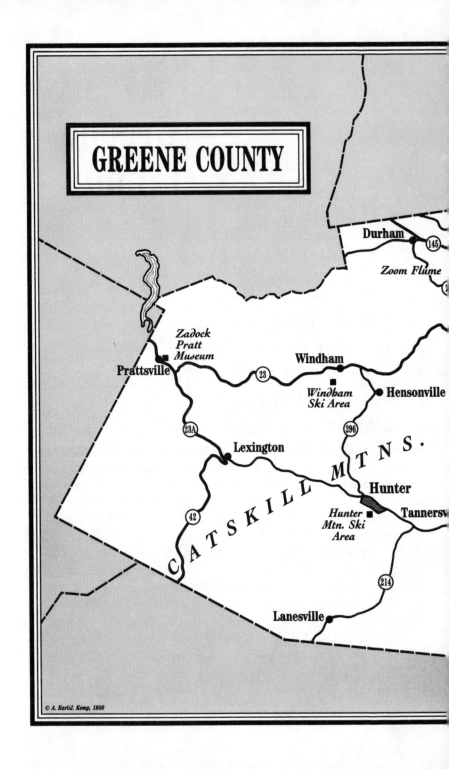

GREENE COUNTY

Durham

(145)

Zoom Flume

Zadock
Pratt
Museum

Windham

Prattsville

(23)

Windham
Ski Area

Hensonville

(23A)

(296)

Lexington

C A T S K I L L M T N S.

Hunter

Hunter
Mtn. Ski
Area

Tannersv

(42)

(214)

Lanesville

© A. Karl/J. Kemp, 1988

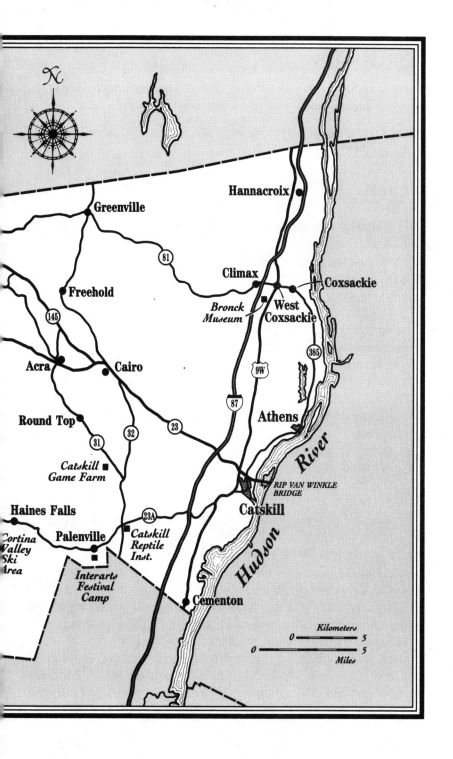

death by her master and his horse. There are also hiking trails, museums, country auctions, breathtaking waterfalls, festivals, waterfront villages and fine restaurants to enjoy.

Catskill

Catskill Reptile Institute If snakes and reptiles interest you, visit this incredible display. The institute houses hundreds of rare snakes and reptiles, from the Yellow Spitting Cobra and Eastern Diamondback Rattler to Nile Monitor Lizards and the 15-foot-long African Rock Python. There are local snakes to wonder at as well as exotic creatures right out of a Rudyard Kipling story, and all are housed in glass cases that duplicate the animals' natural environment. Visitors get an up-close look at these amazing creatures. Tour guides are available if you want to really learn something of the reptiles' history, and guests are encouraged to take photographs throughout the institute. You can even hold a python and have your picture taken. Even people who are frightened of snakes often leave the institute with a better understanding of these remarkable creatures.

> DIRECTIONS *Located on Route 32, two miles north of Catskill.*
> INFORMATION *Open May 15 through September 15—10 A.M. to 6 P.M. daily; winter and spring weekends by appointments. Tel. (518) 678-5590. Admission fee charged. There are guided tours and outdoor demonstrations, and visitors are allowed to touch some of the snakes.*
> FACILITIES *Gift shop, rest rooms.*

Lost Treasure of Rip Van Winkle For those who don't know the story of Rip Van Winkle, it started when he got lost on a Greene County mountain. He joined the ghostly crew of Hendrik Hudson in a drinking party and awoke 20 years later, to the amazement of his friends and relatives. During the party, Rip stole a priceless ninepin from the Halfe Moone's crew and hid it somewhere in Greene County. But he forgot where he put it. The ninepin was "discovered" in 1982 and is on display at Schenectady Trust on Main Street in Catskill. It awaits the treasure hunter who can unravel the clues and discover the stone that covers the spot where the jewel-encrusted object was found. Valued at over $100,000, the pin has more than ninety precious stones on its surface—including diamonds, moonstones and garnets—and so far no one has come across the stone engraved with Rip's initials that will allow them to claim the prize. Clues to the location of the treasure are found in **The Lost Treasure of Rip Van Winkle**, a book that was written by a mystery writer and sponsored by the Kaaterskill Foundation, a non-profit agency that promotes Greene County. While you can follow the book's clues, this much will get you started: it is above ground, on public land, somewhere in Greene County. And it could make you rich.

DIRECTIONS *Taking place all through Greene County.*
INFORMATION *The clue book can be purchased from The Kaaterskill Foundation, P.O. Box 551, Catskill, 12414. It costs $5.95, plus $1.20 shipping and handling. Or call the Greene County Council on the Arts at (518) 943-3400.*

Walking Tour The town of Catskill has long served as a river stop for ships and sailors who worked on the Hudson River, and it boasts many fine homes and public buildings. Walking through the area today, you'll see that many structures have been restored during the last 150 years, and some of the buildings offer interesting bits of history. The **Palmer-Willsey Ice House** at 40 Bushnell Avenue is one of the few surviving nineteenth-century commercial ice houses. The **1797 Catskill Inn**, 251 West Main Street, was once a private house and has seen visitors like Martin Van Buren and the original Uncle Sam. At **Cherry Hill**, located at 47 Division Street, you will find one of the puzzling octagon houses, which were so popular in the 1850s, while the **Catskill Public Library** at 1 Franklin Street was one of the "Carnegie Libraries," erected through the generosity of Andrew J. Carnegie. Several other nineteenth-century architectural styles can be seen throughout the town, especially Italianate, Art Deco, Romanesque Revival and Victorian Gothic. A walk along Prospect Avenue, William Street, Main Street or Bridge Street, to name only a few, will also give a glimpse of the magic of an old river town. Or you may want to write to the Greene County Promotion Department, Box 467 TG, Catskill, 12414, for a copy of "A Guide to Catskill's Architectural History."

DIRECTIONS *Take the N.Y. Thruway to exit 21 or Route 9W into the town.*

Coxsackie

Bronck Museum Once home to nine generations of the Bronck family (who also gave their name to the Bronx), the museum's collection traces the history of the Upper Hudson Valley. Visitors should begin with the original structure, a 1663 stone house that contains an Indian lookout loft—from a time when settlers were not welcomed. Remodeled in the late eighteenth century, a wing was added to the house along with fine paneling and fireplaces. Displays include an impressive exhibit of local textiles, looms and spinning wheels that chronicle the production of Bronck cloth and clothing. An earlier addition, the 1738 Brick House, was connected to the stone house through a hyphen-hall. This part of the family home is now used to display, among other household items, a fine collection of paintings by eighteenth- and nineteenth-century artists, including Ammi Phillips, John Frederick Kensett, Frederic Church and Thomas Cole. Outside is a kitchen, which is set apart from the main house in the style of plantations. The displays here consist of furniture and kitchen tools, and the building itself is a charming, tiny house. Farm buffs will enjoy the three barns that are found at the complex, each representing a different era. The Dutch barn, with its huge beams; the center-pole-supported, thirteen-sided Liberty Barn; and the Victorian horse barn each offer the visitor a look at the tools, carriages and wagons of the day. A walk through the family and slave cemeteries will bring you even closer to the people who made the Bronck complex a working and living farm.

DIRECTIONS Located off Route 9W on Pieter Bronck Road in Coxsackie.

INFORMATION Open the last Saturday in June through the Sunday before Labor Day—Tues. through Sat., 10 A.M. to 5 P.M. (closed for lunch); Sun., 2 to 6 P.M. Closed Mon. Admission fee charged.

FACILITIES Picnic area, gift shop, rest rooms.

Zoom Flume Billed as an "aquamusement park," this playground is set in the Shady Glen canyon, a natural formation of steep walls and running water. Features include the Mountain Coaster, an alpine slide where riders sit on small coasters and zip down through the forests; the Water Slide, where you splash down into a small lake; the Bumper Boats; and the Soak A Buddy, where kids can splash each other to their hearts' content. There are also nature trails, scenic overlooks and waterfalls galore. And parents can leave older kids to enjoy themselves on the rides while they take a break in the observation deck lounges.

DIRECTIONS Located just off Route 145 (Shady Glen Road), two miles north of East Durham.

INFORMATION Open Memorial Day to Labor Day—daily, 10 A.M. to 10 P.M., weather permitting. Admission fee charged. Call (518) 239-4559 for information. Bathing suits are required; no shorts or t-shirts.

FACILITIES Changing rooms, snack stands and restaurant, playground, picnic area, rest rooms.

Lawrenceville

Catskill Game Farm Established in 1933, this is one of the country's oldest and best-known game farms. Visitors can explore a zoological park, where they'll find lions, tigers, monkeys, elephants and giant tortoises. At the nursery, baby animals can be viewed. Another delight is the petting zoo, where tame deer and goats gobble up special snacks you can feed them by hand. A friendly warning: don't leave anything sticking out of your pockets and don't leave small children alone with the animals. Special shows are also offered, and the extravaganzas can include anything from trained bears and elephants to dancing chickens. The Catskill Game Farm is a real institution, and an excellent place to take children.

DIRECTIONS *Located on Game Farm Road near Catskill; take Route 32, 23 or 23A.*

INFORMATION *Open April 15 through October 31 daily, 9 A.M. to 6 P.M. Admission fee charged.*

FACILITIES *Picnic area, gift shop, rest rooms.*

Palenville

Interarts Festival This theater festival, workshop series and summer arts colony is rooted in the nineteenth-century tradition of arts colonies. It all started when the Bond Street Theater Company of New York City stopped in Palenville during a summer tour. The directors discovered a children's camp they felt would serve as the perfect retreat for traditional, ethnic and folk performers; quickly the camp was leased for the next season, and the Interarts group soon began to work with the town in developing an active, popular theater organization. Through workshops and classes, the townspeople—both adults and children—join in each year as entertainers and behind-the-scenes workers. The acts vary each summer, with recent offerings including Circus Arts, the Magicians of Taipei, modern dance, the Odyssey Theatre and the Brubeck-LaVerne Trio. Special children's shows are offered each Saturday morning, and most of the productions are imaginatively staged and exciting to watch. Arrangements to stay at the Interarts camp for a weekend can be made.

DIRECTIONS *Take Route 9W to Route 23A west into Palenville; or Route 32 to 32A.*

INFORMATION *Runs from July to September; call (212) 206-7564 for schedules. Admission fee charged.*

FACILITIES *Picnic area, limited campsites, rest rooms.*

Prattsville

Zadock Pratt Museum and Pratt's Rocks Born in 1790, genius businessman Zadock Pratt started out as a harness maker and soon went into the tanning business. He became such a prominent community leader that the town of Prattsville was named in his honor. His tanning facilities were among the largest in the state, and he built many of Prattsville's homes for his workers. In later years, Pratt served in both the state and federal governments. Today, Pratt's home is a museum that shows what life in New York was like in the 1850s. Exhibits focus on the tanning industry and the story of Greene County, with a room also devoted to Pratt's foresight and eccentricities and several rooms containing period furniture and decorative arts. Just outside of Prattsville are Pratt's Rocks, a memorial he had carved by an itinerant stonemason. The huge stone reliefs show Pratt's favorite horse, Pratt's son and Pratt himself.

DIRECTIONS *Located on Route 23, between Grand Gorge and Ashland.*

INFORMATION *Open May through October—Wed. through Sat., 10:30 A.M. to 5 P.M., Sun., 2 to 5 P.M. The rocks are in a park and are visible all year. There is a guided tour of the house, and the walk up to Pratt's Rocks takes half an hour. Museum admission fee charged.*

FACILITIES *Picnic area.*

Activities

AIRPLANE TOURS

With its rolling meadows and steep mountain heights, Greene County is a popular place to see through the window of an airplane. Recreational flights are an unusual, exciting way to view the region, and air tours add some adventure to any vacation. A call to any of the three local airports listed here will put you in touch with pilots who specialize in tour flights and lessons. **Freehold Airport** in Freehold, (518) 634-7626, is a full-service airport that offers pleasure flights and a glider school. **Maben's Airport**, Route 23A, Prattsville, (518) 299-8585, will arrange airplane rides, lessons and even parachute-jumping instructions for the more daring. At **Cairo Airport**, Bross Street, Cairo, (518) 622-9736, you can also arrange scenic rides. Also has campgrounds and special fly-in events for pilots.

ANTIQUES

Greene County offers the antique lover everything from the funky to the fabulous, with a wide range of shops, auctions and flea markets. Although many establishments are open all year, their hours tend to be limited in the off season; call before you go.

If you are looking for the light of the world, **American Gothic Antiques**, Route 23A, Hunter, (518) 263-4836, stocks a wonderful array of antique lamps and accessories. Art Deco lovers will enjoy stopping in at the **Stone House Gallery** in Lexington, (518) 989-6755, where jewelry, folk art and early American pieces create an eclectic mix. Another stop for people in search of fine jewelry and antique contemporary art is the **Tiffany House Gallery**, Route 23, Acra, (518) 622-3566, where you may come across an antique carousel horse or a magnificent Victorian brooch; the shop itself is also lovely. **Ipsen Antiques** Route 214, Lanesville, (914) 688-7161, offers a unique collection of American and Scandinavian antiques in addition to their general line. Two truly unusual shops cater to the collector who knows exactly what he or she is looking for: at **Mudge's Gun Shop**, Route 296, Hensonville, (518) 734-3517, buyers will discover the best in antique guns, from black powder rifles to finely engraved hunting pieces; if music is more your style, a trip to the **Old Piano Roll Store**, Route 23, Acra, (518) 622-3160, is in order. Here old player pianos still plink out tunes from the past, and there is an incredible selection of player piano rolls from which to choose. And if all that shopping makes you hungry, stop in at the **Last Chance Antiques Cafe**, Main Street, Tannersville, (518) 589-6424, where you can have a gourmet snack and then buy the furnishings right out from under the other diners.

Auctions are also popular throughout the county, and they attract buyers from all over the state. If you go to one, be sure to bring along a box or two and some newspaper to store your finds in. If you have them, toss some folding chairs into the car; auctions can become standing-room-only affairs very quickly. And remember to inspect all merchandise before you buy, because the auctioneer won't return your money if you don't like what you get. Auctions are usually announced in local newspapers, and the advertisements often indicate whether or not there are the additional buyer's premiums. If you are not sure, call before you go, or ask before you bid.

A solid collection of fine antiques can be found at many auctions held at the **Savoia & Fromm Auction Gallery**, Route 23, South Cairo, (518) 622-8000; **Athens Antique Center & Auction Gallery**, Athens, (518) 731-2800; and the **Lincoln Auction Service**, Lincoln Center, Route 9W, West Coxsackie, (518) 943-2704. In the village of Leeds, two auction houses worth visiting are: **Brekel Auction Gallery** on Main Street, (518) 943-3323, and **Leeds Auction Barn**, Route 23B, (518) 943-9143. Fine antiques, household goods and lots more can be discovered at the auctions held at the **Durham Auction Barn**, Route 145, Durham, (518) 239-8475 (open Saturdays, all year), and at **Tannersville Auctions & Sales**, Main Street, Tannersville, (518) 589-5554. **Junior's Auction Barn,** Route 23, Prattsville, (518) 229-3546, has real old-fashioned auctions, filled with gems of all kinds.

FARM STANDS AND PICK-YOUR-OWN FARMS

Greene County could be called the mushroom capital of the Hudson River region, with several farms in the county that produce some of the freshest, most luscious mushrooms around. **Bulich Mushroom Company,** Greenport Road, Catskill, (518) 943-3089 (open all year), and **Osborn Mushroom Farm**, Route 9W, Coxsackie, (518) 731-8730 (open all year), will sell you mushrooms and also answer any questions you have about cooking them. If berries are more to your liking, you can head out to the fields to pick your own. **Bennett's Berry Farms**, Independence Lane, Hannacroix, (518) 756-9472, has strawberries only, and is open during June and July. **Story Farms**, Route 32, Catskill, (518) 678-9716, allows you to pick your own strawberries, peas and tomatoes, but they also offer lots of other local produce at their large farm stand. Apples are the specialty at **Henry Boehm**, County Road 26, Climax, (518) 731-6196, and pick-your-own is the rule from September on. At the **Kaatskill Cider Mill**, Route 32, Catskill, (518) 678-5529 (open year-round), apples, cider, honey and maple syrup make this one sweet stop for regional food lovers. And two large, well-stocked farm stands that offer everything from blueberries to parsnips should be included on any Greene County trip: **Black Horse Farms**, Route 9W, Athens, (518) 943-9324 (open May to October), and **Hamilton's Farm Stand**, Route 145, Cairo, (518) 622-3713 (open July through mid-December). Of course, lots of small, local farm stands and farmers' markets sprout up all over the county during growing season; don't pass them by.

FISHING

Fishing in Greene County can be a lazy day spent pondside or an exciting, nerve-ripping hour fighting a sturgeon in the Hudson. There are more than fifty-eight streams that shelter wild trout here, as well as lakes, ponds and, of course, the Hudson River. A state fishing license is required in Greene County and town permits are also needed for the Potuck Reservoir in Catskill and the Medway Reservoir in Coxsackie. Permits and licenses can be obtained at many of the bait and tackle and sports shops across the county, as well as in town clerks' offices and the county clerk's office in Catskill. Seasons and limits vary with the species of fish; check with the Department of Environmental Conservation for specifics. In Greene County, public fishing areas are marked by yellow signs, and parking spaces are available, although they're sometimes limited. If you want to catch one of the more than 150 species of fish that are found in the Hudson River—shad, perch, herring and sturgeon among them—you may want to use the public boat ramps that can be found in Athens, Coxsackie and Catskill. Route 23A will take you past Rip Van Winkle Lake in Tannersville, the Schoharie Creek and the Schoharie Reservoir, all of which are great fishing areas. Route 145 leads to the Lower Catskill Creek, the Upper Catskill Creek and Ten Mile Creek, while Route 296 provides access to the Batavia Kill boat launch and the East Kill Trout Preserve. BASSmaster Invitational fishing tournaments have been held in Greene County, and you can write to the Greene County Promotion Department (Box 467FF, Catskill, 12414) for information on upcoming fishing events, or call them at (518) 943-3223.

HIKING

Greene County's mountains provide some of the best hiking—and views—in the Catskills. You don't have to be a seasoned hiker to enjoy a day walking on these clearly marked trails, and the magnificent views here have inspired Thomas Cole and other painters of the Hudson River School. A few suggested routes follow.

Although **The Escarpment Trail** runs from Kaaterskill Creek on Route 23A to East Windham on Route 23 (24 miles in all), there are several short hikes to take in this area, to Kaaterskill High Peak, North Point and Mary's Glen. The trails in the North Lake area are renowned for their waterfalls and fantastic views of the entire Hudson Valley. Kaaterskill Falls and the Catskill Mountain House are particularly noteworthy sites. The easy-to-find entry point for these trails is at the junction of Route 23A and Kaaterskill Creek on the north side of the highway. These hikes are usually very popular on summer weekends, so you might want to go during the week, to avoid the crowds, especially if you enjoy solitude in the woods. North Lake and good campgrounds are nearby for those who want to take a swim or stay overnight.

For more experienced and adventurous hikers, there is **The Devil's Path**, named for its steepness and relative isolation. The path passes over much rugged terrain, particularly **Indian Head Mountain**, and also includes **Hunter Mountain** and the **West Kill Mountain Range Trail.** To reach the trailhead, turn south off Route 23A at the only light in Tannersville. Go 1⅓ miles, until the road intersects with Bloomer Road. Turn left and after about half a mile, bear left onto Platte Clove Mountain Road. Stay on this road for one mile to Prediger Road, then go a quarter of a mile further to find the trail. Each single mountain on the Devil's Path can be hiked in a day or less.

At 4,040 feet, **Hunter Mountain** is the second highest peak in the Catskills and is best hiked on the trail that starts on Spruceton Road. To get there, take Route 42 north from Lexington, and go four miles to Spruceton Road. The trailhead and trail are well defined.

Another pleasant day hike takes you to **Diamond Notch** and **West Kill Falls.** Located five miles north of Phoenicia, near Route 214, it is also easy to find. From Route 214, take Diamond Notch Road about one mile to a bridge, cross it and park. The hike is about 4½ miles, and should take 4 hours at most.

SCENIC DRIVES

Mountains, deep gorges, valleys and waterfalls can all be seen during a leisurely car drive through Greene County, and the tours can take all day or only a few hours. Some of the roads are narrow and winding, though, so use the designated parking areas for viewing scenic areas. Also, be careful to check driving conditions if you take a drive in winter or early spring.

Some lovely parts of the county can be seen from Route 28 as you head west toward Route 42. Drive north on Route 42 over the Deep Notch, which is cool even on the hottest summer days. At Route 23A, head east through Hunter, Haines Falls and Palenville. Along the road, you will see Hunter Mountain, breathtaking waterfalls and the Amphitheatre, a natural bowl-shaped rock formation. Follow Route 23 into Catskill, where you can pick up the N.Y. Thruway at exit 21. This drive takes approximately 3 hours.

Starting at the junction of Routes 23A and 23C, follow 23C east to Jewett. The large and elegant homes that line the roads were part of Onteora Park, a "cottage" colony where many wealthy families summered during the nineteenth and early twentieth centuries. The junction of Routes 25 and 23C shelters the Old Stone Church, in which there are some magnificent murals. (The church is closed in the winter.) At Route 17, head south to Route 23A, where you can pick up the route of the scenic drive above into Catskill.

To see some exceptional churches, begin on Route 23A in Jewett Center. Here you will see the St. John the Baptist Ukrainian Catholic Church, which was built in 1961. The church was constructed in the traditional Ukrainian style, with large wooden beams held together by carved wooden pins instead of nails. The interior of the church is decorated with wood carvings and panels, and the education building has displays relating to Ukrainian history. Continue on Route 23A to Haines Falls, where you'll find the Grotto of Our Lady of the Mountain. This shrine was constructed in the 1920s, and was meant to recall the miracle at Lourdes. The Grotto is open to the public, and small, colorful flower gardens mark the walkways. Continue on 23A to Palenville, where the Gloria Dei Episcopal Church is open for tours on Saturdays from 10 A.M. to 2 P.M. Take Route 23A to Route 32 north into Cairo, then Route 24 to South Cairo. There you will find the Mahayan Temple, a Buddhist retreat complete with Chinese temple, dragon decorations and fine artwork. While there are no formal tours, the walkways are open to the public and offer a contemplative way to spend an hour. From South Cairo, you can take Route 24 east to the N.Y. Thruway.

SKIING

Downhill skiers will discover in Greene County a place where they can enjoy excellent snow conditions, the most modern facilities and some of the most spectacular views anywhere. Greene lies right in the New York State snow belt, where sudden spring storms can dump inches of powder in an hour. Skiing here lasts for at least six months of the year. At **Hunter Mountain**, Route 23A, Hunter, (518) 263-4223 (also toll free, 1-(800)-548-6648 in New York, and 1-(800)-FOR-SNOW outside New York), the reputation as the snowmaking capital of the East is well deserved. The three different mountains—Hunter One, Hunter West and Hunter Mountain—offer skiers of all skill levels a chance to test themselves on dozens of different trails. Runs at Hunter can extend more than two miles, with vertical drops of 1,600 feet, and there are some extremely difficult areas for the expert. Double and triple chair lifts cut some of the lines down to size, but this is such a popular area that you should be prepared to wait in line if you go on a weekend or holiday. Hunter offers ski lessons for all levels, including children, and a wide variety of amateur and professional races during the season. Hunter also offers 100 percent snowmaking capability, so the season sometimes begins as early as early November and lasts into May. You will find complete facilities here, including babysitting, cafeterias, a lodge, ski shop and even a small ski museum. There is plenty of parking, but again, Hunter can get very crowded. At **Ski Windham**, Route 23, Windham, (518) 734-3400 (also toll free, 1-(800)-342-5116 in New York, and 1-(800)-833-5056 outside New York), you will be greeted by "Courtesy Bears," who are there to promote safety and courtesy. There are twenty-seven trails at Windham, which has a vertical elevation of 1,500 feet at the base, and 3,050 at the summit. Trail difficulty ranges from easier to most difficult, and there is a 97 percent snowmaking capability. The longest trail at Windham is more than two miles and is fine for novice and intermediate skiers. Even with the huge lift capacity that Windham offers, this is a busy slope and lines will form on weekends. A full line of services is available, including restaurants, ski school, rentals, a ski shop, a nursery and picnic tables. The lodge offers a wonderful view of the mountains, and there is even an area for RV hookups if you make reservations. **Cortina Valley**, off Route 23A in Haines Falls, (518) 589-6500, has a base elevation of 2,000 feet, the highest in the Catskills. They have wide snowmaking capabilities, night and day skiing and even camping and RV facilities, along with restaurants, motel accommodations, ski rentals, lessons and shops. A broad range of special events and fun races are scheduled during the ski season. Cortina's popularity can result in long lift lines, but the pace is a little less hectic than at some of the larger slopes.

For those who cross-country ski, Greene County is home to some of the best areas in the state. Well over 1,000 acres of groomed and ungroomed trails snake their way through the county's forests and fields, and many of the areas are patrolled by Nordic Ski Patrol members, a comforting thought for beginners. **Hyer Meadows**, Onteora Road, Tannersville, (518) 589-5361, is a place where expert skiers, novices and families can all find a place to enjoy the outdoors. The 350 acres of trails are all groomed and well marked according to level of difficulty. The scenery here is magical, especially after an early spring snowstorm. Full facilities are found at Hyer Meadows, including rentals, lessons, tours, cafeteria and babysitting; night tours are also available with advance reservations. **White Birches**, Route 23 in Windham, (518) 734-3266, has 17 miles of groomed, marked trails for all ski levels and services that include a lodge, rentals, ski shop, tours and races. **Winter Clove**, Route 31, Round Top, (518) 622-3267), is located on the grounds of a fine country inn, but the skiing is open to the public and rentals are available. Plan to stay at the inn if you want to enjoy a unique weekend of skiing and fine dining.

Where to Eat

Bell's Coffee Shop (387 Main St., Catskill, (518) 943-4070) An old-fashioned luncheonette, with large portions and low prices. Open every day. A favorite among local residents.

Chalet Fondue (Intersection of Route 296 and South St., Windham, (518) 734-4650) There are three dining rooms here—a greenhouse, a rathskeller and a garden room. The cuisine is Swiss-German, and the fondue is the specialty. Children are welcome.
OPEN *Mon., Wed. through Sat., 5 to 11 P.M.; Sun., 1 to 11 P.M. Closed Tues.*

Chateau Belleview (Route 23A, Tannersville, (518) 589-5525) Fine Continental cuisine and spectacular mountain views. Open every day for dinner.

La Conca D'Oro *(440 Main St., Catskill, (518) 943-3549)* The name means "the golden bay," and this unpretentious Italian restaurant offers fine food at exceedingly reasonable prices. The veal entrées, chicken dishes and homemade mozzarella are house specialties. For dessert, there are excellent cannolis. Children are welcome; special menu provided.

OPEN *Mon., Wed. and Thurs., 11:30 A.M. to 10 P.M. and Fri. until 11 P.M.; Sat., 3 to 11 P.M.; Sun., 2 to 10 P.M. Closed Tues.*

La Griglia *(Route 296, Windham, (518) 734-4499)* Located in a 125-year-old building and lovingly filled with antique paintings and furniture, this restaurant is on the ninth hole of Windham's golf course. The chef-owner, Vito Radelich, is recognized throughout the region for his culinary expertise. House specialties include osso buco Milanese, roast duck with fig and honey sauce, and brodetto. Desserts are prepared fresh daily by the restaurant's own pastry chef. Children are welcome; special menu provided.

OPEN *Daily except Mon., 4:30 to 10 P.M.*

Last Chance Antiques and Cheese Café *(Main St., Tannersville, (518) 589-6424)* A retail gourmet shop, antiques store and café all in one. Items such as cheese or chocolate fondue, homemade soups, quiche, chili and duck liver pâté can also be taken out. There are sixty different beers in addition to an extensive wine list. Sandwiches are super-thick and filled with superb meats and salads. Children are welcome.

OPEN *Mon. through Fri., 10 A.M. to 7 P.M.; Sat. and Sun., 10 A.M. to 9:30 P.M.*

Luigi O'Neill's *(Route 23A, Tannersville, (518) 263-4936)* Fine northern Italian cuisine; a perfect stop after skiing or hiking. Open every day for dinner.

Mike's Catskill Point *(7 Main St., Catskill, (518) 943-5352)* On the Hudson River, and renowned for their pizza. Closed Mondays.

Redcoat's Return (Dale Lane-Platte Clove, Elka Park, (518) 589-6379/9858) A taste of England in the Hudson Valley. British chef-owner Tom Wright serves up fine prime ribs, steak and kidney pie, as well as duck or shrimp curry. For the kids, try the fish and chips, a refreshing change from hamburger. In the Catskill Forest Preserve, this farmhouse-turned-restaurant is filled with plenty of fine antiques and paintings. Dinner is served in a cozy library–dining room, with rows of books lining the walls. Children's menu available.
   OPEN Daily for dinner, 6 to 10 P.M.

Red's (Route 9W, West Coxsackie, (518) 731-8151) The specialty here is seafood at reasonable prices. Open every day for lunch and dinner.

La Rive (R.D. 1, Box 322, Old Kings Rd., Catskill, (518) 943-4888) Can be hard to find; call for directions. Located in a farmhouse off a winding dirt road, no detail has been spared. The hors d'oeuvres plate here includes samples of thirteen different dishes—salads, pâté, fish mousse, pasta and many more delicious creations. Not recommended for children, especially on weekends.
   OPEN May through November only—Tues. through Sat., 6 to 9 P.M.; Sun., 2 to 8 P.M.

Town and Country Restaurant (Route 23B, Catskill, (518) 943-2581) Located in a cozy log cabin, this restaurant has a large, reasonably priced menu that ranges from Yankee pot roast to chateaubriand. Specialties also include the veal and duck dishes. All entrées are accompanied by a relish tray, fresh baked breads, salad, vegetables and potato or rice. Reservations suggested on weekends. Children are welcome; special menu provided.
   OPEN Mon. through Sat., 4 to 9 P.M.; Sun., noon to 8 P.M. Closed Wed.

Vesuvio (Goshen Rd., Route 296, Hensonville, (518) 734-3663) The warm atmosphere and provincial charm make this family-run Italian restaurant worth a stop. The veal is a specialty and all desserts—tortoni, spumoni, cannoli, cheesecake and custard tart—are prepared on the premises. Everything is à la carte; the prices are reasonable. Children are welcome.

OPEN Sun. through Fri., 4:30 to 10 P.M.; Sat., 4:30 to 11 P.M. Closed Wed.

Where to Stay

Albergo Allegria Bed and Breakfast (Route 296, Windham, 12496, (518) 734-5560/4499) Step up on the wickered porch here and feel the grace and beauty of days gone by. The Victorian theme is continued throughout this bed and breakfast with antique furnishings, period wallpaper and accessories. A Continental breakfast consisting of fresh fruit, home-baked muffins, croissants and local honey and jams is served daily. In summer enjoy these treats out on the porch. The main lounge, with its fireplace and overstuffed couches, and the library, with its rows of books, are especially warm and inviting. Open all year. Four suites and twelve rooms, all with private baths.

The Barn Bed and Breakfast (Onteora Rd., Tannersville, 12485, (518) 589-6239) All of the large rooms here have wood-burning fireplaces and lovely views of the surrounding mountains. You will find a fruit basket upon your arrival, as well as flowers in season. The Steinway piano downstairs just begs to be played, and all breads and pastries served at the full breakfast are home-baked. With two days' notice, your hosts will prepare dinner; an additional fee is charged. Open all year. One room has a private bath; two others share a bathroom.

Eggery Inn (County Road 16, Tannersville, 12485, (518) 589-5363) Nestled amidst the majestic ridges of the Catskill Mountains at an altitude of 2,200 feet, this rustic inn offers sweeping views. The wood-burning Franklin stove and antique player piano make for a cozy atmosphere, and the dining room has a handcrafted oak bar and an abundance of indoor plants. During the hearty breakfast, enjoy an unobstructed view of Hunter Mountain. Dinner is served on Saturday nights, December through mid-March and July through October. Open all year, except during April. Eleven rooms have private baths; two share a bathroom.

Greenville Arms (South St., Greenville, 12083, (518) 966-5219) Special care is taken to provide a quiet retreat for guests at this gem of a Victorian home built by William Vanderbilt in 1889. Each room is decorated with antiques, and the seven acres of lush lawns and gardens are beautiful in spring. Old-fashioned country cooking, featuring homemade breads, pies and cakes baked daily, adds a special accent to their hearty breakfast. Greenville is a low-key town with lots of charming Victorian homes. Open May through October. Thirteen rooms have private baths; six others share two baths.

Prink Hill Bed and Breakfast (Susquehanna Turnpike, Durham, 12422, (518) 239-6590) Surrounded by 144 acres of woods and meadows, this 1791 home was once the residence of *New York Times* critic and author Brooks Atkinson. Family heirlooms and antiques decorate this tranquil inn, which is also an operating dairy goat farm specializing in cheese products. There is also a small antiques shop on the premises. A Continental breakfast is served featuring strawberries in June, quiche with homegrown vegetables in summer and pancakes cooked on the woodstove in winter. A variety of homemade breads and muffins are baked year-round. Open all year. Two rooms with private baths; two share one bath. No pets, smoking or alcohol allowed.

Redcoat's Return (Dale Lane-Platte Clove, Elka Park, 12427, (518) 589-6379/9858) The picturesque locale of this 1850s farmhouse will delight outdoors lovers. There is fishing in the nearby Schoharie Creek and skiing at nearby Hunter Mountain. The owners here are British, and they cook a first-class English breakfast, complete with eggs, bacon, sausage, jams and pancakes. The inn also has a fine restaurant. Open Memorial Day through November 1, and November 20 through April 1. Seven rooms have private baths; seven others share four baths.

Scribner Hollow Lodge *(Route 23A, Tannersville, 12485, (518) 263-4211)* For people who enjoy a full-service lodge, this is the place to stay. The main building can accommodate 110 people, and an additional 36 town houses can hold another 350 guests. Every room is different, with a distinct personality and an appropriate name. There is also a sauna and whirlpool. Open all year.

Winter Clove Inn *(Winter Clove Rd., Round Top, 12473 (518) 622-3267)* Located on 400 lovely acres adjoining the Catskill Mountain Wilderness Preserve. Originally opened in 1830, the inn is now run by the fifth generation of the Whitcomb family. There are two swimming pools, a tennis court, a nine-hole golf course, cross-country skiing trails, hayrides and even six regulation-sized bowling alleys. All desserts and muffins are homemade, and many of the recipes have been passed down through the family for generations. Open all year. All meals are included in the rates unless special arrangements are made in advance. All fifty-one rooms have private baths.

City of Albany

The city of Albany recently celebrated the 300th anniversary of its city charter, which was granted on July 22, 1686 by Governor Thomas Dongan. A river stop since Henry Hudson visited the region in 1609, Albany's fertile valleys and abundant game soon attracted Dutch traders, who established a trading post here. It was to become a city of tremendous contrasts—stagecoaches and steamboats, muddy roads and medical colleges, farmers and politicians. But through a combination of pride, pluck and foresight, Albany has made the best of it all. A visit to the area today can focus on many things—history, politics, art, architecture—and can be made at any time of the year. Spring brings the blossoming of thousands of tulips all over the area, pools of color that reflect Dutch origins. The Pinksterfest, a weekend of celebration in May, welcomes the warmer weather in the Dutch tradition, and the city parks come alive with fairs and shows. In the summer, the great Empire State Plaza becomes a unique combination of outdoor park, art gallery and seat of government—a mélange symbol-

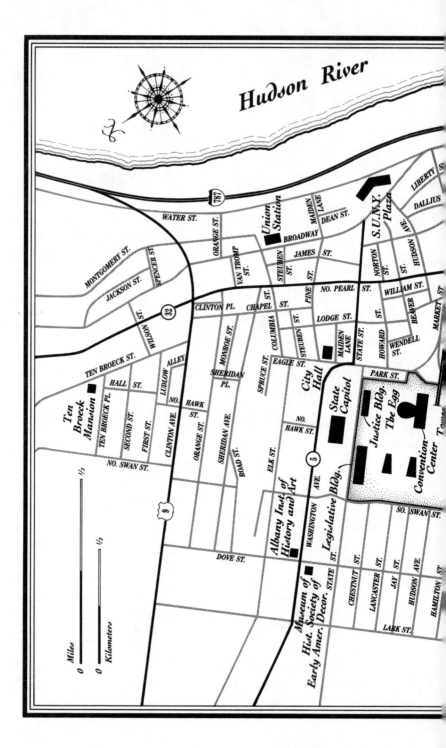

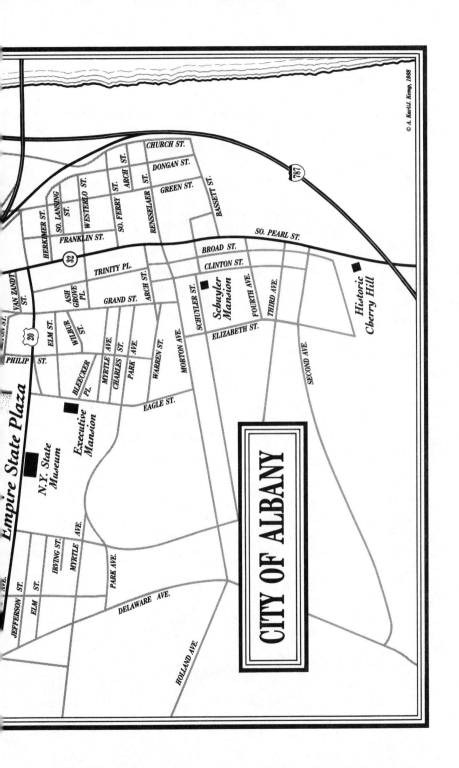

CITY OF ALBANY

Empire State Plaza

N.Y. State Museum

Executive Mansion

Schuyler Mansion

Historic Cherry Hill

CHURCH ST.
DONGAN ST.
GREEN ST.
BASSETT ST.
SO. PEARL ST.
BROAD ST.
CLINTON ST.
TRINITY PL.
GRAND ST.
ELIZABETH ST.
EAGLE ST.
FRANKLIN ST.
DELAWARE AVE.
HOLLAND AVE.

HERKIMER ST.
SO. LANSING ST.
WESTERLO ST.
SO. FERRY ST.
ARCH ST.
RENSSELAER ST.
VAN ZANDT ST.
ASH GROVE PL.
ELM ST.
WILBUR ST.
BLEECKER PL.
MYRTLE AVE.
CHARLES ST.
PARK AVE.
WARREN ST.
MORTON AVE.
ARCH ST.
SCHUYLER ST.
FOURTH AVE.
THIRD AVE.
SECOND AVE.
PHILIP ST.
IRVING ST.
MYRTLE AVE.
PARK AVE.
JEFFERSON ST.
ELM ST.

32
20
787

© A. Karl/J. Kemp, 1988

ized by the blazing fourth of July fireworks display. Autumn offers a perfect time to walk around the city and neighboring towns, and get to know the tiny side streets and shops that keep the small-town feeling alive here. And winter ushers in Victorian greenery displays, snow festivals and the lighting of the state Christmas tree. Whatever the season; be prepared to discover an area where the past and future work together.

The Albany Institute of History and Art Founded in 1791, this exceptional museum is one of the oldest in the United States, and it is still providing visitors with a chance to see varied, changing exhibits that focus on the Hudson Valley region's cultural history. The building itself is a graceful collection of individual galleries and sweeping staircases, and there is even a small display area in the entrance hall. Some of the institutes' collections include fine European porcelain and glass, Dutch furniture, paintings and decorative arts from the early settlement period in Albany, pewter and silver produced by local smiths in the eighteenth century, and breathtaking examples of the Hudson River school of painting. The Dutch Room offers an interesting look into early Albany family life, and be sure to get to the lower level to see the Egyptian Room, where several mummies are on display, along with some of their prized belongings. Changing exhibits are featured throughout the year, as well as special events such as the Noontime Presentations, a lecture and slide series, and the colorful Festival of Trees. The Luncheon Gallery, located across the walkway from the museum, is a popular place for a fast snack. It is run by the museum volunteers, and the desserts there are homemade.

DIRECTIONS *Located at 125 Washington Avenue in downtown Albany.*

INFORMATION *Admission is free. Open all year—Tues. through Sat., 10 A.M. to 4:45 P.M.; Sun., 2 to 5 P.M. Closed legal holidays. Wheelchair accessible. Parking is limited.*

FACILITIES *Gift shop, lunchroom, rest rooms.*

Capitol Building This fairy-tale building, with its red towers and hundreds of arched windows, is one of the few state capitols in the country that isn't topped by a dome. Construction of the building took more than 30 years, ending in 1899, and cost the then-unheard-of sum of $25 million. This is where the state senate and assembly meet, and where you'll find the governor's offices once used by Charles Evans, Theodore Roosevelt, Nelson Rockefeller and Franklin Roosevelt. Throughout the building there are thousands of fine stone carvings, a tradition that can be traced back to the great churches of the Middle Ages. Many were caricatures of famous politicians and writers, others were of the families and relatives of the artisans, still others were self-portraits of the stonecarvers themselves. But the most compelling carvings are the ones that form "Million Dollar Staircase," which took many years to complete and is the best known of all the capitol's embellishments. Another unusual architectural feature is the senate fireplaces; the huge chimneys did not draw well, so their original function was abandoned in favor of using them as private discussion "nooks." Tours of the capitol are given daily, every hour from 9 A.M. to 4 P.M.; they leave from the Capitol Guide Center. If you enjoy military history, don't miss the small military museum here; it traces the history of the state militia and National Guard. And flower lovers should make a special point of visiting the Capitol Park in the spring, when thousands of tulips blaze into red and yellow bloom.

DIRECTIONS *Located at the State Street end of the Empire State Plaza.*

INFORMATION *Open daily, year-round, 9 A.M. to 4 P.M. Closed Thanksgiving, Christmas and New Year's Day. Tours leave from the Guide Center, inside the capitol. Admission is free.*

FACILITIES *Book store, rest rooms.*

Empire State Plaza Popularly called the Plaza, this is really a government complex that includes office buildings, a convention center, a performing arts center—known as "The Egg"—a concourse and the state museum. Built at an extraordinary cost of more than $2 billion and finished in 1978, the Plaza has fulfilled then-Governor Rockefeller's dream of a government center that would draw visitors and allow them to feel in touch with their state government. Tours of the Plaza are given several times a day, but if you want to walk the quarter-mile-long site yourself, there are several points of particular interest. The esplanade area is wonderful to explore on a warm day, with tranquil reflecting pools, one of which is used for ice-skating in the colder months. An environmental sculpture called the Labyrinth offers benches and a play area, while the Sculpture Garden displays the work of artist David Smith. At the Vietnam War Memorial, there is an indoor exhibit as well as a simple, quiet garden for meditation. The strange, UFO-shaped building is the Performing Arts Center, where you'll find a theater and a concert hall. For a bird's-eye view of Albany and the distant Adirondack Mountains, go to the Corning Tower (next to the Labyrinth) and take the elevator to the observation deck (open from 9 A.M. to 4 P.M.; on weekends, enter on the lower concourse level). Inside the concourse can be found one of the most intriguing art collections in the world. The largest publicly owned and displayed art collection in the United States, it is all the work of New York artists. More than ninety-two sculptures, tapestries, paintings, mobiles and constructions are displayed, among them works by such artists as Calder, Nevelson, Frankenthaler and Noguchi. Special art tours are available free of charge on Wednesdays, or stop in and ask for the self-guided tour brochure. Another spot that hosts art shows is in the Legislative Office Building on the concourse level (opposite the Justice Building) in an area known as the "Well." An atriumlike area, it is used for small concerts and art shows. Art exhibits and special events are also held on the concourse; check with Visitor Services for upcoming activities. The state museum is also located here, as is the state capitol (see separate entries).

DIRECTIONS *Take N.Y. Thruway exit 23 to I-787 or I-87 to I-90 east; there is an Empire State Plaza exit on both roads.*

INFORMATION *Open all year, except Thanksgiving, Christmas and New Year's Day; tours are conducted hourly from 9 A.M. to 4 P.M. Wheelchair accessible. Admission is free.*

FACILITIES *Restaurants, information booths, fitness information area, rest rooms.*

Executive Mansion Originally built in 1850 as a private house, this forty-room mansion has been home to New York's governors since Samuel Tilden. Located near the state museum at 138 Eagle Street, the mansion has several public rooms, including the reception hall, the dining and drawing rooms and the County Room, which contains artwork depicting each of New York State's sixty-two counties. Tour guides help you find your way and can tell you about the varied personalities of past governors.

DIRECTIONS *Located near the state museum at 138 Eagle Street.*
INFORMATION *Open for tours Thurs. only at 1, 2 and 3* P.M. *Reservations must be made in advance by calling (518) 474-2418. Call at least a month before you plan to visit. Admission is free.*
FACILITIES *Rest rooms.*

Historic Cherry Hill Built in 1787 by Philip Van Rensselaer in order to replace what was called the "Old Mansion," this Georgian-style house was the centerpiece of a 900-acre farm. Cherry Hill remained in the family for five generations, until 1963, and provides the visitor with a rare opportunity to see the growth and care of a home over 176 years. The farm has, of course, disappeared under Albany streets, and the view across the road is of oil tanks instead of orchards, but the house itself still offers a sense of grace and elegance. A visit begins in the basement orientation center, where a wall chart untangles the complicated knot of marriages and relationships that kept Cherry Hill in the family. Upstairs, many of the thirty-one rooms have not been restored to match one particular period, but contain the designs, belongings and personal touches of their inhabitants. The collections found here are irreplaceable as a record of America's social history. There are more than 150 chairs, 30 tables and thousands of decorative objects, which include eighteenth-century paintings, nineteenth-century oriental export ware, and even twentieth-century clothing. Although the house was modernized over the years, things such as heating ducts and plumbing are carefully hidden away. Cherry Hill is a special place, chockful of New York history and spirit.

DIRECTIONS *Located at 523½ South Pearl Street. Take I-787 to Route 32 south, turn left at the exit stoplight.*
INFORMATION *Open February through December—Tues. through Sat., 10 A.M. to 3 P.M.; Sun., 1 to 3 P.M. Guided tours offered every hour. Admission fee charged.*
FACILITIES *Gift shop, rest rooms.*

The Museum of the Historical Society of Early American Decoration (HSEAD)

Despite its unwieldy name, HSEAD is a small museum. They have a magnificent collection of ornamented tin, papier-mâché and wood, and the museum is considered one of the world's foremost repositories for the decorated items popular in many European and American homes during the eighteenth and nineteenth centuries. Probably the most familiar pieces are the tin pots, trays and boxes that were covered with paintings of bright flowers and birds. But painted tin is not the only major collection at HSEAD; there are fine examples of stenciling and metal leaf painting as well. The objects themselves are often as fascinating as their decorations, and the well-lighted displays will guide you through special exhibits and permanent collections. If the museum isn't too busy, ask if you can see the storage area, which contains hundreds of other items that are awaiting restoration or display space. The tours here are self-guided, but there are lots of explanatory notes and histories to read. And if you see things you like, don't worry—the gift shop is stocked with finely crafted and decorated objects that were made by HSEAD's guild members.

DIRECTIONS *Located at 19 Dove Street (just across the street from the Albany Institute of History and Art).*
INFORMATION *Open all year—Wed. through Fri., 9:30 A.M. to 4 P.M.; Sat., noon to 3 P.M. Call (518) 462-1676 for exhibit schedules. Admission is free.*
FACILITIES *Gift shop, rest rooms.*

New York State Museum

Anchoring one end of the new Empire State Plaza, the museum has nonetheless been a part of the state's history since 1836, making it one of the oldest state museums in the country. It is not, however, a dusty old repository with outdated displays of rocks and unidentified bones. This museum is alive with multi-media presentations that allow you to experience everything from a thunderstorm to a Lower East Side pushcart alley of the 1920s. The permanent exhibits include "Adirondack Wilderness," which explores the natural history of that region; "New York Metropolis," which focuses on New York City and the surrounding counties (here you'll find an Ellington-era A Train and a set from "Sesame Street"); "Gems of New York State" and "Birds of New York State," two dazzling exhibits that emphasize New York's wealth in these areas; and "Fire Fighting," a look at the brassy way in which fires were once fought. Changing exhibits may feature folk art, contemporary art, and shows in the new video theater. Special events are scheduled all year, so a trip may include a Victorian Holiday, a movie festival, a Chanukah celebration, even a visit with an American artist.

DIRECTIONS Located at the Madison Avenue end of the Empire State Plaza, in the Cultural Education Center.

INFORMATION Open all year, except Thanksgiving, Christmas and New Year's Day, 10 A.M. to 5 P.M. Wheelchair accessible; interpretation aids available for the hearing and sight impaired. Admission is free.

FACILITIES Gift shop, rest rooms.

Schuyler Mansion Once home to Philip Schuyler, a general in the Revolutionary War, the Schuyler Mansion was completed in 1764 on a rolling plot of land known as the Dutch Church Pasture. Schuyler was an important figure during the war, and many well-known statesmen, including Washington, Franklin and the defeated English general, John Burgoyne, visited the mansion over the years. During the war, Schuyler's daughter married Alexander Hamilton there, and a kidnap attempt was later made against her by the Tories; a gash on the wooden staircase bannister is said to have been made by a kidnapper's tomahawk. The house did not remain in the family after Schuyler's death but passed through a succession of owners before being purchased by New York State in 1912. Although the exterior of the house has changed greatly over the years, including the removal of all the outbuildings, visitors today can still see many examples of eighteenth-century furniture, glassware, pottery and art, as well as Schuyler family possessions. An herb garden has been added to replace the original paintings.

> DIRECTIONS *Located at the corner of Catherine and Clinton Streets, two blocks west of South Pearl Street.*
> INFORMATION *Open April through December—Wed. through Sat., 10 A.M. to 5 A.M., Sun., 1 to 5 P.M. Winter hours by appointment only. Handicapped accessible, but call ahead for assistance. Tel. (518) 474-3953. Admission is free.*
> FACILITIES *Gift shop, rest rooms.*

Tulip Festival and **Pinksterfest** Usually held the second weekend in May, the festivities include outdoor craft and food fairs, a children's festival, the crowning of the Tulip Queen and a dance. Tel. (518) 434-2032 for further information.

Activities

ART GALLERIES

Many publicly sponsored and privately owned galleries are scattered throughout the city, offering the best in the fine arts. At the **Nelson A. Rockefeller Empire State Plaza Art Collection** (see pages 171–72) free tours are given to enhance the appreciation of the great treasures found there. At the state university campus, the **University Art Gallery**, 1400 Washington Avenue, Fine Arts Building, Albany, (518) 457-3375, focuses on contemporary art with a variety of changing exhibits, some drawn from the gallery's own holdings, others from the works of both established artists and university students. The gallery's hours change during the school year, so call before you go. At the **Harmanus Bleecker Center**, 19 Dove Street, Albany, (518) 465-2044 or 463-4478, you will find changing displays of the works of regional artists. The center is associated with the Albany Institute of History and Art, so classes and special events are held there as well. The **Rice Gallery** at the Albany Institute of History and Art, 125 Washington Avenue, Albany, (518) 463-4478, offers changing shows by New York State artists and craftspeople. A small gallery at the College of Saint Rose, the **Picotte Gallery**, 324 State Street, Albany, (518) 454-5185, offers drawings, photographs and paintings by well-known contemporary artists, including some, like Christo, who are better known in other media. If you enjoy marine art, then stop at **The Albany Art Gallery**, Stuyvesant Plaza, Western Avenue, (518) 482-5374, which carries both nineteenth- and twentieth-century art, along with regional work. Other nineteenth-century works, including Hudson River School paintings, can be found at the McLean Gallery, 231 Lark Street, Albany, (518) 465-8959; the gallery exhibits twentieth-century art as well.

WALKING TOURS

There is so much to see in this historic city that a walk down just about any street will give you a glimpse of Albany's colorful past. The following are not specific tours, therefore, but suggestions for starting points on an Albany exploration.

An example of a nineteenth-century row house community, the **Pastures Historic District** is bounded roughly by Morton and Second avenues and Elizabeth and Pearl streets. Here you will also find the Schuyler Mansion (see pages 175–76) as well as many impressive private homes. The **Mansion Historic District**, bounded by Eagle, Dongan, Hamilton and Ferry streets, is a kaleidoscope of building styles, Italianate, Federal and Revival being only a few. Although the area became run down earlier in this century, people have been rediscovering the richness of the district, and there is a sense of renewal here. The largest historic area is found in the **Center Square–Hudson Park Historic District**, bounded by South Swan, Madison Avenue, South Lake and Spring streets. This district's centerpiece is Washington Park, a 90-acre area that once served as parade ground and cemetery. Throughout the park you will find statues, lovely flower beds and a lake. The district itself has scores of restored houses and commercial buildings.

Where to Eat

L'Auberge *(351 Broadway, Albany, (518) 465-1111)* Fine French cuisine. Open for lunch and dinner daily, except Sun. (No lunch served Sat.)

Cafe Capriccio *(49 Grand St., Albany, (518) 465-0439)* Fine northern Italian cuisine, with a classical guitarist on Thursdays. Open every night for dinner.

Caffe Italia Ristorante *(662 Central Ave., Albany, (518) 482-9433)* This family-run Italian restaurant is a popular spot with members of the state legislature. Everything is prepared to order, and of the specialties, the veal Antica is worth a mention. Not for younger children.
  OPEN *Lunch—Mon. through Fri., 11:30 A.M. to 2:30 P.M.; dinner—Mon. through Sat., 5 to 11 P.M. Closed Sun.*

Cavaleri's *(334 Second Ave., Albany, (518) 463-9047)* Steak is the specialty here. Open for dinner Wednesday through Sunday.

Dahlia Ice Cream *(858 Madison Avenue, Albany, (518) 482-0931)* One of the best ice cream "restaurants" anywhere. More than two dozen flavors are made on the premises, including Sunkissed Chocolate, Truffle and Moonshine. Belgian waffles and home-baked brownies are also specialties here.
  OPEN *Sun. through Thurs., noon to midnight; Fri. and Sat. until 1 A.M.*

Jack's Oyster House *(42-44 State St., Albany, (518) 465-8854)* Albany's oldest restaurant, and for 75 years it has been run by the same family. A tradition here, the steak and seafood specialties are consistently excellent. Children are welcome; special menu provided.
  OPEN *Daily, 11:30 A.M. to 10 P.M.*

Justin's *(301 Lark St., Albany, (518) 436-7008)*   Located in Albany's answer to New York's Greenwich Village, part of this restaurant dates back to the 1700s, and there has been an inn or tavern on this site since that time. All soups are made fresh daily, and the crab, mussel and tomato-dill bisques are excellent. There are daily specials and a light menu of gourmet sandwiches and hamburgers is also offered. A great stop for lunch. Jazz is featured three nights each week. Not appropriate for children.

> OPEN *Lunch—Mon. through Fri., 11:30 A.M. to 2:30 P.M., until 4 P.M. on Sat.; Sunday brunch—noon to 3 P.M.; dinner— Sun. through Thurs., 5 to 10 P.M., until 10:30 P.M. on Fri. and Sat.*

El Loco Mexican Café *(465 Madison Ave., Albany, (518) 436-1855)* This funky, lively café is in a nineteenth-century building that has a pressed-tin ceiling. Renowned for their chili, vegetarian meals and one of the largest selections of Mexican beers in the state. The "Banana Changa" for dessert is heavenly.

> OPEN *Lunch—Wed. through Fri., 11:30 A.M. to 4:30 P.M.; dinner—Tues. through Thurs., 4:30 to 10 P.M., until 11 P.M. on Fri. and Sat.*

Lombardo's *(121 Madison Ave., Albany, (518) 462-9180)*   Traditional Italian fare in a setting that offers a taste of old Albany. Open Wednesday through Sunday for lunch and dinner.

Mamoun's Falafel *(206 Washington Ave., Albany, (518) 434-3901)* A perfect stop for a delicious vegetarian meal. Open 11 A.M. to 11 P.M. every day.

Ogden's *(42 Howard St., Albany, (518) 463-6605)*   Featuring fresh seafood specialties. Open for lunch and dinner every day except Sunday. (No lunch on Sat.)

Quintessence *(11 New Scotland Ave., Albany, (518) 434-8186)* An Art Deco diner featuring nightly international themes, and live entertainment on weekends. Open daily, brunch served on weekends.

La Serre Restaurant *(14 Green St., Albany, (518) 463-6056)* This glass and wood restaurant specializes in Continental cuisine and is housed in a historic nineteenth-century building with bright awnings and windowboxes. Some of the specialties here are bouillabaisse Marseillaise, Selle de Veau (loin of veal with Bearnaise sauce), poached salmon and steak au poivre. Desserts are made fresh daily and include a sumptuous rum cake with apricot brandy. Children are welcome; smaller portions will be served upon request.
    OPEN *Lunch—Mon. through Fri., 11:30 A.M. to 2:30 P.M.; dinner—Mon. through Sat., 6 to 10 P.M.*

Sitar *(1929 Central Ave., Albany, (518) 456-6670)* Indian specialties prepared to your taste. Children's menu, and buffet on Sun. Open for lunch and dinner Tues. through Sun.

Yates Street *(492 Yates St., Albany, (518) 438-2012)* A mahogany front bar and dark green pressed-metal ceilings and walls set the tone here. Specializing in nouvelle cuisine, everything on the imaginative menu is prepared to order. Children are welcome.
    OPEN *Dinner—Mon. through Thurs., 6 to 10 P.M., until 10:30 P.M. on Fri. and Sat. Reservations required on weekends.*

Where to Stay

Albany Marriott Hotel *(189 Wolf Rd., Colonie, 12205, (518) 458-8444)* Near four major shopping malls, a 5-minute drive from the airport and less than 20 minutes from downtown Albany. Each room in this luxury hotel is equipped with a color television, HBO and other modern amenities. There is an indoor and an outdoor pool, a sauna, a whirlpool and exercise and game rooms. A Continental breakfast is served, and the nightclub offers hors d'oeuvres and a raw bar over-flowing with fresh shellfish. Open all year; 302 rooms. Children are welcome.

Desmond Americana Inn *(660 Albany Shaker Rd., Albany, 12211, (518) 869-8100)* All the charm and style of a luxurious Colonial manor, with antiques, paintings and handsome wood paneling. Vaulted ceilings and sunlit gardens that bloom year-round highlight two eighteenth-century courtyards. The ambiance combines the best features of an inn and hotel. All rooms have custom-made furniture with authentic colonial fabric and wall-covering designs. Exercise-minded guests can choose from two heated pools, a health club, saunas, exercise room and billiard/game room. Open all year; 310 rooms, with 4 suites. Children are welcome.

Mansion Hill Inn *(115 Philip St., Albany, 12202, (518) 465-2038 or 434-2313)* Albany's only downtown bed and breakfast establishment, located within walking distance of the state capitol and downtown business district. This inn won a Preservation Merit Award from the Historic Albany Foundation in 1986. Each suite includes a living room, study, kitchen, large bedroom and deck. Choose from a wide range on the breakfast menu. Very reasonable rates. Open all year. Three suites with private baths. Children are welcome.

Columbia County

Home first to the Native Americans who greeted Henry Hudson, Dutch, German and New England settlers were later attracted to Columbia County by the river and the fertile land. Whaling became a major industry, and cities echoed with the noises of shipping and trading. Homes were built that resembled the widow-walked extravaganzas of Maine and Massachusetts. Columbia was home to some of the day's leading politicians and merchants. Well-kept farms were always a mark of the region, with neat rows of apple and pear orchards lining the banks of the Hudson. The unusual is really the rule here; a colorful museum filled with firemen's memorabilia is located here, as is a library that once served as a lunatic asylum and a seminary for young ladies. Washington Irving is said to have been so inspired by the region that "The Legend of Sleepy Hollow" was born of a visit here. Across the county, fine antiques glow in the windows of well-appointed shops, while the simplicity

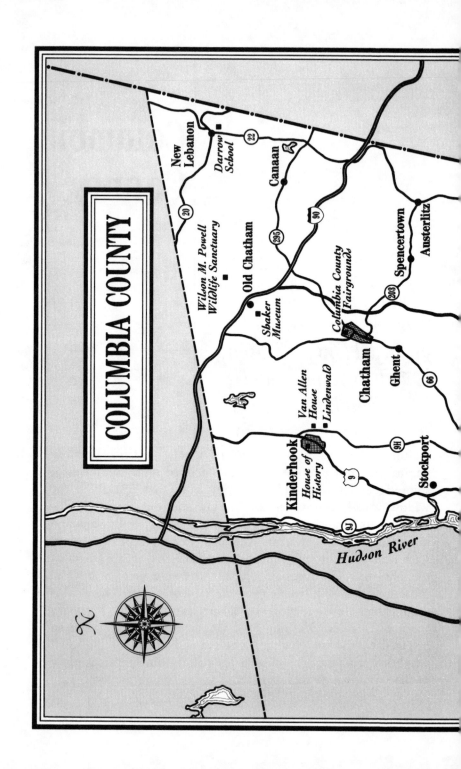

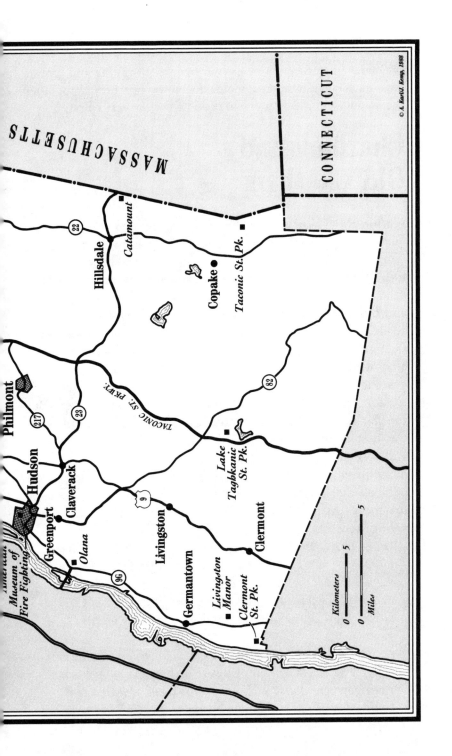

MASSACHUSETTS

CONNECTICUT

© A. Karl/J. Kemp, 1988

22

Hillsdale

Catamount

Copake ●

Taconic St. Pk.

82

Philmont

TACONIC ST. PKWY.

217

23

Hudson

Claverack

Lake
Taghkanic
St. Pk.

9

Greenport

Olana

Livingston

Clermont

American
Museum of
Fire Fighting

9G

Germantown

Livingston
Manor

Clermont
St. Pk.

Kilometers

0   5

Miles

0   5

of Shaker furniture offers its own comment on life and living. And each year, the state's oldest county fair brings together the young and old in a celebration of the harvest's best.

Chatham and Old Chatham

Columbia County Fair The oldest in New York State, this fair is nearing its 150th birthday, and it's as lively and entertaining as ever. Held on the weekend nearest Labor Day, this five-day celebration is less raucous and somewhat smaller than other county fairs, but just as much fun. Horses, sheep, cows and other animals are all displayed proudly by 4-H members, while prize-winning vegetables and fruits are shown off in the Grange buildings. Handmade quilts and needlecrafts also make a colorful display. Sheep-to-shawl demonstrations and antique gas engines enliven the fairgrounds throughout the week, although modern farm machinery has its place here as well. But the fair is more than just exhibits—it's also entertainment in the best country tradition. Bluegrass, country and western, and folk singers perform to large crowds, while the popular demolition derbies draw huge crowds in the evening. And because the fairgrounds are the winter training headquarters for more than 100 trotters and pacers, you'll see some fine racing, too.

DIRECTIONS *Held at the fairgrounds on Route 203 in Chatham.* INFORMATION *Held near Labor Day; the grounds are open from 9 A.M. until late evening. Admission fee charged. Tel. (518) 828-4417, or write the Columbia County Chamber of Commerce, 729 Columbia Street, Hudson, 12534 for further information.*

Since the exhibits are both indoors and outdoors, dress accordingly. The length of your visit here will depend on how much you enjoy agricultural fairs, but plan to spend at least 2 to 3 hours, more if you stay for the entertainment. Children will love

the animals and the fair has one of the best selections anywhere of rides for very young kids.
FACILITIES Food concessions, midway, rides, rest rooms.

Mount Lebanon Shaker Village On the site of a former Shaker settlement and now part of the Darrow School. A visit here includes an introductory slide show about the Shakers and a walking tour through some of the remaining buildings, including the original meetinghouse and the stone dairy barn.
DIRECTIONS On Route 20 near the town of New Lebanon; follow signs to the Darrow School.
INFORMATION Open from mid-June through Labor Day—daily from 9:30 A.M. to 5 P.M.; from May to mid-June and for the month of October, on Sat. and Sun. only. A small fee is charged. Tel. (518) 794-9100, or write to The Darrow School, Shaker Road, New Lebanon, 12125.
FACILITIES Gift shop, rest rooms.

The Shaker Museum In the late eighteenth century, a group of English men and women immigrated to the colonies with the hope of being allowed to practice their communal religion. Called "Shakers" because they danced and moved during worship services, the group established settlements throughout the new country and became as well known for their crafts and innovations as for their unusual life-style. Industry, thrift and simplicity were their bywords, and the Shakers produced many items in their workshops. Chairs, seed packets, tin milk pails and jams were made with equal amounts of care and skill, and today Shaker-made items are valued for their beauty and grace. At the Shaker Museum, visitors can see hundreds of items made and used by the Shakers. Located in a barn and several outbuildings, the museum collections were gathered by both Shakers and non-Shakers with the goal of preserving a way of life that is almost gone. All the major Shaker industries are represented at the museum—trip-hammer and washing machine manufacturing as well as clothing and broom making. The Shakers are credited with inventing the circular saw and the revolving bake oven, although they rarely took out a patent, preferring that the world benefit from their work. The museum also houses one of the finest collections of furniture and household items from the various settlements.

DIRECTIONS *Located on Shaker Museum Road. Take Route 295 east to the East Chatham Post Office and make a left; follow county Road 13 south to the museum.*

INFORMATION *Open May 1 to October 31—daily, 10 A.M. to 5 P.M. Admission fee charged. Tel. (518) 794-9100, or write Shaker Museum, Old Chatham, 12136.*

Plan on spending at least 1½ hours in the exhibits, more if you attend a special events day. On the first Saturday in August there's an antiques festival. A harvest and crafts fair is held on the third Saturday in October. Limited access for disabled visitors; call before you go. Older children may enjoy the exhibits, but the simplicity of Shaker life may not please younger kids.

FACILITIES *Refreshments, picnic area, gift shop, rest rooms.*

Germantown

Clermont Standing on land that was awarded to the Livingston family in 1686, this Georgian mansion remained in the family until the 1960s. The Livingstons' illustrious history—Judge Robert Livingston wrote the letter of protest to King George just before the Revolutionary War and Chancellor Robert R. Livingston helped to draft the Declaration of Independence—is evident throughout the house. Although Clermont itself was burned by the British during the war, it was later rebuilt around the old walls and foundation. Additional changes and additions were made into the late nineteenth century, so the house today reflects changes wrought by several generations. Clermont's thirty-five rooms are furnished with family heirlooms and fine examples of period furniture and decorative accessories. A crystal chandelier from 1700 hangs above the drawing room, where you can also find a French balloon clock, made to commemorate the Montgolfier brothers' ascent. Family portraits decorate the hallways and help visitors sort out the confusing Livingston family tree, and there are exquisite examples of cabinetmaking throughout the mansion. But as lovely as Clermont is, the setting makes it more so. The views up, down and across the nearby Hudson River are magnificent, and the early Livingstons purchased as much land as they could see to be sure the view never changed. Tradition holds that the black locust trees which flank the houses were planted by the builder of Clermont in the mid-eighteenth century. The roses in the English box garden transform the month of June into an enchanting time. There are special events from April to December at Clermont, including a sheep-shearing festival, which recalls Chancellor Livingston's interest in agriculture; a croquet day complete with musical entertainment; a fabulous Independence Day celebration, with hot air balloons and costumed Colonial-era soldiers; the annual Hudson River steamboat days; a pumpkin festival; and a Christmas open house.

DIRECTIONS *Located just off Route 9G on county Route 6, in Germantown.*

INFORMATION *The mansion is open Memorial Day through Labor day—Wed. through Sat., 10 A.M. to 5 P.M.; Sun., 1 to 5 P.M. The grounds are open all year, from 8 A.M. to dusk. Admission is free. For seasonal hours and special events, call (518) 537-4240, or write Clermont State Historic Park, R.R. #1, Box 215, Germantown, 12516.*

The tour of the house takes approximately 35 minutes and is given every 20 minutes beginning at noon: Sundays at 1 P.M. Plan to spend at least 1 hour on the grounds, especially if the roses are in bloom. The site is partially accessible to the handicapped; call ahead. Children interested in American history will enjoy the mansion; all kids will enjoy any of the special events.

FACILITIES *Picnic area, hiking trails, rest rooms.*

Hudson

American Museum of Fire Fighting For a step back in time to the glory days of fire fighting, stop at this fascinating museum. Here, in a building located next door to the Firemen's Home, you will discover hundreds of pieces of fire memorabilia dating back to the eighteenth century. To greet you as you enter the museum is a wooden statue of a volunteer fire chief, dressed in patriotic red, white and blue, complete with stars and a golden trumpet. From there the museum is divided into two "Engine Halls," which house fire fighting pumpers, mobile apparatus and engines, as well as paintings, clothing, banners and other memorabilia. There is a Newsham Engine, which was used to quench flames on Manhattan in 1731, and saw more than 150 years of use. A silver parade carriage from Kingston, New York, is a delicate example of the carriage maker's art, and is topped by a statue of firemen holding a rescued baby. Throughout the museum you will see lots of gleaming brass, and bright red paint, as well as an oddity or two, like the ornate firemen's parade trumpets, the hand–grenade–style glass fire extinguishers and the brass fire markers, which indicated which fire company had the right to fight a particular fire.

DIRECTIONS Located on Harry Howard Avenue in Hudson, next to the Firemen's Home.

INFORMATION Open April 1 to October 31—Tues. through Sun., 9 A.M. to 4:30 P.M. Closed Mon. Admission is free. Tel. (518) 828-7695, or write Firemen's Home, Harry Howard Avenue, Hudson, 12534.

Plan to spend at least an hour here. The museum is mostly on one level, but call ahead regarding handicapped accessibility. Children will love the colorful engines and the statue of the volunteer.

FACILITIES Rest rooms.

Dinosaurs Discover these creatures lurking in Churchtown, at the Louis Paul Jonas Studios. This workshop produced the dinosaurs that were displayed at the New York World's Fair in 1963, and they still make full-size and smaller versions of the reptilian wonders.

DIRECTIONS Call for directions; the studio is on a back road outside the city.

INFORMATION A perfect stop if you have children. Tours by ap-

pointment only. Tel. (518) 851-2211, or write to Louis Paul Jonas Studios, Box 193, R.D. 4, Hudson, 12534.
FACILITIES *Rest rooms.*

Hudson Walking Tour The city of Hudson is rich with the traditions and cultural heritage of its settlers: first the Dutch, then seamen from Massachusetts and Rhode Island, Quakers and whalers. Carefully designed in the 1780s as a shipping center, with straight streets and "gangway" alleys, ropewalks, wharves and warehouse sections, Hudson was the first city to receive a charter after the Declaration of Independence. Soon, whaling and industry took over as the mainstays of the economy, and although Hudson has had its ups and downs since then, the city is again going through a renaissance. A walking tour of Hudson will reveal dozens of architectural styles and hundreds of commercial buildings and homes that have been maintained or restored to their nineteenth-century glory. A visitor to the city may want to stop in at the **Chamber of Commerce**, 729 Warren Street, and pick up a detailed walking guide, which describes many of the houses in Hudson. But a walk around several main streets will at least show the architectural heritage of the area. From Route 9G, follow Warren Street to Front Street and park. At Front Street, you will see the **Parade**, an eighteenth-century park that was kept open for use by the city's inhabitants. From the park you can see a dazzling view of the Hudson, the Athens Lighthouse and the Catskill Mountains. Inside the park you will find a statue of **St. Winifred**, which was donated to the city by a man who felt that Hudson needed a saint. The easiest walk in Hudson is along **Warren Street**, which is also an antiques mecca. The architectural styles to be found here include Greek Revival, Federal, Queen Anne and Victorian. At the **Curtiss House** (#32), look up at the widow's walk, which was built by the whaling owner in the 1830s to provide a magnificent view of the river. Some of the houses here sport "eyebrow" windows, narrow windows that were tucked under the eaves and often appear at floor height from within the houses. The Adam-style house at 116 Warren is considered a rare remnant from the early nineteenth century and boasts an enclosed, private garden. One house on Warren Street is open to the public, the 1811 **Robert Jenkins House**, 113 Warren Street, (518) 828-5240 (open April through August—Wed., 1 to 4 P.M. and Sun., 1 to 3 P.M., or by reservation; admission fee is charged), which serves as headquarters for the local DAR chapter. This building was constructed by an early mayor of Hudson, and offers local history displays that span the last two centuries. There are quilts, paintings by Hudson River artists and whaling items that recall the town's role in the industry. Another good walking area is around **State Street.** At the **Hudson Area Library Association** (#400), you will find an 1818 stone building guarded by proper library lions. The structure has served also as an almshouse, a lunatic asylum, a young ladies' seminary and a private home. If the building is open, look in at the second floor History Room, which has some local memorabilia, prints and books. When you come to North 4th Street, notice the **Register Star** newspaper building (#354), with its tiny park. Like many others places here, the building served several purposes: as a dance hall, opera house, county jail and assembly hall. Now continue south down Warren Street and spend some time looking at the fine eighteenth- and nineteenth-century buildings there, many of which are undergoing restoration. Other walking areas include **Union Street, Court Street** and **East Allen Street.**

If you are in Hudson in June, you might get to see the **Hudson River Shad Festival**, which is held annually to commemorate the importance of this river fish to the area's early economy and diet. There is a giant shad bake, music and entertainment at the Hudson Boat Launch Site. Call (518) 828-2252 for more information.

DIRECTIONS Route 9G north will take you into town. Or take the N.Y. Thruway to exit 21, then Route 23 east across the Rip Van Winkle bridge.

Olana Frederic Edwin Church was one of America's foremost nineteenth-century artists, a painter who captured the grandeur and mystery of the expanding nation. Church first gained acclaim for his vision of Niagara Falls, a painting which won a medal at the 1867 Paris International Exposition. In 1870, Church and his wife, Isabel, returned from their travels in the Middle East and Europe to their farm in Hudson and began the planning and building of the Persian fantasy which would become known as Olana, "our place on high." The thirty-seven-room mansion features hand-painted tiles on the roof and turrets, adding touches of pink and green to the sky. Garden paths and carriage roads wind through the property, presenting a perfect place from which to watch the Hudson below. Inside, you will discover hand-carved, room-sized screens, rich Persian rugs, hundreds of pieces of decorative pottery and china and even a pair of gilded crane lamps that resemble Egyptian wall paintings. Olana is also rich in examples of Church's paintings, including "Autumn in North America" and "Sunset in Jamaica." His studio is still set up as it was in his time. During the winter holiday season, there are special events days.

DIRECTIONS Located on Route 9G, five miles south of Hudson. INFORMATION Open late May through Labor Day—Wed. through Sat., 10 A.M. to 5 P.M.; Sun., 1 to 5 P.M. Closed Mon. and Tues. Labor Day through late October—Wed. through Sat., 12 to 5, and Sun., 1 to 5 P.M. Open Memorial Day, Independence Day and Labor Day. Admission fee charged. Tel. (518) 828-0135, or write Olana State Historic Site, R.D. 2, Hudson, 12534.

Olana is open by guided tour only, and the tours last 45 minutes. Only twelve people admitted on each tour, and tickets may sell out early, especially during summer weekends. You can reserve tickets by calling ahead, but if you fail to pick up the tickets at least 15 minutes before the tour, they will be sold. Olana's grounds are quite beautiful, and the park is open all year, from 8 A.M. until dusk, so if you do miss a tour, you can still enjoy the house and the view. Call ahead if handicapped accessibility is a concern. Older kids may be intrigued by the castlelike atmosphere of Olana, but the tour is not recommended for younger children.

FACILITIES Walking trails, rest rooms.

Kinderhook

James Vanderpoel House Also called "The House of History," and indeed it does present some fine exhibits of life in Columbia County, especially the era when the area was a bustling industrial and whaling center. Built around 1819 for lawyer and politician James Vanderpoel, the house is characterized by delicate ornamentation, including plasterwork ceilings, graceful mantelpieces and a wide staircase that seems to float to the second floor. A blend of American pride and European style, fine examples of the works of New York's cabinetmakers are displayed throughout the rooms. A fine selection of paintings, including many by country artists, depicts Columbia County life. The Vanderpoel House holds several special events throughout the year, among them a Christmas greens show and a coaching competition.

DIRECTIONS *Located on Broad Street in Kinderhook.*
INFORMATION *Open Memorial Day through Labor Day—Tues. through Sat., 10:30 A.M. to 4:30 P.M., and Sun., 1:30 to 4:30 P.M. In September and October, weekend hours only. A small admission fee is charged for the tour. Tel. (518) 758-9265.*

History buffs may also want to visit the **Van Allen House***, which is maintained by the same group that cares for the Vanderpoel. Located on Route 9H, one mile south of town, it is now a museum of the early Dutch period, with furnishings and art of the era.*
FACILITIES *Rest rooms.*

Lindenwald This Federal-style house, built in 1797, was purchased in 1839 as the retirement home of Martin Van Buren, eighth president of the United States. Van Buren was born in Kinderhook, and from there embarked on a 30-year political career. At Lindenwald, visitors will see the house that offered Van Buren a restful place to look back upon three tumultuous decades of public service. Named after the trees on the property, the graceful building—complete with shutters, double chimneys and arched windows—is today a National Historic Site and has recently undergone a major restoration that removed or lessened the impact of certain Victorian "improvements." Outside, the grounds offer an escape to the peace of rural nineteenth-century America. But it is inside Lindenwald that the amount of work which went into the 13-year-long restoration is most evident. A center stairway winds upward through the house, the hundreds of turned spindles polished so they gleam. The old wallpaper was stripped and replaced with new paper more appropriate to the era, and furniture and decorative objects look as if they finally belong to the home. The house contains a fine collection of Van Buren memorabilia, and is an excellent way to become acquainted with the president who was also known as the "Little Magician," both because of his size and his political acumen.

DIRECTIONS *Located on Route 9H, two miles southeast of Kinderhook.*

INFORMATION *Open from Memorial Day through September— Wed. through Sun., 9 A.M. to 4:30 P.M. Admission is free. Tel. (518) 758-9689, or write Lindenwald, P.O. Box 545, Kinderhook, 12106.*

There is a short tour, which runs every half hour. Call ahead if handicapped accessibility is a concern. Recommended only for older children who are interested in American history.

FACILITIES *Rest rooms.*

Activities

AIRPLANE TOURS

There is no better way to see Columbia County than from the air. The area's ever-changing lakes, parks and even the Hudson River take on a new magnificence when viewed from an airplane window. To arrange a flight, call the **Columbia County Airport** in Ghent at (518) 828-9461.

ANTIQUES

Searching for antiques in Columbia County, expect to discover rare and lovely items at shops that are often as well-stocked as many museums. You'll see everything from severe Shaker rockers to ornate English sideboards here, from fine examples of American folk art to the just plain odd. Quality antiques and shops are located throughout the county, but since the area has become a favorite weekend stop, many items are imported and/or pricey. This is not to say that an English hunt table isn't worth the several thousand dollar price tag; but you can forget about picking up a Shaker table at a house sale for peanuts. Many sellers and the shop owners in Columbia have become savvy, experienced experts in their fields.

In the city of Hudson, Warren Street and nearby blocks have become the antiques center of the county. If English antiques are your dream, stop in at the **English Antiques Centre,** Union and South 4th streets, (518) 828-7855/0968 (call ahead for hours). Here you will discover more than eighteen rooms filled with the finest furniture, accessories, prints, china, pottery and more from England, Ireland and France. The pieces here are beautiful and expensive, but the proprietors are right in pointing out that you would pay far more for their stock in a major city, and they will arrange for delivery of the items anywhere in the U.S. Both English and Irish antiques can be seen at **The Irish Princess**, 612 Warren Street, (518) 828-2800 (open Fri. through Tues., 11 A.M. to 5 P.M.; except Sun., when the hours are 12 to 4 P.M.). The stock here includes furniture, jewelry and silver, as well as some lovely gift items. Down the road, the **Hudson Antiques Center**, 536 Warren Street, (518) 828-9920 (hours change with the seasons; call ahead), houses the wares of more than a dozen dealers. You'll find everything from clothing and jewelry to toys, games and even cast iron garden furniture. At **Watnot Shop II,** 525 Warren Street, (518) 828-1081 (open Mon. through Fri., 10 A.M. to 4:30 P.M., Sat. till 5:30 P.M.), the emphasis is on home furnishings, and their ever-changing stock is sure to suit all tastes and budgets; the same is true of **Bobbie's Flea Market**, 510 Warren Street, (518) 828-1274 (open year-round 10 A.M. to 4 P.M.; closed Wed. and Sun.). **Townhouse Antiques**, 306 Warren Street, (518) 828-7490 (call for days and hours), is a funky selection of antiques and collectibles housed in a Hudson Valley townhouse. Those collectors who are looking for Shaker furniture can try **Greenwillow Farm Shaker Gallery**, Raup Road, Pawling, (518) 392-9654 (call for directions and hours). They offer fine Shaker furniture and accessories, like wooden boxes and sewing baskets, but the demand for Shaker antiques is extremely high so their stock changes often. In East Chatham there are at least three notable specialty shops. The **Librarium,** Route 295, one mile east of East Chatham, (518) 392-5209 (open Sat. and Sun., but call ahead), is a book barn that stocks more than 20,000 used books at great bargains. **Betty Ann and Richard Rasso**, Route 295, (518) 392-4501 (call for directions and hours), carry Shaker items and American folk art. **Robert and Mary Lou Sutter**, 59 Frisbee Street, (518) 392-4690 (call for hours), carry eighteenth- and nineteenth-century decorative items; they also have a small tool museum that is open by request only. Fine antiques from area homes and estates are carried at **Spencertown Art and Antique Company**, Route 203, (518) 392-4445 (call for hours), and more Shaker pieces can be had at **John Sideli Art and Antiques**, Shaker Museum Road, Malden Bridge, (518) 766-3065. And if you are in Kinderhook, stop at the **Kinderhook Antique Center**, Route 9H, (518) 758-7939 (open daily, year-round), and **Hardscrabble Antiques**, 44 Broad Street, Route 9, (518) 758-1807 (call for hours), both of which offer fine collections of American antiques.

Auction-goers can also enjoy a day in Columbia, and the times and dates of these exciting sales can be found listed in local papers. Remember to get to the auctions early enough to examine the merchandise and ask any questions you may have; generally, if you buy it, you keep it unless you can show that the auctioneer misled you. Watch for **Copake Country Auctions**, Copake, (518) 326-1142; **Watnot Auctions**, Churchtown, (518) 828-1080; **Niverville Exchange Auction**, Niverville, (518) 784-4451; and **Mesick's Country Auctions**, Spencertown, (518) 392-3505/4705.

FARM STANDS AND PICK-YOUR-OWN FARMS

The lush, rolling farmlands of Columbia County provide not only a lovely place to visit, but a remarkably large variety of farm stands and pick-your-own farms as well. Along with the traditional apple orchards and berry fields, discover the county's vineyards, melon patches and cherry orchards, where the selection of the fruit is left up to you. If you go to a pick-your-own farm, bring along a container for the fruits and vegetables, a hat to shade you from the sun and a long-sleeved shirt to protect you from insect bites, sunburn and scratches. The delightful thing about the smaller farm stands, which sprout as fast as corn in the summer, is that many of them will carry unusual or hard-to-get varieties of corn, apples and tomatoes.

In Germantown, **Hettling Farmlands**, Route 9, (518) 537-4152 (open year-round), lets you pick your own grapes, while **Wintje Farms**, Route 9G, (518) 537-6072 (open June through November), lets you buy or pick apples, cherries, melons, berries, squash, tomatoes, pears and plums. A truly special farm is found in Ghent on Route 9H, five miles north of Hudson: **Loveapple Farm**, (518) 828-5048 (open July through November), lets you pick your own apples, but they also sell pears, prunes, cherries and more than a dozen varieties of peaches at the roadside market. Kinderhook is home to **Samascott Orchard**, Sunset Avenue, (518) 758-7224 (open June to November), which has more than a dozen pick-your-own harvests, including grapes, pears, plums, strawberries, corn and a dozen varieties of apples. Near Claverack are the large farm markets like **Hotalings**, Route 9H, (518) 851-9864 (open all year), which lets you pick cherries, apples and strawberries; **Phillips Orchards**, Route 9H, (518) 851-6351 (open mid-August to November), with pick-your-own apples and pears; **Cardinales Orchard**, Route 9H, (518) 851-7390 (open August through October) for apple and plum picking; and **Bryant Farms**, Route 9H, three miles south of Claverack, (518) 851-9061 (open May through November), which is strictly a roadside market, but offers a huge selection of fruits, vegetables and local products including honey and maple syrup. The region around the city of Hudson is filled with farm stands during the season, including **Taconic Orchards**, Route 82, eight miles south of Hudson, (518) 851-7477, where you can pick berries and buy everything else imaginable; **Meisner's Farm Stand**, at the junction of Routes 9 and 23, with another huge selection of pre-picked goodies; **Kleins Kill Fruit Farm**, Route 10, (518) 828-6082, which has sweet, deep-red cherries; and **Phillip S. Egan Apple Farm**, Gahbauer Road, near the intersection of Routes 9H and 66, (518) 828-6056 (open September and October), an apple-lover's delight.

If goat cheese, known as chevre, is your delight, then you should be aware that three outstanding producers of the cheese are here in Columbia County, and sell their wares in local gourmet shops. **White Birch Farm**, (518) 325-3527, and **Little Rainbow Chevre**, (518) 325-3351, are both located in Hillsdale; a larger operation, **The Coach Farm,** is near Pine Plains, and welcomes visitors if you call in advance at (518) 398-5325.

HIKING
Wilson M. Powell Wildlife Sanctuary, Hunt Club Road, Old Chatham, (518) 794-8811, a small nature site also known as the ABDC Bird Sanctuary, is located on Route 13 near the Old Chatham Shaker Museum and offers a lovely view of the surrounding mountains. A marked trail leads you on a half-mile walk to the observation area; the sanctuary is particularly appealing for hiking in the fall, although it is open all year.

SCENIC DRIVES
It's difficult to avoid taking a scenic drive in Columbia County—wherever you look, you can see rolling, bright green meadows, misty ponds and quiet villages that look the same as they did a century ago. A drive through this county may lead you to a bluff overlooking the Hudson River or to a city that recalls the glory of the whaling industry. The roads are well-maintained, it's almost impossible to get lost.

For a sampling of the county's charms, start at Route 9 near

Clermont and head north to 9H, following the road through small towns until it again becomes Route 9. Stop in Kinderhook, then follow Route 9 south to Hudson, a "city" worth exploring. You can then take Route 9 back to Clermont or follow the signs to 9G and spend the afternoon at Olana. If you stop at all the restorations along the way, this 40-mile drive will take a day or so.

To see the western portion of the county, which runs along the Massachusetts border, take Route 9 to Route 82, which leads you through parklike country. Follow Route 7 north to Route 22, along Taconic State Park (a nice picnic stop); I-90 will take you west, back to N.Y. Thruway or to the Taconic Parkway (take the latter for a scenic drive.) This trip is particularly pretty in the fall, and will take approximately 4 hours.

SKIING

Skiers may want to visit **Catamount** in Hillsdale, (518) 325-3200, for a day on the slopes. Straddling the borders of New York and Massachusetts, the ski center is popular with all ages and skill levels and offers many services, including snow-making capabilities, dining, lessons, rentals and even RV and camping facilities. In the summer, Catamount still offers outdoor attractions in the form of grass skiing and mountain coasters, a sort of bobsled on tracks.

Cross-country skiing in Columbia County is centered in the state parks, which offer well-marked, uncrowded trails, free skiing and breathtaking natural surroundings. You must bring your own equipment. **Lake Taghkanic Park**, Route 82 at Taconic Parkway, 11 miles south of Hudson, (518) 851-3631, has skiing and ice-skating. **Clermont State Park**, Route 6 off Route 9G, (518) 537-4240, has skiing, as does **Taconic State Park**, east of Route 22 in Copake, (518) 329-3993; **Rudd Pond**, off Route 22 near Millerton, (518) 789-3059; and **Olana State Historic Site** in Hudson, (518) 828-0135. Ice fishing is also allowed at Lake Taghkanic and Rudd Pond.

THEATER

In Columbia County, there are two places to watch for good summer stock and concerts: the **Mac Haydn Theatre**, Route

203, Chatham, (518) 392-9292, specializes in musicals, while the **Spencertown Academy**, in the center of Spencertown near Chatham, (518) 392-3693, has concerts that range in scope from classical music to folk.

Where to Eat

Bucci's *(517 Warren St., Hudson, (518) 828-4990)* Good Neapolitan and Italian cuisine, this spot is open for both lunch and dinner.

Carolina House *(Route 9, Kinderhook, (518) 758-1669)* This log cabin restaurant has a large, fieldstone hearth in the dining room. The cuisine here is southern-style, and specialties include ribs, Chesapeake crab cakes, blackened beef steak and crispy catfish. For those who enjoy warm biscuits and other traditional southern favorites, this is the place to go. Children are welcome; all menu items half-price.
    OPEN *Dinner served daily, from 5 P.M. on.*

Chatham Bakery and Coffee Shoppe *(1 Church St., Chatham, (518) 392-3411)* An institution in Chatham, this family-run restaurant is famous for wonderful baked goods of all kinds. Other specialties include "Wallyburgers," served on homemade bread and Pumpkin Donuts in the fall. The soups, sandwiches and coffee are great. Moderate prices. The perfect stop for breakfast or lunch. Children are welcome; smaller portions available.
    OPEN *Mon. through Sat., 5 A.M. to 6:30 P.M., until 8:30 P.M. on Fri.; Sun., 5 A.M. to noon (breakfast menu only).*

The Claverack Food Mart *(Route 9H, Claverack, (518) 851-9164)* The place to go for enormous sandwiches made with high quality meats and salads. Open every day.

The Columbia Diner *(717 Warren St., Hudson, (518) 828-9083)* For a taste of vanishing Americana, stop here for breakfast or lunch. Open every day.

The Cottage Restaurant *(Route 295, East Chatham, (518) 392-4170)* Enjoy the peaceful country atmosphere and friendly service at this restaurant where all soups, breads and desserts are prepared fresh every day. Specials include stir-fry shrimp, Cottage chili and pastrami surprise (hot pastrami, mushrooms and muenster cheese on rye bread). Prime ribs served on Saturday nights only. Children are welcome; special menu provided.
OPEN *Daily, from 8:30 A.M. Closed Tues.*

Country Cuisine Catering and the Bakery *(1 Broad St., Kinderhook, (518) 758-7247)* The ambiance here is Victorian— stenciled walls, antique oak cabinets and glass display cases. Sample Scottish scones, Ellen's famous cranberry crunch pie, chocolate mousse cake and a huge selection of donuts daily. Also a great stop for gourmet take-out picnic treats like pâté, chicken divan, cheeses and sandwiches of all kinds. Children are welcome.
OPEN *Tues. through Sat., 6:30 A.M. to 5:30 P.M.; Sun., 6:30 A.M. to 3:30 P.M.*

L'Hostellerie Bressane *(Routes 22 and 23, Hillsdale, (518) 325-3412)* Classical French cuisine is the specialty here. Located in a 1783 brick Dutch Colonial house, this restaurant's warmth and character is the result of meticulous refurbishing. For the seafood lover, there's fillet of sole with puree of scallops and celery or fresh salmon with tomato butter sauce. Meat and poultry entrées include veal chop Orloff, roasted pheasant and rack of lamb with garlic confit. Not recommended for children.
OPEN *Wed. and Thurs., from 6:30 P.M.; Fri., Sat. and Sun., from 5:30 P.M. Also open on Tues. in July and August. Closed during March and April.*

Old Dutch Inn *(Route 9, Village Square, Kinderhook, (518) 758-1676)* The dining room here has ruffled country curtains and overlooks the Kinderhook village square. Colonial print wallpaper and tables set with linen cloths and napkins adds to the nineteenth-century atmosphere at the inn, and specials include shrimp and chicken Provençale, veal scaloppine Dijonais or steak au poivre and many fresh seafood dishes. For those seeking lighter fare, the tavern room features live music on Fri. and Sat. nights starting at 9:30 P.M. Well-behaved children only; smaller portions available.

OPEN *Lunch—Tues. through Sat., 11:30 A.M. to 3 P.M.; Sunday brunch—noon to 3; dinner—Tues. through Thurs., 5 to 9 P.M., until 10 P.M. on Fri. and Sat. 1 to 9 P.M. on Sun.*

The Red Barn (*Route 9H, West Ghent [no telephone]*) This old-fashioned ice cream parlor has a soda fountain and serves the best homemade ice cream sodas around. The sundaes come with real fresh fruit toppings, which are made on the premises. For those who don't have a sweet tooth, the homemade soups and seafood salads (shrimp, crabmeat and lobster) are other specialties. Children are welcome.

OPEN *May through Sept.—daily, except Wed., noon to 10 P.M.; April and October—Fri. through Sun., noon to 9 P.M. Closed November through March.*

St. Charles Hotel (*14 Park Place, Hudson, (518) 828-4165*) A good place to stop for cocktails, with an excellent oyster bar. Open every day.

Spencertown Country Store (*Main St., Spencertown, (518) 392-3577*) For great homemade sandwiches, salads and pies. Open every day.

Sweet Times (*12 Park Place, Hudson, (518) 828-6388*) Great ice cream and desserts.

Swiss Hutte (*Route 23, Hillsdale, (518) 325-3333*) Overlooking the slopes at Catamount ski area, the dining rooms here are wood-paneled and the three fireplaces make them warm and cozy. The Swiss chef-owner is both a master chef and a ski racer; the menu features Swiss-French dishes and home-baked pastries. Children are welcome.

OPEN *Lunch—Mon. through Sat., noon to 2:30 P.M.; Sunday brunch—noon to 4 P.M.; dinner—Mon. through Thurs., 5:30 to 9 P.M., until 9:30 P.M. Fri. and Sat., and 5 to 9 P.M. on Sun.*

The Vanderbilt Inn *(Main St., Philmont, (518) 672-9993)* Open every day for dinner, this establishment serves a variety of home-cooked American favorites.

Where to Stay

Good Earth Farm Bed and Breakfast *(Route 23B, Claverack, 12531, (518) 851-9808)* This 1850s Victorian farmhouse was built by the Bushnell family in the nineteenth century and is known for once hosting Marilyn Monroe. All bedrooms are large and airy, and horses graze on the farm's 80 acres of land. For breakfast, enjoy the farm fresh eggs and homemade baked goods from the on-premises bakery, Our Daily Bread. Open all year. One suite and one room with private bath; four other rooms share two baths. Children are welcome.

Hilltop Bed and Breakfast *(62 Hogel Hill Rd., Chatham, 12037, (518) 392-4985)*

L'Hostellerie Bressane *(Routes 22 and 23, Hillsdale, 12529, (518) 325-3412)* An outstanding example of Dutch Colonial architecture, this inn was built in 1783 by an officer in the Revolutionary War. There are three Palladian windows, a museum-quality corner cupboard and eight fireplaces with the original mantlepieces. Each of the six guest rooms on the second and third floors is decorated differently. The furnishings include beds with Hanover headboards, Windsor rocking chairs, Colonial mirrors, candle stands and pine chests, all finely crafted reproductions of museum pieces. A Continental breakfast of croissants and fresh juice is served from 8:30 to 9:30 A.M. The gourmet restaurant on the ground floor serves dinner daily. Open year-round, except March and April. Four rooms share a bath; two others have private bathrooms.

The Inn at Oliver House *(Route 7, Ancram, 12502, (518) 329-2166)*

The Inn at the Shaker Mill Farm *(off Route 22, Canaan, 12029, (518) 794-9345)* On a quiet dirt road, this restored Shaker gristmill made of fieldstone sits beside a hillside waterfall. A perfect romantic spot, the inn is surrounded by woodland trails just right for long walks. You can opt for breakfast only or take the MAP package. Dining is informal and provides an opportunity to meet other guests. A specialty of the house is sushi; the cuisine is a variety of dishes from around the world. Open all year. Twenty rooms with private bath; two suites. Children are welcome.

The Lace House *(Route 22, Canaan, 12029, (518) 781-4669)*

Locust Tree House *(P.O. Box 31, Old Chatham, 12136, (518) 794-8651)*

Riverview House *(Stuyvesant, (518) 758-7347)*

Spencertown Guests *(Box 122, Spencertown, 12165, (518) 392-2358)*

Wolfe's Inn *(R.D. 2, Box 22, Ghent, 12075, (518) 392-5218)* A white nineteenth-century farmhouse with black trim and red doors, this inn is nestled on ten acres and has a large pond for fishing. A hearty breakfast is served, featuring home-baked breads and muffins. Open all year, except Christmas Day. One suite and one double room with a private bath.

Dutchess County

Dutchess County was described by one of Henry Hudson's crew as ". . . as pleasant a land as one can tread upon." The generous forests, impressive mountains and abundance of wildlife attracted the Dutch first, but the county was eventually named in honor of the Duchess of York, later Queen Mary of England. Early landholders in the region belonged to several powerful families who controlled the area's major industries—milling, farming, lumbering and iron mining—and who built elegant stone and wood manors overlooking the rivers and mountains.

Today much of the county's past remains alive; many of the area names are the same as those of three centuries ago. A visit to Dutchess County is time spent in a more gracious era, a time when whitewashed houses clustered around neat village greens, and huge personal fortunes could, and did, build castles on the Hudson.

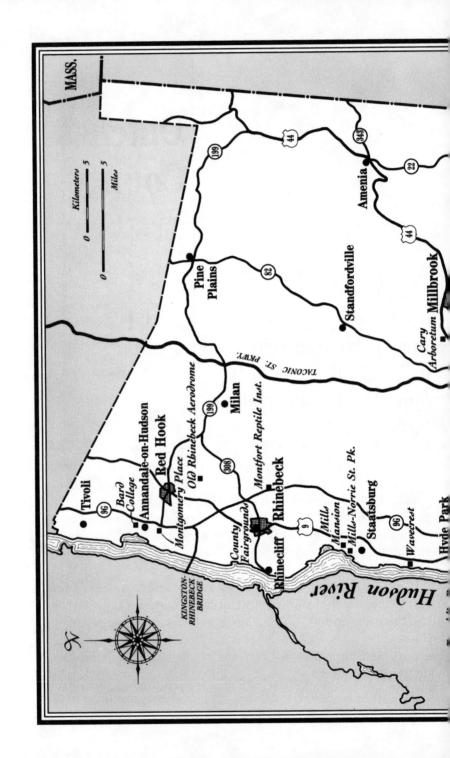

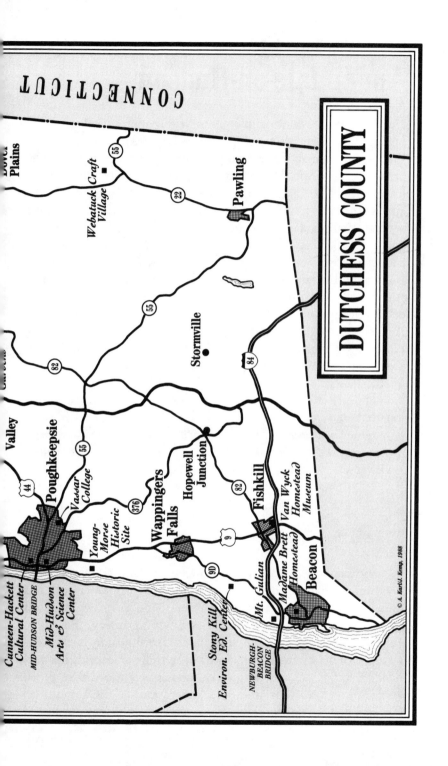

CONNECTICUT

Plains

Webatuck Craft Village

Pawling

Stormville

Valley

Poughkeepsie

Vassar College

Young-Morse Historic Site

Wappingers Falls

Hopewell Junction

Fishkill

Van Wyck Homestead Museum

Cunneen-Hackett Cultural Center

MID-HUDSON BRIDGE

Mid-Hudson Arts & Science Center

Stony Kill Environ. Ed. Center

Mt. Gulian

Madame Brett Homestead

Beacon

NEWBURGH-BEACON BRIDGE

© A. Karl/J. Kemp, 1988

DUTCHESS COUNTY

Annandale-on-Hudson

Bard College Founded in 1860 as St. Stephen's College, Bard began life as a men's school; today it is a coeducational facility that is renowned for its support and encouragement of the creative arts. Special programs open to the public include lecture series, art and philosophy seminars, concerts, art shows and performances. The Edith C. Blum Art Institute offers several exhibits a year in their gallery, along with workshops and slide shows; the Avery Center for the Arts focuses on modern artists and their techniques. At the Chapel of the Holy Innocents, the summer program features concerts by the Hudson Valley Chamber Music Circle. Other sites on campus offer photography exhibits, plays and musical performances. A mélange of architectural styles and buildings, the centerpieces of the campus are two Hudson River estates, Blithewood and Ward Manor. There are also lovely gardens, a Victorian gatehouse, and Dutch farmhouses nearby.

DIRECTIONS *Located on Route 9G, north of Rhinebeck.*

INFORMATION *The campus is open all year; the Blum Gallery is open Tues. through Sun., 12 to 5.* P.M. *Most programs are free; admission charged for some concerts. Tel. (914) 758-6822, or write Bard College Center, Annandale-on-Hudson, 12504.*

Hour-long campus tours are available, or you can walk around the campus yourself. Some gallery shows offer special presentations for children; call ahead for information.

FACILITIES *Bookshop, rest rooms.*

Montgomery Place This magnificent Federal-style mansion, with more than twenty rooms and situated on 400 acres, was once the home of Janet Livingston Montgomery, wife of Revolutionary War General Richard Montgomery. Begun in 1802 and completed three years later, the mansion is the centerpiece of an estate that includes waterfalls, footbridges, gardens, river views and an orchard containing more than 5,000 apple, peach and pear trees. Six generations of the Livingston family lived at Montgomery Place, and when it was purchased in 1986 by Historic Hudson Valley, personal possessions and family memorabilia were included in the sale. The interior is filled with fine decorative objects, rare furniture and artwork from the last three centuries. Gilbert Stuart portraits, Persian tile chairs, Czechoslovakian chandeliers, family china and rare books only hint at the treasures to be seen on a tour of the house. Montgomery Place is meant to show a family's history rather than the history of one specific era, so the interior displays the collections of many former inhabitants. On the grounds outside, visitors can view the Hudson or imagine themselves having tea in a "ballroom" of evergreens. And if a walk through the orchards whets your appetite, Montgomery Place fruit is sold at a stand outside the main gates.

DIRECTIONS *Located on River Road. From Route 199, take River Road north for 2 miles.*

INFORMATION *Admission fee charged. Tel. (914) 758-5461, or write Historic Hudson Valley, Montgomery Place, Box 32, Annandale, 12504.*

The guided tour of the house takes approximately 45 minutes; you can spend at least an hour walking on the grounds. Recommended for older children who are interested in history.

FACILITIES *Gift shop, restaurant, rest rooms.*

Beacon

Madame Brett Homestead When Catheryna and Roger Brett moved to the area now known as Beacon in 1708, they built a homestead graced by native stone, scalloped red-cedar shingles and sloped dormers. When Catheryna was widowed by a sailing accident, she continued to manage and maintain the 28,000-acre estate and gristmill while raising a family. During the Revolutionary War, the homestead was believed to have been a storage place for military supplies, as well as a stopping point for such luminaries as Washington, Lafayette and the Baron von Steuben. The house remained in the family until 1954, when it was purchased by the DAR. Today it offers a glimpse into the time when Beacon was a wilderness area.

Although the house has changed over the centuries, much of the original structure remains, along with some interesting stories. The upstairs once provided lodgings for slaves, and the front door was originally the rear door; as the town grew around the house, the main street formed at the back of the building, so the doors were switched for the convenience of callers. A cupboard in the dining room was brought to this country as ship ballast, and its top was trimmed off when it was discovered that it wouldn't fit through the door. There was even a well that could be reached from inside the house—a major comfort in the eighteenth century.

DIRECTIONS *Located at 50 Van Nydeck Avenue in Beacon.*

INFORMATION *Open May through October—Fri. through Sun., 1 to 4 P.M. Admission fee charged. Tel. (914) 831-6533.*

The house tour takes 30 minutes; make certain you visit the herb and formal gardens.

FACILITIES *Rest rooms.*

Fishkill

Van Wyck Homestead Museum Built in 1732 by Cornelius Van Wyck in the Dutch Colonial style, the house remained untouched by further changes after the 1757 addition of the West Wing. During the Revolution, the house was used as an officer's headquarters, a supply depot and a courtroom. It is also believed to have been the setting for James Fenimore Cooper's novel, *The Spy*. Now administered by the Fishkill Historical Society, the homestead is furnished with eighteenth-century pieces, and visitors can watch demonstrations of Colonial crafts and skills or examine artifacts recovered from the surrounding archeological explorations.

DIRECTIONS *At the intersection of Route 9 and Interstate 84, one mile south of Fishkill.*

INFORMATION *Open from Memorial Day to Labor Day—Sat. and Sun. only, from 1 to 5 P.M., or by appointment. Tel. (914) 896-9560. Admission fee charged.*

FACILITIES *Rest rooms.*

Hyde Park

Culinary Institute of America Founded in 1946 as a place where returning veterans could learn useful culinary job skills, today the school is regarded as a premier training institute for those in the food service and hospitality industries. Housed in a former Jesuit seminary, the grounds of the institute provide visitors with a sweeping view of the Hudson. Although the school itself does not have tours, you can walk the grounds and stop in at the bookstore, which has a dazzling array of cookbooks and kitchen accessories, as well as a selection of pastries and breads baked by the students.

DIRECTIONS Located on Route 9 in Hyde Park.

INFORMATION Open to the public year-round. Tel. (914) 452-9430. Award-winning food displays are in glass cases in the lobby. Wonderful restaurants, see pages 235–36.

FACILITIES Rest rooms.

Franklin Delano Roosevelt Home and Library Embellished with Georgian touches, the Victorian home here was the birthplace and lifelong home of Franklin Delano Roosevelt. Known as "Springwood," it was on this Hudson River estate that he and Eleanor raised their family and shaped world history. The site was designated a National Historic Site in 1944, and now includes the house, the first presidential library and the rose garden, where the Roosevelts are buried. A museum on the grounds has special exhibits drawn from the life and times of the family. In the house itself there's the office, jokingly referred to by Roosevelt as the Summer White House, where the agreement that provided the world with the first atom bomb was signed. Throughout the house, the rooms hold furniture and paintings gathered by Roosevelt's parents during their travels, including Aubusson rugs and Dresden chandeliers. In the Snuggery, visitors can see the retreat of Mrs. Sara Roosevelt, the president's mother, an iron-willed woman who adored her son and sometimes made life difficult for her daughter-in-law. F.D.R.'s bedroom is a very private look at a complex man, with favorite books and personal photographs in evidence. Outside, walk around the grounds and don't miss the rose garden in June. There is also a path to an environmental study area which swings down toward the Hudson River.

DIRECTIONS *Located on Route 9 in Hyde Park.*

INFORMATION *Open all year—daily, 9 A.M. to 5 P.M. Closed Tues. and Wed. from December to February, as well as Thanksgiving, Christmas and New Year's Day. Admission fee charged. Tel. (914) 229-9115, or write F.D.R. Home, c/o National Park Service, 249 Albany Post Road, Hyde Park, 12538.*

The tour takes about 45 minutes; plan to spend at least an hour in the library and on the estate. Add more time if you want to take the nature walk. The Park Service warns that there are some steep slopes and poison ivy along the trail, so stay on the walk itself. The house is wheelchair accessible.

FACILITIES *Rest rooms.*

Val-Kill The only National Historic Site dedicated to the memory of a president's wife, although Eleanor Roosevelt was quite famous in her own right. Val-Kill began as a favored spot for Roosevelt picnics, and in 1924, F.D.R. deeded the land to Eleanor for a personal retreat. A Dutch-style stone cottage was built (it now serves as a conference center), and an existing, small stucco building was converted into a factory, as part of Mrs. Roosevelt's attempt to encourage rural economic development. The factory later was remodeled into her house, and is now the Val-Kill Museum. Visitors here will see a biographical film about Mrs. Roosevelt, tour her home and have a chance to walk along the many hiking trails on the site.

DIRECTIONS *Located on Route 9G in Hyde Park.*

INFORMATION *Open March through November—daily from April to October; Thurs. through Mon. in March and November. Closed Thanksgiving. Admission fee is charged. Tel. (914) 229-9115, or write: Eleanor Roosevelt National Historic Site, c/o National Park Service, 249 Albany Post Road, Hyde Park, 12538. Allow at least 1 hour for the tour and film; more time if you walk any of the surrounding trails. Also note that from April through October, access is by shuttle bus from the F.D.R. Museum only.*

FACILITIES Hiking trails, rest rooms.

Vanderbilt Estate This imposing Beaux-Arts mansion was used by Frederick Vanderbilt, the grandson of Commodore Vanderbilt, as a summer and autumn "retreat." Designed and built by McKim, Mead and White, the estate was visited by the wealthiest people in America and Europe. There they enjoyed the fine art, furniture and other luxurious appointments at the mansion. The surrounding acres were used as a family farm by the Vanderbilts, and the gardens were planted in the formal Italian style with fountains, terraces and statues forming a grand backdrop for the flowers and shrubs themselves. Here the views of the Hudson River stretch far up and down the river, and there are few better ways to spend an afternoon than watching the sloops and cruise ships as they pass.

DIRECTIONS Located on Route 9 in Hyde Park.

INFORMATION Open March through November—daily from April through October; Thurs. through Mon. during November and March. Closed December through February. Hours are 10 A.M. to 6 P.M. Admission fee charged. Tel. (914) 229-9115, or write Vanderbilt Estate, c/o National Parks Service, 249 Albany Post Road, Hyde Park, 12538.

The tour takes about 45 minutes; plan to spend at least 1 hour walking on the grounds and watching the river.

FACILITIES Picnic areas, rest rooms.

Wavecrest A privately owned home overlooking the Hudson, Wavecrest has a permanent exhibit of the paintings and drawings by the Waugh family. Edward Ulrich, Wavecrest's owner, assembled the most complete collection of the works by this American art dynasty; here you will see portraits by Samuel Waugh (1814–1888), marine paintings by Frederick Waugh (1861–1940) and paintings and cartoons by Coulton Waugh (1896–1973.) Mr. Ulrich takes you around himself, and his stories about the Waughs are fascinating.

DIRECTIONS Located on Route 9 in Hyde Park.
INFORMATION Open on weekends in July and August; at other times by appointment only. Tel. (914) 229-7107. Small admission charge.
FACILITIES Rest rooms.

Millbrook

Innisfree Gardens Unlike the lush floral designs of many other formal plantings, you will discover a world here that is guided by the philosophy of the East, where harmony and placement is valued far more than color or species. Walter Beck began his garden in 1930, although his studies of Eastern art began at the end of the nineteenth century. Inspired by the powerful scroll paintings of Japanese artists, Beck—who never visited the Orient—set to work sculpturing his lands. Innisfree is planned around individual garden pictures or "cup gardens," each a unique scene, and all connected by a series of paths. Using natural formations as well as the additions of terraces and walls, Beck spent more than twenty-two years shaping the landscape to fit a precise vision; so specific was he with the designs that he believed the movement of certain rocks only an inch or so could totally destroy the effect. The garden was meant as a visual laboratory and notebook to be used by other gardeners, but it's worth a stop even if you don't have a green thumb.

DIRECTIONS Located on Tyrrell Road, one mile from Route 44.

INFORMATION Open May through October—Sat. and Sun., 11 A.M. to 5 P.M.; Wed. through Fri., 10 A.M. to 4 P.M. A fee is charged on weekends; free weekdays. Tel. (914) 677-8000.

FACILITIES None.

Mary Flagler Cary Arboretum More than 1,900 acres of nature trails and plant collections are found on this educational and research facility. There are special horticultural displays throughout the year, guided ecology walks and driving tours.

DIRECTIONS *On Route 44 in Millbrook.*
INFORMATION *Open year-round, except major holidays—Mon. through Sat., 9 A.M. to 4 P.M.; Sun., 1 to 4 P.M. Tel. (914) 677-9747/5343 for special event information. No charge, but stop at Gifford House Visitor Center to pick up a free access permit.*
FACILITIES *Gift shop, visitor center, picnic area, rest rooms.*

Trevor Teaching Zoo Started as a teaching zoo in 1936 with the hope that children would better appreciate wildlife if they were familiar with it, the zoo is now a four-acre site that offers close-up looks at a variety of animals. Red-tailed hawks, coati, otters, swans, badgers and snakes are only some of the guests at the zoo, which the Millbrook School students maintain. There is a 1¼-mile self-guided nature walk, and a boardwalk that overlooks a marsh.
DIRECTIONS *Located at the Millbrook School, six miles east of Millbrook on Route 44.*
INFORMATION *Open every day during daylight hours; tours available. Tel. (914) 677-8261/3704.*
FACILITIES *Rest rooms.*

Poughkeepsie

Driving Tour The town has several historic districts that are fascinating to drive through. **Garfield Place** (go south off Montgomery Street) began as a residential area in the 1850s and has been a popular area ever since. The houses are glorious, with turrets, towers, cupolas and Hudson River bracketing, and they span several design periods. **Academy Street** (from Montgomery to Holmes Streets) is a gracious residential area, with lawns, trees and ornate Victorian houses, as is the **Union Street Historic District** (cross Market Street and continue down Union to Grand Street). In the 1760s, Union Street was a dirt path that tied the town to the river, and by the nineteenth century a neighborhood popular with Irish and Germans had grown up around it. Today watch for cast-iron details on the brick and clapboard houses and churches. The area covers several square blocks, and is worth a walk on a spring day. Clinton House, at the corner of Main and North White Streets, is the headquarters of the **Dutchess County Historical Society**, where visitors can see collections of furnishings and decorative arts that detail New York life over the last three centuries. Tel. (914) 471-1630, for more information.

Vassar College and Art Gallery
When Matthew Vassar founded the college that bears his name in 1861, he not only broke new ground by making it a women's college, he also gave it the distinction of being the first American college to include an art gallery and museum as part of its holdings. The gallery now owns some 8,000 works of art, including Hudson River landscapes, prints by Rembrandt and Whistler, and European paintings, sculptures, coins and even armor. In addition to its permanent exhibits, the museum has changing exhibits and lectures; the gallery has up to twenty different shows each year. After enjoying the art, take a walk around the Vassar campus, where more than 100 buildings and an observatory grace the grounds. A stop in at the chapel to see the Tiffany glass windows is a rare treat.

DIRECTIONS Located on Raymond Avenue, off Routes 44/55, in Poughkeepsie.

INFORMATION The gallery and museum are open throughout the academic year; other times by appointment. Call ahead for specific times. Admission is free. Tel. (914) 452-7000.

Plan to spend a couple of hours at the museum and gallery, and on the campus. Wheelchair accessible.

FACILITIES Book store, golf course, snack shop, restaurant, lodgings, rest rooms.

Young-Morse Historic Site
Just outside of Poughkeepsie, on the old stagecoach route, is the summer home of Samuel Morse, the artist and scientist who changed the way the world communicates. In 1847, he purchased a country residence for his family, and under the guidance of architect Alexander Jackson Davis, he transformed the house into a Tuscan villa complete with extensive gardens. The octagonal house boasts

a four-story tower, a skylighted billiard room and a false stone exterior. Visitors who take the guided tour will see paintings by Morse, George Caitlin and various European artists, as well as a hand-colored copy of John James Audubon's *Birds of America*. Later owners of the home filled it with a diverse collection of decorative arts, as well as an odd but fascinating chair collection; one chair is covered in an elegant nineteenth-century cloth known as denim. In the basement gallery you will find a collection of telegraphs, Morse's most famous invention. Along the paths outside, huge iron urns bloom with fuschias and the air is scented with herbs from the formal herb garden. If you are up for a longer ramble, follow the 1½-mile trail through the adjoining Young Memorial Wildlife Sanctuary, which includes 88 acres of woodlands, ravines and ponds. The trail is clearly marked for recreational hikers.

DIRECTIONS *Located 2 miles south of the Mid-Hudson Bridge, on Route 9 in Poughkeepsie.*

INFORMATION *Open Memorial Day through September—Wed. through Sun., 10 A.M. to 4 P.M. Last tour at 3 P.M. Open on holidays; admission fee charged. Tel. (914) 454-4500.*

FACILITIES *Gift shop, picnic tables, nature trail, rest rooms.*

Rhinebeck

The village of Rhinebeck is rich in architectural delights, and a walk through town can make the history of families like the Roosevelts, Livingstons and Beekmans come alive. The post office on Main Street was reconstructed in 1938 under the direction of Franklin Delano Roosevelt; it's a replica of a 1700 Dutch house and contains murals and local history artifacts. A walk down Market Street and along Route 9 will take you past many lovely churches and other fascinating buildings. For more information, contact the Rhinebeck Chamber of Commerce, Route 9, Rhinebeck, 12572, (914) 876-4778.

Dutchess County Fair For the biggest—and according to many, the best—county fair in New York State, a stop at the

Dutchess County Fair is in order. The fair takes place during the two weeks before Labor Day and is eagerly anticipated by the entire Hudson Valley every year. The fairgrounds include large, comfortable display buildings, an outdoor horse-racing track, food stands, a picnic area and even an "old-fashioned" village where children can play. Because the fair began as an agricultural display, there are plenty of livestock shows and events; some of the top area breeders bring their prized cows, chickens, horses and hogs for judging. Kids will love the colorful, noisy midway, and the rides are equal to any of those found at larger amusement parks. Top-name entertainers appear for several shows during the fair's run, and there are fireworks at night. The fairgrounds also hosts a major crafts fair in June and two large antiques fairs—one on Memorial Day weekend and one on Columbus Day weekend—which draw dealers and buyers from all over the country.

DIRECTIONS The fairgrounds are located on Route 9 in Rhinebeck.

INFORMATION Shows and fairs held from May through October. Admission fee charged. Tel. (914) 876-4001, or write Dutchess County Fair, P.O. Box 389, Rhinebeck, 12572.

Plan to spend several hours at the fair or any of the special shows. Since many exhibits are outdoors, bring a sunhat, sweater or umbrella, depending upon the weather. Almost everything is at ground level, and the walks are paved so it's accessible to wheelchairs.

FACILITIES Snack stands, picnic tables, rest rooms.

Montfort Reptile Institute Snake and reptile fans will be fascinated by this incredible display. The institute consists of two floors of modern, glass-enclosed exhibit areas, and the collection of live snakes will charm even the most nervous visitors. Both poisonous and nonpoisonous species live at the institute, including boa constrictors, rattlers and benign black snakes. The tour guide helps dispel any fears you may have about these misunderstood reptiles. You can even handle a snake if you wish, a rare opportunity for young and old alike.

DIRECTIONS Located on Schultz Hill Road, off Route 9G in Rhinebeck.
INFORMATION Open all year—Sat. and Sun., 11 A.M. to 4 P.M.; weekdays by appointment. Admission fee is charged. Tel. (914) 876-3769 or 229-9595.
The tour takes about 45 minutes. This is the perfect place for anyone to make friends with these fascinating reptiles.
FACILITIES Rest rooms.

Old Dutch Christmas Experience the Dutch customs that were traditions in the Rhinebeck of the 1600s. This annual festival of St. Nicholas has been revived and is now celebrated with such ongoing events as open house at all stores, pony rides, hayrides, Morris dancers and clowns throughout town. See *The Nutcracker* performed on stilts. The local school is open for children to decorate tree branches and crowns for the evening parade. Musical entertainment continues all day in town hall featuring a variety of acts. The candlelight parade and tree lighting ceremony, with Santa on horseback, enormous floats, stiltwalkers, dancers and music, make this parade the Mardi Gras of the Hudson Valley. Don't miss this event if you have children.
DIRECTIONS Located throughout the village of Rhinebeck.
INFORMATION The festival is held the first Saturday in December from noon to 10 P.M. Admission to all events is free. Pick up a program listing the day's activities in the Beekman Arms hotel. Call (914) 876-4778 for information.
FACILITIES Food vendors, rest rooms in restaurants, schools and churches.

Old Rhinebeck Aerodrome One of the most unusual history museums around, the Aerodrome is the site for airshows, displays and demonstrations of aeronautic history. But the finely restored airplanes (or copies with original engines) are not earthbound; they are frequently taken up for a spin over the valley, or a make-believe dogfight over the nearby fields. And visitors can participate in the fun, too. There is a museum here, with guided tours that illustrate the history of flight.

You'll get to see Fokkers, Sopwith Snipes and Curtiss airplanes, old engines and antique cars up close. On weekends, you can thrill to the daring men and women in their flying machines as they reenact flights from the pioneer and Lindberg eras on Saturdays, and battles from World War I—complete with nefarious villains and brave fighter pilots—on Sundays. You can even take a ride in an open-cockpit plane, but these jaunts are not for the faint of heart.

DIRECTIONS *Located off Route 9 on Stone Church Road in Rhinebeck; watch for signs.*

INFORMATION *Open May 15 to October 31—10* A.M. *to 5* P.M.*; tours Mon. through Fri. during July and August at 1* P.M. *Sat. and Sun. airshows at 2:30 and 4* P.M. *Tours and rides are available before the shows. Admission fee charged. Tel. (914) 758-8610, or write R.D. 1, Box 89, Rhinebeck, 12572.*

Plan at least 2 hours here if you take the tour and stay for the show. The viewing stands are outside, so bring appropriate clothing. Great for photographers, and kids will remember the Red Baron and the airshow long after it ends. Wheelchair accessible.

FACILITIES *Picnic tables, rest rooms.*

Omega Institute Proponents of a holistic approach to people, civilization and nature, the center offers special lecture series and seminars. Topics have included folk music, spiritual studies, fitness and personal transformation. World-famous composers, writers and philosophers participate in the programs. Family visits are encouraged.

DIRECTIONS *Take Route 9G to Slate Quarry Road; located at 2 Long Pond Road off Slate Quarry Road.*

INFORMATION *Tours are given, usually by appointment. Tel. (914) 266-4301 for tour and seminar information.*

FACILITIES *Picnic area, snack bar, rest rooms.*

Staatsburg

Mills Mansion One of the grand, old Hudson River estates, the Mills Mansion had its origins in the eighteenth century, when Morgan Lewis and his wife, Gertrude Livingston Lewis, built a home on the site. A disastrous fire destroyed the structure in 1832, and a Greek Revival home was built as a replacement. It was this house that served as the center for the remodeling and enlargement of the estate by the firm of McKim, Mead and White. The owner at the time, Ruth Livingston Mills, commissioned the massive job, which was completed in 1896. What had been a large home was transformed into a vast mansion filled with fine European antiques and decorative objects. Rooms were gilded and plastered with ornamental balustrades, ceilings and pilasters. The sheer size of the rooms is almost overwhelming; one dining hall table has more than twenty leaves and is still dwarfed by the space around it. Much of the furniture is carved and gilded and covered with floral fabric in the rich styles of Louis XV and Louis XVI of France. Throughout the house, the walls are hung with costly, elaborate tapestries and fine paintings. Ironically, for all its size and wealth, the house was used primarily during the autumn months and stood empty for much of the year.

DIRECTIONS *Located near Staatsburg, off Route 9 on Old Post Road.*

INFORMATION *Open Memorial Day through Labor Day—Wed. through Sat., 10 A.M. to 5 P.M. and Sun., 1 to 5 P.M.; Labor Day through the last Sunday in October—Wed. through Sat., 12 to 5 P.M. and Sun., 1 to 5. Admission is free. Tel. (914) 889-4100.*

The guided tour takes approximately 30 minutes; grounds open for walking anytime. Special events are held here May until December; call ahead for information.

FACILITIES *None.*

Wappingers Falls

Stony Kill Environmental Education Center Part of a seventeenth-century estate owned by Gulian Verplanck, this nature center was later used as a practice farm by the New York State University system. Today Stony Kill is fulfilling its mission to provide agricultural and natural history programs to the public, and several different environments can be studied here. The trails are relatively short (the longest is two miles) and allow all ages to explore pond life, deciduous forests, swamps and farm fields. The bird observation area is a wonderful place to view both migrating and native birds, and in the farm education area there is a livestock barn that will be opened if you make an appointment. A map is available at the interpretive center, and special events are scheduled throughout the year.

DIRECTIONS *Located on Route 9D in Wappingers Falls.*

INFORMATION *Open year-round, dawn to dusk. Admission fee for special programs. Tel. (914) 831-8780.*

A lovely place to spend an afternoon, especially in the summer or fall. Wear suitable walking shoes, and bring binoculars if you enjoy watching birds and wildlife. If you have children, try to schedule your visit to coincide with some of the weekend special events that are usually held on Sunday afternoons.

FACILITIES *Picnic tables, rest rooms.*

Wingdale

Webatuck Craft Village A cluster of crafts shops and studios, the village is situated along the Ten Mile River. Crafts demonstrations, music festivals and special events are also offered. Here craftspeople show visitors how to make musical instruments, fine jewelry, stained glass and weavings, among other things.

DIRECTIONS *On Webatuck Road, between Pawling and Dover Plains off Route 22.*

INFORMATION *Open from March 1 to January 31—Wed. through Sat., 10 A.M. to 4:30 P.M. and Sun., noon to 4:30 P.M. Festivals run throughout the summer. Tel. (914) 832-6464.*

FACILITIES *Gallery, restaurant, rest rooms.*

ACTIVITIES

ANTIQUES

Lovers of antiques and collectibles will have a hard time leaving Dutchess County once they discover the wide selection of general-line and specialty shops here. Clocks, vintage clothing, fine old jewelry, rare painted cupboards and Hudson River paintings are all waiting for a home, and it's easy to spend an afternoon looking for that one-of-a-kind treasure. Antiques centers offer a cluster of dealers under one roof and usually have regular hours all year; auction houses generally have regularly scheduled sales throughout the year; individual shops vary widely in their hours and seasons. If you are driving a long distance or looking for something in particular, call before you go.

In Rhinebeck, the **Beekman Arms Antique Market and Gallery**, Beekman Square, (914) 876-3477, is home to more than two dozen dealers, and the wares here range from modern paintings to nineteenth-century china. The stock changes regularly and there is something here for all price ranges. Down the road at **Silhouette**, 15 East Market Street, Rhinebeck, (914) 876-4545, textile enthusiasts will discover an ever-changing selection of lovely vintage clothing, including many Victorian whites, table linens, quilts and accessories. Poughkeepsie offers something unusual at the **Clock Man Gallery**, Poughkeepsie Plaza Mall, (914) 473-9055, where antique clocks, watches and music boxes share space with other collectibles. Or change into period clothing at **Madame Bovary**, 5½ Garden Street, Main Mall, (914) 471-1015. In the Red Hook Antique District, along Route 9 in Poughkeepsie, seekers of antique fashions, furniture, decorative pieces and glass can choose from among several shops, including **Casey's Antiques, Reid's Antique Center, Traditional Details, 1770 House** and **Howson & Ross.** Just out of town on Route 9G in Tivoli, you can find **White Clay Kill Antiques**, (914) 757-3041, which specializes in early examples of American glassware and lamps. Another fine antiques center is found on Route 9 in Hyde Park. The **Hyde Park Antiques Center**, (914) 229-8200, is located in a rambling old building at the side of a pond. The prices here range from a few dollars for a kitchen tool, to thousands for a piece of Hudson River school art. Millbrook has the **Village Antique Center**, Franklin Avenue, (914) 677-5160, where specialty dealers offer American Indian art, sterling silver, formal and country furniture, cut and Victorian glass. **The Millbrook Antiques Mall**, Franklin Avenue, (914) 677-9311, has an excellent selection of furniture, rugs, quilts and collectibles at reasonable prices.

Auctions here can be formal or informal, pricey or filled with dollar buys, and the best place to find them is in the local newspaper. At least two, however, offer year-round sales and are worth a stop. The **Country Fare Antiques, Arts Center and Auction Barn**, Route 82, Stanfordville, (914) 868-7107, is a combination antiques shop, concert hall, art gallery and auction barn, where you can catch a concert of early American music or jazz and then buy the chair you're sitting on. In Pleasant Valley, the **Pleasant Valley Auction Hall**, on South Avenue, (914) 635-3169, also has a shop on the premises and sells at auction the contents of area estates.

ART GALLERIES

The Cunneen-Hackett Cultural Center, Vassar Street, Poughkeepsie, (914) 471-1221 (open all year, except major holidays—9 A.M. to 5 P.M.), offers theater, dance and art shows to the public. Both buildings at the center have been restored and provide a wonderful glimpse of the elaborate taste of Victorian America. The art gallery sponsors exhibits of regional artists' work throughout the year, and the ballroom and theater are put to use for concerts, lectures and plays produced by Hudson Valley theater companies. At the **John Lane Gallery**, 31 Collegeview Avenue, Poughkeepsie, (914) 471-2770, there are more than 3,000 square feet of display space filled with original paintings, prints and bronzes from around the world. But the highlight here is the collection of works by local and western artists. Paintings by the former group offer views of the Hudson, the towns and mountains; the latter gives us magnificent interpretations of the natural world, cowboys and Native Americans. One of the best galleries in the area. **The Mid-Hudson Arts & Science Center (MASC)**, 228 Main Street, Poughkeepsie, (914) 471-1155, is housed in the old city hall, which once had fish stalls and an open air market on the first floor. Today MASC has restored the building for use as a showcase and gallery for the visual arts. They also offer lectures, demonstrations and special events to the public. Shows may include food art, self-made books and other craft. A lively place to stop. **Artscape** is a festival of the arts held throughout Dutchess County each fall. Dozens of special performances by mimes, musicians, folksingers, artists and more are made extra special by the autumn foliage. Special events are held at many historic sites. Write to the Dutchess County Arts Council, 39 Market Street, Poughkeepsie, 12601, for performance schedules. Rhinebeck and Red Hook have seen the growth of several art galleries within the past few years. The following list will make a walking tour of the galleries easier. All are open on weekends and most have hours from 11 A.M. to 6 P.M. during the week. In Rhinebeck, visit **The Connoisseur Gallery**, 9 Mill St., (914) 876-6994/5; **Joe Aaron's Gallery**, 28 Montgomery St., (914) 876-6248; **The Bell Gallery**, 31 West Market St., (914) 876-4744; **John Lane Gallery**, 28 East Market St., (914) 876-2441; **The Monarch Gallery**, 19 West Market St., (914) 876-1810; **Rhinebeck Artist's Shop**, 36 East Market St., (914) 876-4922; and **The Hummingbird**, 14 East Market St., (914) 876-4585. In Red Hook, don't miss **The Hamlet of Fine Craft and Art**, 6B Tobacco Lane, (914) 758-5000 and **Chrisjohn's Trading Post**, Northern Dutchess Mall, south on Route 9, (914) 758-0224.

BICYCLING

A forty-mile bike hike in October that takes in some of the best scenery around, the **Hudson Highlands Fall Foliage Bike Tour** begins and ends in Beacon and takes in West Point, Cold Spring, Bear Mountain and Newburgh. The pace is slow, but there are some hills along the route. Stops are made for picture taking. Call organizer Fred Schaeffer at (914) 635-2242 for dates and details.

BOAT CRUISES

Spend a day on the Hudson River passing by elegant old estates, being dazzled by autumn's paintbox and stopping at a riverside festival or two. There's a cruise for all budgets, from 1-hour introductory sails to daylong extravaganzas complete with champagne. **Shearwater Cruises**, R.D. 2, Box 329, Rhinebeck, (914) 876-7350, leaves from the marina at Norrie Point in Staatsburg. Barbecues, picnics, blueberry tastings and breakfasts can all be enjoyed when you sail aboard the 28-foot yacht, *Genesis*. Tours can be arranged for morning, afternoon or early evening. Only two to eight people can be accommodated per cruise. **Riverboat Tours**, P.O. Box 504, Pleasant Valley, (914) 473-5211, allows you to explore the Hudson on a motor launch with a decorative sternwheel. The *River Queen* is available for special tours, which can include trips to West Point for the Army Cadets football games or to riverside festivals in Greene County. One of the most famous of the ships plying the river is the sloop **Clearwater**, 112 Market Street, Poughkeepsie, (914) 454-7673. Dockside festivals are the ship's specialty, but tours and private sails are available.

FARMS

Ace Polled Herefords, Overlook Farm, Millbrook, (914) 677-8258, is a dairy farm, which also has llamas. Visitors are welcome at **Westview Farms**, Quaker Hill Road, Pawling, (914) 855-9055, a horse-breeding farm (Peruvian Pasos). Call before you go. If you love the pure, rich colors of anemones, be sure to stop at **Battenfeld Greenhouses**, Route 199, Milan, (914) 758-8018, one of the largest anemone growers on the East Coast. **Pitcher's Nursery**, Middle Road (off Route 9G), Rhinebeck, (914) 876-3974, is an anemone grower open for retail business, but call ahead for hours.

FARM STANDS AND PICK-YOUR-OWN FARMS

June's ripe strawberries, summer blueberries and jewellike raspberries are three of the most popular crops in Dutchess County. But the harvest doesn't end with the berries; there are peas, asparagus, apples, pears, squash and big-bellied orange pumpkins. Farm stands sprout like corn along the back roads, many of them are homey little places where freshly baked goods lure you inside. And if you have a taste for doing it yourself, check out the area's pick-your-own farms.

The **Kohlmaier Farm**, Route 376, Hopewell Junction, (914) 226-5068 (open March through December), carries a broad line of vegetables and fruits, including cherries, melons and grapes from local producers. The farm also specializes in German yellow potatoes and offers tours by appointment. Another stand that has a wide selection of local harvests is **Piggot's Farm Market**, Spring Road, Poughkeepsie, (914) 297-3993 (open July through November). This family farm stocks dozens of fruits and vegetables, along with maple syrup, eggs and local honey. Tours of the farm can be arranged by calling ahead. In Rhinebeck, **Wonderland Farm**, Hilltop Road, (914) 876-4981 (open July through November), is a roadside stand packed with only the best, including the coveted springtime asparagus.

Pick-your-own farms are often indicated by a roadside sign saying which crop is ready to be harvested. For your own comfort, bring along a sunhat and sunscreen, as well as a container for the harvest; if you need to, you can buy containers at most of the farms. And if you are after a particular crop, it's best to call ahead; even though strawberries are a June fruit, you never know exactly when the berries will be at their peak. **Secor Strawberries, Inc.**, Robinson Lane, Wappingers Falls, (914) 452-6883 (open June, July and October), has pick-your-own peas, strawberries and pumpkins, as well as hayrides in the fall. **Fishkill Farms**, East Hook Cross Road, Hopewell Junction, (914) 897-4377 (open May through December), offers a farm stand with luscious tomatoes, corn, plums, beans and berries. The apples are pick-your-own, and they have more than a dozen varieties to choose from. Freshly pressed cider and hot-malt cider can be sampled, along with outrageously good donuts. Also in Hopewell Junction, **Johnson Farms**, Carpenter Road, (914) 221-7940, lets you harvest snap peas and raspberries on your own. **Montgomery Place** (see pages 210–11) lets you harvest apples from an orchard that has been producing for two centuries. Open from Labor Day to November 1. **Greig Farm**, Pitcher Lane, Red Hook, (914) 758-5762 (open May through October), has acres of fields that are available for pick-your-own harvesting. Asparagus, peas, blueberries, raspberries and strawberries, apples and pumpkins are all there for the enthusiastic harvester; you can also purchase boxes and bags to put the harvest in. Near the Greig fields is the Herb Farm and Tea Room, where you will find more than 150 varieties of plants for sale in the spring, and over 200 varieties of plants in the eighteen gardens. In the Tea Room, which overlooks the gardens, you can enjoy an herb-based snack, choosing from dishes like calendula buns, blueberry soup or lemon rose geranium cake. The Herb Farm is open Thursday through Sunday; the Tea Room on Saturday and Sunday.

HIKING

Dutchess County lies along part of the Appalachian Trail, 30 miles of which is open to hikers. The trail passes through the southeastern portion of the county and is a comfortable hike for day visitors or people staying overnight. There are several public parks along the trail. **Edward R. Murrow Park**, Lakeside Drive and Old Route 55 in Pawling, (914) 855-1131, has hiking trails, camping for Appalachian trail hikers only and picnic facilities. **Wilcox Park** in Stanfordville, (914) 758-6100, is open all year and has all the amenities of a large park, along with marked hiking trails suitable for a family day outing. **Pawling Nature Reserve**, Quaker Lake Road, Pawling, (914) 855-1569, spans more than 1,000 acres and contains several trails, including part of the Appalachian trail; they also offer guided nature walks. **Mills-Norrie State Park**, Old

Post Road near Staatsburg (the Mills Mansion is actually part of the park), (914) 889-4646, offers a wonderful place to spend a day outdoors in the Hudson Valley. The park has hiking trails, campgrounds, a well-marked fitness trail, a large playground, picnic areas, a golf course and clubhouse, a yacht basin and the Dutchess Community College Environmental Museum. The museum has natural history displays and a freshwater aquarium. Visitors can take part in special events like lectures and nature walks. The park is open all year, dawn to dusk.

SCENIC DRIVES

In Dutchess County almost any drive is breathtaking. Even the Taconic Parkway, which is now over 50 years old, is more a country drive than a major highway and reveals commanding views of distant mountains and lovely spring vistas along its length. The roads of Dutchess County are well marked, and the tourism council publishes a series of detailed, drive-yourself tours that are keyed to numbered roadside markers. (Write to Dutchess County Tourism, P.O. Box 2025, Hyde Park, 12538, or call (914) 229-0033.) The following drives are lovely during any season.

Starting from Route 9G in Tivoli, take county Route 79 to the Tivoli Bays Area, where you'll find a scenic overlook. This is where Henry Hudson was believed to have anchored while exploring the area. Next, drive south on Route 9G, also called River Road, which connected many of the great estates to one another. Near the Mid-Hudson Bridge, 9G will become Route 9; follow it south, past the stone walls that mark many of the estates, to Route 44 and take 44 to the Taconic Parkway north; exit at Route 308 west and follow it into the village of Rhinebeck. This drive will take approximately 2½ hours.

For a shorter drive, start in the village of Rhinebeck. This is a circular drive that takes you past some of the original farms of the county's founding families. Follow Mill Road South to Fishing Ground Road (county Route 85) to Charles Street, then take Market Street east back to Rhinebeck. This 15-mile drive was designated as the first scenic/historic landscape in New York. Some of the things to watch for along the road include stone walls, graceful private drives, farm outbuildings and tenant buildings, entrance gates and well-tended fields.

If you want to see New York's wine country, this drive is a little bit lengthy but worth the time. There are also several picnic grounds and nature preserves where you can stop along the way. Beginning at Red Hook, follow 199 east to Pine Plains. Stop here at the Hammertown Barn, a country store chockful of fine crafts and antiques. Continue southeast on county Route 82 and pass the Clinton Vineyards; then take Route 44 south through Pleasant Valley and into Poughkeepsie. If you want to return to Red Hook, Route 9 north will take you there.

SKIING

Dutchess County was made for cross-country skiing, with low hills that slope down toward the river, open meadows turned into liquid silver by moonlight, secret paths that cross streams and disappear into the pines. Many of the area's trails are maintained by the towns and villages, and they are often quiet even on a perfect winter's day. Multiple-use sites dot the Dutchess countryside, offering camping and hiking in the summer and skiing in the snowy months. Be sure to know the area where you are planning to ski so you'll avoid being caught on private property. **Mills-Norrie State Park**, Route 9, Staatsburg, (914) 889-4100, has several miles of well-marked trails, all of which offer magnificent views of the Hudson and the surrounding countryside. The park also offers picnic areas, and for the kids, sledding hills near the Mills Mansion. **Wilcox Park**, Route 199, Stanfordville, (914) 758-6100, offers more than 600 acres of land to explore on skis; there are no marked trails. **Bowdoin Park**, Sheafe Road, Poughkeepsie, (914) 758-6100, is a 300-acre site that allows skiing and sledding throughout the winter; special outdoor education classes are also held there. **James Baird Park**, Freedom Road, Pleasantville, (914) 452-1489, is open all winter for outdoor recreation, as are **Lafayetteville State Multiple-Use Area**, Route 199 and

Wilber Flats Road, Milan, (914) 677-8268; **Roeliff Jansen Kill State Multiple-Use Area**, Taconic State Parkway, Millbrook, (914) 677-8268; **Stissing Mountain State Multiple-Use Area**, Hicks Hill Road, Stanford, (914) 677-8268, and **Ferncliff Forest Preserve**, Astor Road, Rhinebeck. The only drawback to skiing at these sites is the lack of ski rentals, although **Cassidy's Cross Country**, Route 9, Rhinebeck, (914) 876-7161, has rentals, tours and lessons available.

THEATER

The **Bardavon Opera House**, 35 Market Street, Poughkeepsie, (914) 471-5313, was built in 1869 and is one of the oldest theaters in the country. The building now stands on the site of former lumber and coal yards, and was remodeled in 1921 in response to the public's desire for a grand-style movie palace. Today it is a major center for the performing arts of the region, including dance, drama and vaudeville. Tours of the theater are available by appointment; it is wheelchair accessible and has a special listening system to assist hearing-impaired patrons.

WINERIES

Two award-winning wineries in Dutchess County welcome visitors with tours, demonstrations and tastings. **Cascade Mountain**, Flint Hill Road, Amenia, (914) 373-9021 (open daily all year, 10 A.M. to 6 P.M.), was founded by novelist Bill Wetmore in 1972. At first a family-run business where everyone did a little of everything, Cascade has grown into a respected concern that has won best-of-class awards in the New York Wine Competition. Visitors to the winery can tour the facility and judge the wines for themselves. A gourmet picnic lunch is available for indoor or outdoor enjoyment or try the intimate restaurant, where local foods highlight the menu. **Clinton Vineyards**, Old Post Road, Marlboro-on-Hudson, (914) 266-5372 (open year-round, Sat. and Sun., 9 A.M. to 5 P.M.), recalls the small, family-run vineyards that dot the countryside of France. The winery specializes in seyval blanc, and their product has been cited as one of the best of its kind. A tour is available, and the grounds are lovely, with large pots of flowers and picture-book buildings dotting the hill. It is a small operation, so please call before you go and let them know you're on your way. A new winery, **Veraison Wine Cellars**, Shunpike Road, Millbrook, (914) 677-5098, (open June to September by appointment), produces chardonnay, claret and pinot noir. The owner of Veraison is John S. Dyson, industrialist and exchairman of the New York State Power Authority.

Where to Eat

The Beekman Arms *(4 Mill St., Rhinebeck, (914) 876-7077)* This Hudson Valley institution is housed in the oldest inn in America and dates back to 1766. The hearty breakfasts and weekend brunch are particularly good and include excellent home-baked muffins and eggs cooked to perfection. Children are welcome; no special menu provided.
OPEN *Breakfast—8 to 10* A.M.*; lunch—11:30* A.M. *to 3* P.M.*; dinner—5 to 10* P.M. *every day.*

Caesar's Ristorante *(2 Delafield St., Poughkeepsie, (914) 471-4857)* Located in a historic district of the city, this first-rate Italian restaurant has Art Deco decor and a piano bar. Specialties include the homemade pasta, veal, chicken, beef, antipasto and caesar salad. Not recommended for children.
OPEN *Daily, 4 to 11* P.M.

Le Chambord Restaurant *(Route 52 and Carpenter Rd., Hopewell Junction, (914) 221-1941)* Located in a gracious 1863 Colonial manor house, each dining room here has a fireplace and is furnished with Oriental rugs, antiques, crystal chandeliers and fine paintings. Chef Henri Benvenista prepares a wide range of award-winning nouvelle cuisine specialties. Children are welcome; half portions served.

OPEN *Lunch—Mon. through Fri., 11:30 A.M. to 2:30 P.M.; dinner—Mon. through Fri., 6 to 10 P.M., until 11 P.M. on Sat. and from 5 to 9 P.M. on Sun.; Sunday brunch—11:30 A.M. to 2:30 P.M.*

Cherry Blossom Restaurant *(150 Main St., Fishkill, (914) 897-9691)* The specialty here is sushi and sashimi prepared by a chef who once cooked for Japan's Emperor Hirohito. Located in a shopping plaza, the fare is definitely some of the best Japanese cuisine in the region. Children discouraged.
OPEN *Tues. through Sat., 11:30 A.M. to 3 P.M.; Sun., 4 P.M. on; closed Mon.*

Chez Marcel *(Route 9, Rhinebeck, (914) 876-8189)* Continental cuisine with a French accent. Open every day except Mon., for dinner.

Coppola's Restaurant *(825 Main St., Poughkeepsie, (914) 452-3040)* Serving Italian cuisine, both lunch and dinner, from noon on Tues. through Sun.

Culinary Institute of America *(Route 9, Hyde Park, (914) 471-6608)* There are four first-rate restaurants on the 75-acre campus overlooking the Hudson River. On the site of the formerly Jesuit seminary, St. Andrew's-on-Hudson, the institute now turns out some of the best chefs in the world. The CIA was founded in 1946 and now has 1,850 full-time students from all across America. Don't miss dining at one of these restaurants. Reservations are essential (call between 8:30 A.M. and 5 P.M.), except during the week at St. Andrew's Cafe. The months of January through March are usually less crowded; all weekend reservations should be booked several weeks in advance.

American Bounty Restaurant Here you can sample American regional cuisine at its best. The menu changes daily and might include smoked turkey with black pepper pasta and cream for an appetizer, poached salmon with oysters and dill sauce or sautéed tenderloin of beef with Creole mustard sauce for an entrée and fresh fruit cobbler with wild turkey sauce or a Mississippi riverboat for dessert. Not recommended for children.

OPEN *Lunch—Tues. through Sat., 11:30 A.M. to 1 P.M.; dinner—6:30 to 8:30 P.M.*

Caterina d'Medici Restaurant A relatively new student-staffed restaurant specializing in northern Italian cuisine, the pasta here is superb and so are the entrées. Try the tricolor large pasta diamonds with prosciutto, mushrooms and cream sauce or fillet of flounder with artichoke butter sauce, chopped eggs and basil. Not recommended for children.

OPEN *Lunch—Mon. through Fri., one seating at noon; dinner— one 6 P.M. seating.*

Escoffier Restaurant & Rabelais Grille Escoffier was the king of chefs and the chef of kings. This is the restaurant where final semester students practice preparing and serving classical haute cuisine. Examples of luncheon entrées are: pheasant with morels and sage or fillet of sole with lobster mousseline and saffron sauce. There is a prix fixe lunch and dinner; tax, gratuity and drinks are not included. Not recommended for children.

OPEN *Lunch—Tues. through Sat., noon to 1 P.M.; dinner—6:30 to 8:30 P.M.*

St. Andrew's Cafe This restaurant offers an informal atmosphere and features healthful dishes that are delicious as well. For lunch there is farmer-style lentil soup and mesquite-grilled salmon fillet with tomato-horseradish sauce. For dinner, enjoy fillet of beef with bleu cheese and herbs. Desserts include chocolate bread pudding soufflé or apple strudel. The prices are incredibly reasonable and the food is excellent. Well-behaved children permitted at lunch; not encouraged at dinner.

OPEN *Lunch—Mon. through Fri., 11:30 A.M. to 1 P.M.; dinner— 6 P.M. Closed on certain Mondays; call ahead. Some vacation periods also during July and August.*

La Fonda Del Sol *(100 Old Route 9, Wappingers Falls, (914) 297-5044)* Enjoy authentic Spanish cuisine in a charming Mexican-style restaurant. Downstairs is La Cantina, with live entertainment six nights a week. The menu here is extensive and prices are exceedingly reasonable. A couple of specialties are paella Valenciana (chicken and seafood with saffron rice) and guachenago a la Veracruzana (red snapper with tomatoes, onion, olives and pepper sauce). There are also a number of Mexican combination platters to choose from. Not encouraged for children; but small portions will be served.
OPEN *Lunch—Mon. through Fri., 11:30 A.M. to 3:30 P.M.; dinner—Mon. through Fri., 3:30 to 10:30 P.M., and 1 to 10 P.M. on Sat. and Sun.*

Foster's Coach House Tavern *(22 Montgomery St., Rhinebeck, (914) 876-8052)* A terrific place to stop for a hamburger and homemade fries. Open every day for lunch and dinner.

Guidetti's *(Pleasant Ridge Rd., Wingdale, (914) 832-6721)* Fine northern Italian cuisine, open Wed. through Sun. all year, except February.

Harrald's *(Route 52 [R.R. 2, Box 950], Stormville, (914) 878-6595)* Set in a 200-year-old Tudor-style house and recipient of several culinary awards, this restaurant is superb. Dine by candlelight, with classical music in the background. All baking is done on the premises and some house specialties are Maryland jumbo lump crabmeat cakes, baby pheasant in casserole and trout meuniere. Well-behaved children only; no special menu provided.
OPEN *Wed. through Sat., for dinner only.*

Maharaja Room *(Main St., Millerton, (518) 789-4808)* Indian cuisine. Dinner served daily from 5 to 10 P.M. Lunch on weekends only, from noon to 3 P.M.

Mariko's Japanese Restaurant *(Route 9, Rhinebeck, (914) 876-1234)* There is live shakuhach (Japanese bamboo flute) music on Sundays at Mariko's. Specialties include a sushi bar and several enticing entrées (all with detailed translations) that are sure to tempt even the least adventurous. If traditional Japanese favorites don't intrigue you, there is also grilled Norwegian salmon with vegetables, Tokyo steak and Peking duck. Children are welcome; no special menu provided.

OPEN *In summer, dinner served every day except Tuesdays. In winter, dinner served on weekends only, from 6 P.M. on.*

Old Drovers Inn *(Dover Plains, (914) 832-9311)* Once a tavern catering to cattle drovers on their way to market in New York City, the building that houses this appealing restaurant dates back to 1750. Some of the specialties include Old Drovers' cheddar cheese soup, duck liver pâté with pistachios, breast of pheasant in champagne sauce and chocolate truffle cake. Children permitted only if very well behaved; no children's menu.

OPEN *Lunch—Mon., Thurs. and Fri., noon to 3 P.M.; dinner— Mon. and Thurs., 5:30 to 8:30 P.M., until 9:30 P.M. on Fri. Sat. open noon to 9:30 P.M.; Sun., 1 to 8 P.M.*

The Pastry Garden *(199 Dutchess Turnpike, Poughkeepsie, (914) 473-5220)* For the best cakes, cookies and pies in town. Open every day.

Le Pavillon *(230 Salt Point Turnpike [Route 115], Poughkeepsie, (914) 473-2525)* This 200-year-old brick farmhouse outside the city of Poughkeepsie provides an elegant setting for a restaurant. Serving French country-style cuisine, the specialties are game, fish and seasonal dishes. Not for children.

OPEN *Lunch—noon to 2 P.M. (reservations required); dinner— daily, 5:30 to 10 P.M.*

The Red Hook Inn *(31 South Broadway, Red Hook, (914) 758-8445)* Serving Continental cuisine. Open all year for lunch, dinner and Sunday brunch.

Schemmy's Ltd. *(19 East Market St., Rhinebeck, (914) 876-6215)* An old-fashioned ice cream parlor serving breakfast and lunch every day. The homemade soups and salads are also a treat.

Taste Buds *(139 South Broadway, Red Hook, (914) 876-1606)* A gourmet food shop and restaurant specializing in imaginative homemade salads, pasta dishes and quiches. A great stop for brunch or picnic supplies.
OPEN *Wed. through Sun., 10 A.M. to 6 P.M.*

Tivoli Garden *(10 South Broadway, Red Hook, (914) 758-6902)* Specialties here include homemade soups, salads, quiches and sandwiches. Breakfast, lunch and dinner served daily, all year.

Towne Crier Cafe *(366 Beekman Rd., Hopewell Junction, (914) 223-5555)* Located in the historic hamlet of Beekman, this restaurant is in a building that dates back to 1716 and served as a stagecoach stop, inn and general store. Since 1972, the Towne Crier has been presenting fine folk and jazz—Tom Paxton, Melanie and Country Joe McDonald are just a few of the top-name talent who have performed here. An international menu features fresh seasonal foods and desserts are the specialty. Pastry chef Mary Murphy makes exquisite tortes; the chocolate truffles are heavenly. Not recommended for children.
OPEN *Dinner—6:30 to 9 P.M.; entertainment begins 9:30 P.M.*

The Village Diner *(39 North Broadway and Route 9, Red Hook, (914) 758-6232)* The only diner in the state named to the New York State Historic Register, this Art Deco–style structure built in 1927 is family-owned and -operated. They serve hearty home-cooked meals and are known for their breakfast specials, homemade donuts and muffins, soups, freshly brewed iced tea and egg creams.
OPEN *Daily, 6 A.M. to 9 P.M., until 10 P.M. Fri. and Sat.*

Where to Stay

Beekman Arms *(4 Mill St. [Route 9], Rhinebeck, 12572, (914) 876-7077)* The oldest inn in America, the Beekman Arms is steeped in history. The eighteenth-century atmosphere and charm remain today in the building's great mellowed-brown beams. The guest rooms are above the restaurant and occasionally noise can be a problem. If you want a more serene atmosphere, try the **Delamater House**, which is run by the same people. This lovely gingerbread Victorian, designed by Alexander Jackson Davis, dates back to 1844 and offers rooms reminiscent of a country manor. Open all year. Forty-nine rooms with private baths. Children are welcome.

Calico Quail Inn *(Box 748, Route 44, Mabbettsville, 12545, (914) 677-6016)* This lovely, classic 1830 farmhouse is set on a parklike property that has a Chinese bridge and a pond with a 30-foot boat, where guests can enjoy drinks. The emphasis is on personalized service, and you will find freshly cut flowers and period antiques in your room. An intimate breakfast is served in the Tavern Room, and it includes fresh fruits and homemade pastries. Open all year, except during March. Two rooms; one has a reading and dressing area, and a queen-sized bed. Both share one bathroom. Children are not permitted.

Castle Hill Bed and Breakfast, *(Box 325, Wappingers Falls, 12590, (914) 298-8000)* Stone pillars lead to a tree-lined drive at this Victorian-era inn. The "castle" is actually a brick mansion, one of the few in the area. It was once the home of Dr. Henry Yates Satterlee, who later designed the National Cathedral in Washington, D.C. The Victorian atmosphere here has been preserved, and most of the furnishings are genuine antiques. A Continental breakfast is served, featuring fine pastries and exotic teas, and the 50-foot swimming pool is a treat in the summer months. Open from April 1 to November 30. Two rooms share one bath; two others have private bathrooms and there are also two suites. Children not permitted.

Le Chambord Inn *(Route 52 and Carpenter Rd. [R.D. 9, Box 350], Hopewell Junction, 12533, (914) 221-1941)* A charming inn tucked away in the woods, Le Chambord offers elegance and relaxation with the convenience of a first-rate restaurant downstairs. The rooms, located on the second and third floors, all are furnished with fine antiques. A Continental breakfast is served in one of the dining rooms by the fireplace. Open all year. All twenty-five rooms have private baths, telephones and TV upon request. Children are welcome.

Hammertown Inn *(R.D. 2, Box 25, Hammertown Rd., Pine Plains, 12567, (518) 398-7539/7075)* This elegantly restored 1790 Colonial on two acres is filled with antiques. The owners also run an antique and gift shop, The Hammertown Barn, next door. The two guest rooms are furnished with antiques and a country breakfast is served each morning, featuring lemon bread, homemade apple cake and egg soufflé. Guests are also welcome to visit the family-run dairy farm, where prize-winning Holstein cows are raised. Open all year. Two rooms share one bathroom. Children are welcome.

Inn at the Falls *(50 Red Oaks Mill Rd., Poughkeepsie, 12603, (914) 462-5770)* A blend of the luxury of a plush resort and the atmosphere of a country estate. Nestled next to a waterfall, the inn is known informally as simply "The Falls." Some rooms are decorated in an English style, while others have American country and Oriental motifs. A European-style Continental breakfast is delivered to your room each morning, and there is a cocktail bar in the living room. Open all year, except December 31. Twenty-four rooms and twelve suites, all of which have private baths, phones and a TV. Children are welcome.

Montgomery Inn Guest House *(67 Montgomery St., Rhinebeck, 12572, (914) 876-3311)* Located in the heart of the village of Rhinebeck, this well-tended Victorian home has a spacious wraparound porch and a colorful flower garden. The interior has been carefully constructed with oak detailing and each room has been filled with comfortable, old-fashioned furniture. Open all year. Four rooms share two baths; one other has a private bath. Children must be well behaved.

Old Drovers Inn *(Dover Plains, 12522, (914) 832-9311)* Originally opened as a tavern for cattle drovers in 1750. The drovers are gone, but their stopping place remains and offers travelers rooms furnished with antiques and a fine restaurant downstairs. Enjoy breakfast in the Federal Room, where murals depict several area landmarks including Roosevelt's home, West Point and the Old Drovers Inn itself. Open Thurs. through Sun. only; closed December 8 through 30. All three rooms have private baths. Well-behaved children only.

The Pines *(R.D. 1, Box 131, Pine Plains, 12567, (518) 398-7677)* This spacious Victorian mansion, built in 1878 on five acres of land surrounded by huge pine trees, is listed in the National Register of Historic Places. Inside there's rich walnut, cherry and chestnut woodwork. The rooms are furnished with period furniture. Breakfast consists of fresh fruit, homemade bread and an egg dish, accompanied by coffee or tea. Open all year. Two rooms have private baths; three other rooms share one bath. Children not permitted.

The Residence Inn *(Route 9 and Interstate 84, Fishkill, 12524, (914) 896-5210)* These fully modern low-rise suites are designed in the Tudor style and have walks, lawns and lovely landscape. All suites offer wood-burning fireplaces, kitchens, Continental breakfast and a daily newspaper. There is a pool, whirlpool and use of a fully-equipped health club. There are even rooms equipped for handicapped guests. This establishment combines the best features of motel and inn accommodations. Open all year; 104 suites, all with private bathrooms. Children are welcome.

Simmon's Way Village Inn *(Main St. [Route 44], Millerton, 12546, (518) 789-6235)* E. W. Simmons, an educator, lawyer and statesman, built the original house on this property in 1854. In 1892, the president of the Millerton National Bank transformed the house into an elegant Victorian. Five years ago, the property was renovated and the rooms filled with down pillows, plush linens, antiques and canopied beds. Enjoy a Continental breakfast in your suite, the dining room or the front porch. Afternoon tea is served on weekends. There is an excellent restaurant on the premises. Open all year, except for two weeks in March. Eleven rooms all with private baths. Children are welcome.

Troutbeck *(Leedsville Rd., Box 26, Amenia, 12501, (914) 373-9681)* This English country estate on 422 acres is an executive retreat during the week; but on weekends, it's a relaxed getaway. Fronted by a row of towering sycamores and a bubbling brook, the slate-roofed estate has leaded windows, antique furniture, walled gardens, an outdoor pool and tennis courts. Open on weekends only, from 5 P.M. Friday to 2:30 P.M. Sunday. Twenty-six bedrooms and five suites, all with private bathrooms. Six of the bedrooms have fireplaces. Not recommended for children.

Vassar College Alumnae House *(Raymond Ave., Poughkeepsie, 12601, (914) 485-3700)* Set on a hill at the edge of the Vassar College campus, this spacious Tudor-style inn, restaurant and pub are all open to the public. The house, given to the college in 1924 by two sisters who had graduated from Vassar, was designed by the architectural firm of Hunt & Hunt, sons of the famous nineteenth-century architect Richard Morris Hunt. A Continental breakfast, lunch, dinner and late-night meals are served every day in a handsome oak-paneled dining room or on the terrace in warm weather. Open all year. Fifteen rooms with private baths. Children are welcome.

Whistlewood Farm *(11 Pells Rd., Rhinebeck, 12572, (914) 876-6838)* Maggie Myers runs this distinctive bed and breakfast, a working 13-acre horse farm. In addition to the geldings and mares there are geese, cats and a German shepherd. Although it might look at first glance like an ordinary ranch house, the interior will tantalize antiques collectors with an eclectic collection, including a player piano. The living room has a stone fireplace and a beautiful view of the farm's horse paddocks. A hearty farm breakfast is served daily and includes homemade muffins, doughnuts, jams and jellies. Open all year. One master bedroom (queen-sized bed) with private bath; three other rooms share one bathroom. Children are welcome.

Putnam County

One of the gateways to the Hudson Highlands, Putnam County offers splendid river views, lots of outdoor entertainment and a chance to see small-town America before it completely disappears. In Cold Spring, the tiny shops and riverside gazebo are charming reminders of a more leisurely past. And at Garrison's Landing, you'll discover another riverside park. Up north, the Federal-style mansion called Boscobel has been restored to its former elegance after coming within a hairbreadth of being completely demolished. A walk through the gardens there is magnificent in spring, with tens of thousands of flowers filling the air with their colors and scents. Putnam is also home to the huge Fahnestock Park, where untouched wetlands and woods beckon the hiker, and crystal clear lakes cool down a summer's day. A very different outdoor environment is found at Manitoga, which was created by the industrial designer Russell Wright. Here you can visit Dragon Rock, a unique house that was built into the wall of a quarry, or stop by at the Woodlands Indian exhibit, where full-sized wigwams are used

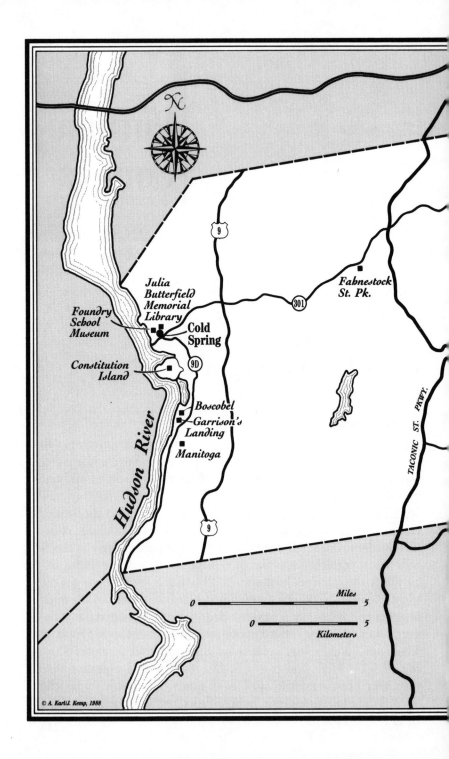

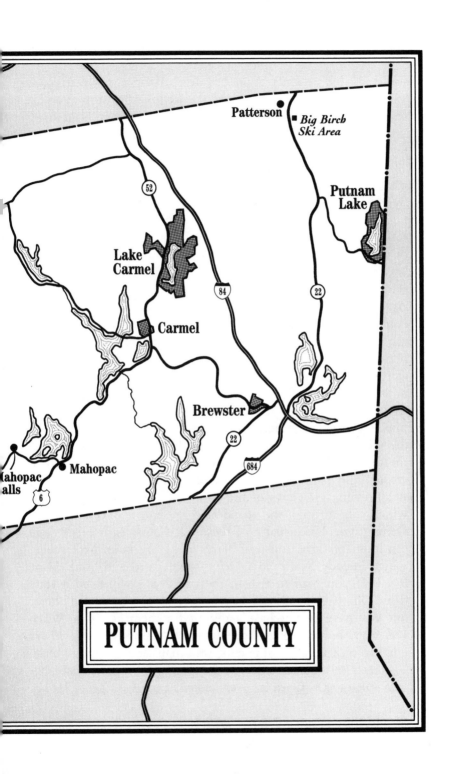

Patterson

■ *Big Birch*
Ski Area

52

Putnam
Lake

Lake
Carmel

84

22

Carmel

Brewster

22

684

Mahopac
alls

Mahopac

6

PUTNAM COUNTY

for study by students. You can drive along rustic dirt roads and see houses that date back to the Revolution, stop at an art show or even dress up for a Victorian fair. Just an hour from New York City, Putnam County can seem a century or more away, with a pace and a grace all its own.

Carmel

Clarence Fahnestock State Park This huge park, consisting of several thousand acres of forest, swamp, lake and meadow, was assembled through donations of land from private and state organizations. Several hiking trails, including part of the Appalachian Trail, weave in and out of the park, which also contains fishing ponds, a lakeside beach, boat rentals, ice-skating areas and cross-country ski trails. The park also sponsors performing arts programs, and it does have provisions for camping, although you must call ahead for reservations. The unusual, 1.5-mile **Pelton Pond Nature Trail** is a self-guided trail that follows the perimeter of a pond formed when an old mine shaft was dammed. You can picnic in this area, or watch the woods from the small pavilion. Hikers will want to look for the **Appalachian Trail**, an eight-mile stretch of which crosses the park; the **Three Lakes Trail**, with its varied wildflowers and views of the park; and **Catfish Loop Trail**, which cuts through the abandoned settlement once known as Dennytown. Since many of these trails cross each other, you can look for signs and trail blazes along the main park roads, which include Route 301, Dennytown Road and Sunk Mine Road. If you plan to fish in the park, you will need a state fishing license (boats can be brought along, or rented there, but you have to purchase a permit for them as well). When you visit, be certain to stop at the park headquarters, where you can pick up a list of events, trail maps and a fishing guide.

DIRECTIONS *Located on Route 301, east of the Taconic Parkway.* INFORMATION *Open all year. Admission is free. Tel. (914) 225-7207.*

It's easy to spend a day or more here, swimming, fishing and

*delighting in an unspoiled outdoor environment. Bring a bath-
ing suit for the lake, and sturdy hiking shoes for the trails; and
remember that early spring and late fall can be much colder in
the woods than you might expect. Cross-country skiers will have
to provide their own equipment, as will ice skaters. Facilities
are handicapped accessible.*
*FACILITIES Bath house, snack stand (in summer), information
office, rest rooms.*

Cold Spring

Julia Butterfield Memorial Library Art buffs, particularly
fans of the Hudson River school, may be interested in this
small, but select, collection of works.
   DIRECTIONS Located at Morris Avenue and Main Street.
   *INFORMATION The library's hours change frequently, so call be-
fore going. Tel. (914) 265-3040.*
   FACILITIES Rest rooms.

***The Foundry School Museum of the Putnam Historical
Society*** A small museum dedicated to preserving local history
through various permanent and changing exhibits, there are
displays here of portraits, furniture, models, paintings and
Hudson River memorabilia.
   DIRECTIONS Located at 63 Chestnut Street, Cold Spring.
   *INFORMATION Open Wed., 9:30 A.M. to 4 P.M. and Sun. 2 to 5
P.M.*
   FACILITIES Rest rooms.

Walking Tour This lovely river town was founded in the
eighteenth century, and according to local folklore, received
its name after George Washington commented on the water he
tasted at a nearby spring. Cold Spring received an economic
boost during the nineteenth century, when it became the site
of one of the largest iron foundries in the United States.
Production at the town's West Point Foundry covered everything from weapons to some rather unusual furniture, some of

which can still be seen today at the Tarrytown home of Washington Irving. On **Main Street**, you can visit "antiques row," where dozens of dealers own or share shops that specialize in everything from fine vintage clothing to brass beds to odds and ends of all kinds. Be sure to stop in at the **Hudson Valley Visitor Center**, 72 Main Street, (914) 265-3066, which specializes in local crafts, as well as books and maps. If you continue down Main Street to the railroad tracks, you will find a plaque that marks Washington's visit. Also right there is the bandstand, which was constructed to host riverside concerts. Now it provides a wonderful place to look across the river to Storm King Mountain, which gained its current name after someone noticed the mountain was at the center of many storms. At the corner of Main and West Streets, follow West Street south to Market to see **The Chapel of Our Lady** (914) 265-2781. This Greek Revival one-room chapel was built in 1834 for the workers at the foundry; it's the oldest Roman Catholic church in the region. The view from the chapel looks across the river, but you may have to wait to enter on weekends, since this is a popular place for weddings.

DIRECTIONS Located off Routes 9D and 301.

INFORMATION Guided walking tours offered on Sunday afternoons at the Visitor Center, 72 Main Street, or by appointment. Call (914) 265-2111.

Garrison

The Landing, which overlooks the Hudson River at the railroad station, is the town's hub. Walk down to the riverside gazebo, once used as a set in the movie *Hello Dolly*, and a fine spot from which to see the remains of an old Hudson River ferry at low tide. The Landing also houses the **Garrison Art Center**, (914) 424-3960, where you can stop in and peruse the works of local artists. The railroad station house is now the **Depot Theater**, home to the Hand to Mouth Players, a popular theater group that performs musicals during the summer months.

The Alice and Hamilton Fish Library This library contains historical memorabilia of local families, as well as an astounding collection of slides on the Hudson River painters.

   DIRECTIONS *Located at the junction of Routes 9D and 403 in Garrison.*
   INFORMATION *Slides viewed by appointment only. Tel. (914) 424-3020 for hours.*
   FACILITIES *Rest rooms.*

Graymoor The home of the Franciscan Friars, visitors here will be treated to fantastic views, especially during the fall foliage season.

   DIRECTIONS *On Route 9D, near Route 403.*
   INFORMATION *Open to the public from May through October during daylight hours.*
   FACILITIES *Picnic tables, walking paths, snack stand, rest rooms.*

Manitoga, Man with Nature Center The name of this center is taken from the Algonquin word for "Place of the Spirit," and the philosophy of Manitoga lives up to its name. Here people and nature are meant to interact and visitors are encouraged to experience the harmony of their environment. The center was designed by artist Russell Wright, who created a system of trails that focus on specific aspects of nature. The Morning Trail takes advantage of the early day's sunlight, the Spring Trail introduces the walker to wildflowers and the Blue Trail wanders over a brook and through a dramatic evergreen forest. On a walk through Manitoga, you will find a full-sized reproduction of a Native American wigwam, which was constructed with traditional methods and tools. The site is used as an environmental learning center, and many special programs are offered here. There are workshops in art, poetry, photography, anthropology and botany, along with guided nature walks and concerts of music and dance. You can even visit Dragon Rock, the cliff house built by Wright; it has glass walls so visitors can view the forest. Manitoga is a rare site, where human-directed design and the natural world reflect and inspire each other.

DIRECTIONS Located on Route 9D in Garrison.
INFORMATION Open all year, but hours vary; it's best to call ahead. Admission fee is charged. Tel. (914) 424-3812, or write Manitoga, Old Manitou Road, Garrison, 10524.

You can walk for hours along the trails (there are both guided and self-guided tours) or spend time in the workshops and visiting the house. Dress for the outdoors and bring a camera. Older children are usually fascinated by the wigwam and by Dragon Rock; not recommended for younger kids.
FACILITIES Picnic area, rest rooms.

Garrison-on-Hudson

Boscobel Standing on a bluff looking out on the Hudson River, the country mansion known as Boscobel seems as if it has spent its full 180 years in peace and prosperity. But appearances can be deceiving. States Morris Dyckman, a loyalist of Dutch ancestry, began building the mansion in 1805, but he died before it was completed. It was his wife, Elizabeth Corne Dyckman, who was to live there with their family. Designed in the Federal style, Boscobel was furnished with elegant carpets, fine porcelains and furniture from the best workshops in New York. The house remained in the family until 1888; from then on it had various owners, including the federal government. Then, in 1955, the government decided that Boscobel was no longer needed, and the house was sold for $35 to a contractor, who in turn, stripped it of many of its architectural details and sold them off. Local people were so incensed that they tracked down the sections that had been sold, stored the other parts of the house and, finally, purchased land on which to reerect the building. Today, visitors to Boscobel will see the house as it was—complete with elegant staircase, fine decorative objects and period furniture, much of it from the Dyckman family. And Boscobel's grounds are enchanting as well. At the Gate House, you can see the home of a middle-class family of the era or explore the Orangerie, a nineteenth-century greenhouse. In the spring and summer, the gardens at Boscobel blaze with thousands of flowers, including tulips, daffodils, roses, pansies and wildflowers. There is even a special Celebration of Roses Day in June. Concerts are held on the lawn throughout the summer. In the fall, apples from Boscobel's orchard go on sale, and the winter season ends the year with the lovely candlelight holiday tours.

DIRECTIONS *Located on Route 9D in Garrison-on-Hudson.*
INFORMATION *Open March through December—April through October, 9:30 A.M. to 5 P.M.; November, December and March, 9:30 A.M. to 4 P.M. Admission fee is charged. Tel. (914) 265-3638, or write Boscobel Restoration, Inc., Garrison-on-Hudson, 10524.*

The house tour takes 45 minutes; you will want to spend at least an hour on the grounds, especially if the flowers are in bloom or if you walk to the Hudson River overlook. Boscobel recommends that you wear broad-heeled walking shoes for comfort— and to protect the rugs and floors in the mansion. And don't miss the gift shop, which stocks lots of unique gifts. Recommended only for older children, and then only if they enjoy house museums.
FACILITIES *Picnic area, gift shop, rest rooms.*

Activities

BIRD-WATCHING

Constitution Marsh Wildlife Preserve, Indian Brook Road, Garrison, (914) 265-3119, is a National Audubon Society haven for nature lovers who enjoy bird-watching along the river or spotting rare wildflowers in spring. There is a boardwalk to make viewing easier, and a self-guided nature tour. If you call ahead, you can also arrange to take a guided tour by canoe. To find the preserve, take Route 9D to Indian Brook Road and park at the trailhead; walk down to the trails. (Near Boscobel Restoration.)

BOAT CRUISES

A 32-foot ketch, *Claddagh,* will take up to eight people on a cruise of the Hudson River. Piloted by one of the few female Coast Guard captains on the Hudson, *Claddagh* was named after an ancient center for boating in Ireland. Reservations may be made through the **Hudson House**, 2 Main Street, Cold Spring, (914) 265-9355.

FARM STANDS
Salinger's Orchards, Guinea Road off Fields Lane, Brewster, (914) 277-3521 (open all year, except July), lets you go out into the trees to select your own apples. They also stock a good selection of local produce, eggs, honey, maple syrup and cider at their roadside stand.

SCENIC DRIVES
Route 9D begins at the Bear Mountain Bridge, and takes you past many of the historic areas of Putnam County. Route 9 is the old Albany Post Road, and has been in constant use for more than two centuries. In Phillipstown, there are two dirt roads that offer interesting landscape viewing, but watch out for road conditions in questionable weather. The first, Lane Gate Road, is a circular drive that can be picked up along Route 301. You can also take Jaycox Road from Route 301 to Route 9. For a real adventure, pick up the Old Albany Post Road at the Bird and Bottle Inn and take it south where it intersects with a road that goes back to Route 9.

SKIING
Located in Patterson, **Big Birch** ski center, (914) 878-6242, is especially fun for families and beginning skiers. The snow-making here means skiing can go on throughout the winter season, and they offer night skiing as well. Call for further information and hours.

Where to Eat

The Arch *(Route 22, Brewster, (914) 279-5011)* An elegantly decorated, intimate spot, they specialize in Continental cuisine with a French accent here. The menu changes to feature seasonal items; game is the specialty in the fall. Reservations required; men must wear jackets. Not recommended for children.

OPEN Lunch—Wed. through Fri. and Sun., noon to 2:30 P.M.; dinner—Wed. through Sun., 6 to 10 P.M.

L'Auberge Bretonne *(Route 22, Patterson, (914) 878-6782)* This French country restaurant has a wood-beamed dining room and large windows overlooking the foothills of the Berkshires. The menu changes constantly, but some recent specials include breast of duck with honey mustard sauce, roast saddle of lamb in a puff pastry, tournedo of beef forestiere and sea scallops Veronique. Children are welcome; half portions served.

OPEN Lunch—Mon. through Sat., noon to 2:30 P.M.; dinner— Mon. through Sat., 5:30 to 9:30 P.M.; Sunday brunch, noon to 2:30 P.M., then dinner until 8:30 P.M.

The Bird and Bottle Inn *(Old Albany Post Rd. [Route 9], Garrison, (914) 424-3000)* Established in 1761 and originally known as Warren's Tavern, this restaurant was a major stage-coach stop along the route from New York to Albany. The inn still retains the ambiance of the Colonial era with wood-burning fireplaces, beamed ceilings, wide plank floors and authentic antiques. Lunches are reasonably priced and include a tankard of draught beer. Brunch and dinner are both prix fixe; some of the dinner specialties include rack of lamb, pheasant, salmon Wellington and veal medallions served with a blue cheese and Dijon mustard sauce. Reservations suggested; jackets are required for men. Not recommended for children.

OPEN Lunch—daily, noon to 2:30 P.M. and brunch served Sundays; dinner—6 to 9 P.M., and 4 to 7 P.M. on Sun.

Breakneck Lodge Restaurant *(Route 9D, Cold Spring, (914) 265-9669)* This cozy, family restaurant, which has been in business for over 50 years, looks out on the Hudson River and Storm King Mountain. Featuring Swiss-German and Austrian cuisine, specialties include veal, beef, venison and homemade pastries for dessert. Children are welcome; special menu provided.

OPEN Lunch—daily from noon to 2:30 P.M.; dinner—from 5 to 9 P.M., until 10 P.M. on Fri. and Sat.

Capriccio (*Route 22, Brewster, (914) 279-2873*) Enjoy a view of the lake and surrounding countryside while dining at this fine restaurant, which is housed in a large white clapboard house set back from the highway. The specialties at this northern Italian establishment are the pasta, rack of lamb, veal, shrimp scampi, duckling and chicken. Reservations required on weekends; men must wear jackets. Not recommended for children.

OPEN Lunch—daily, noon to 2:30 P.M.; dinner—from 6 to 9:30 P.M., until 10:30 P.M. on Fri. and Sat. Closed Tues.

The Dreamwold Inn (*Gypsy Trail Rd., Carmel, (914) 225-3500*) This restaurant is for people who want to enjoy each course of a gourmet meal in a different dining room of a spectacular forty-eight-room English Tudor mansion.

Hudson House Restaurant (*2 Main St., Cold Spring, (914) 265-9355*) The lounge and entryway here are filled with country-style touches, from the wallpaper and curtains to the napkins and tablecloths. Located in a restored 1832 landmark building, the dining rooms offer fine views of the Hudson. The imaginative menu includes entrées such as seafood sloop and half moon fish, star-spangled salad (pasta with garden vegetables) or nesting chicken and back-roads lamb. The desserts are superb—the peanut butter and chocolate pie, and the chocolate cheesecake are particularly good. And if you can, try the Yankee Doodle Sunday Brunch. Children are welcome.

OPEN Daily, for breakfast, lunch and dinner.

Pastries by Exposure (*142 Main St., Cold Spring, (914) 265-9484*) Pastries like they serve in Vienna. Even if you aren't hungry, do take a look—they are beautiful!

Plumbush Restaurant (*Route 9D, Cold Spring, (914) 265-3904*) Enjoy Continental cuisine in a restored Victorian home with dark oak-paneled walls in one dining room and giant rose-patterned wallpaper in another. Both dining rooms have wood-burning fireplaces and soft candlelight. During the summer months, dine on the spacious porch overlooking acres of grounds. There is a live trout tank, lots of charm and attention to detail. Reservations are suggested; jackets required for men on weekends. Not recommended for children.

OPEN *Lunch—Mon. through Sat., noon to 2:30 P.M.; dinner—Mon. through Sat., 5:30 to 9:30 P.M.; Sunday brunch—noon to 2:30 P.M., dinner, 2:30 to 8 P.M. Closed Tues.*

Rose Peddler Cafe *(129 Main St., Cold Spring, (914) 265-2633)* A small, homey cafe with a fireplace and large porch for outdoor dining in the summer. Specialties include homemade soups, quiche, pancakes, shepherd's pie, large lean hamburgers, omelets and salads. All pies, cakes and muffins are baked on the premises. Great for lunch. Children are welcome.

OPEN *Daily, except Tues., 9 A.M. to 6 P.M. (from 5 to 6 P.M., desserts only).*

Texas Taco *(Route 22, Patterson, (914) 878-9665)* If you love Tex-Mex food, try this restaurant. Open for lunch and dinner.

Xaviar's Restaurant at the Highland Country Club *(Route 9D, Garrison, (914) 424-4228)* One of the finest restaurants in Putnam County, the quality here is consistently high and the ambiance is accented with lots of fresh cut flowers, crystal and silver. The menu changes continually; some special entrées are quail boned and grilled over pasta, medallions of rabbit with white grapes and mustard and grilled Norwegian salmon basted with honey and Chinese mustard. Desserts are equally imaginative. Jackets recommended for men. Not appropriate for children.

OPEN *Lunch—noon to 2:30 P.M.; dinner—Tues. through Fri., 6 to 9 P.M. There are two dinner seatings on Saturday night at, 6:30 and 9:30 P.M. Closed in January.*

Where to Stay

The Bird and Bottle Inn *(Old Albany Post Rd. [Route 9], Garrison, 10524, (914) 424-3000)* For history buffs, this is a great place to stay. Built in 1761, the building has had a romantic and colorful past. Each room has a fireplace and is furnished with period furniture, as well as a canopied or four-poster bed. A full breakfast is served to guests in the lovely restaurant dining rooms downstairs. Open all year, except January 1 through 16. Two double rooms with private bath; one suite and one cottage. Children not permitted.

Golden Eagle Inn *(Garrison's Landing, Garrison, 10524, (914) 424-3067)* Locally famous since it appeared in the movie *Hello Dolly*, this inn was built in 1848 and is listed on the National Register of Historic Places. The rooms are decorated with antiques and two have wonderful river views. Downstairs, the Hudson Room, with its fireplace, wing-backed chairs and old books, is a nice place to meet other guests. A Continental breakfast is served between 8:30 and 9:30 A.M. in the Riverboat Room overlooking the Hudson. If you like being near the river, this is the perfect spot. The railroad station is across the street. Open all year, except February and March. Two rooms with shared bath, two with private bathrooms and two suites. Children allowed, except on weekends.

Hudson House Inn *(2 Main St., Cold Spring, 10516, (914) 265-9355)* The second oldest continuously operating inn in New York State, Hudson House has been completely restored and filled with antiques and Colonial crafts. In addition to the quaint bedrooms, there's a cozy lounge, dining rooms with a spectacular view of the Hudson and an exquisite garden. On the banks of the river opposite the inn is the village gazebo and park. The entire downtown section of Cold Spring has been designated a historic landmark district; it's the perfect place to explore, particularly if you're an antiques buff. Open all year, except during January. Fifteen rooms with private baths, and two suites. Children are welcome.

Olde Post Inn *(43 Main St., Cold Spring, 10516, (914) 265-2510)* Built in 1820, this inn is listed on the National Register of Historic Homes. Restored in 1983 by the present owners, the decor in all rooms is early American. A large comfortable living room, patio and garden are available for use by guests. A Continental breakfast is served in the dining room, which boasts its original open-beamed ceilings and wide-plank floors. A tavern in the stone and brick cellar features jazz groups on Friday and Saturday nights and provides a cozy gathering place to relax at the end of a busy day. Open all year. Six rooms share two baths. Children not permitted.

Pig Hill Bed and Breakfast *(73 Main St., Cold Spring, 10516, (914) 265-9247)* This brick Georgian town house is a most unusual place to stay. Each guest room is furnished in a different style and all have fireplaces. And if you fall in love with the rocking chair (or anything else) in your room you can buy it. Egg dishes are a specialty at breakfast, and all muffins and breads are homemade. The hearty morning meal is served downstairs, but if you're feeling lazy, enjoy breakfast in bed and snuggle down in a four-poster with the *New York Times*, delivered with breakfast. A picnic basket will even be prepared for lunch if you make arrangements in advance. Open all year. Four rooms have private baths and four others share two baths.

West-
chester
County

Home of the unexpected,
Westchester can be a
quiet nature preserve, a
seventeenth-century
Dutch home tucked
alongside an old stage-
coach road, a gentleman's farm where children are welcomed
to meet the animals, a museum that marks the beginning of
circuses in this country. The county has made extraordinary
attempts to preserve both its history and its natural environment. Although Westchester borders New York City and offers
some of the best shopping in the Hudson Valley, it is an area
replete with parks and nature preserves that offer an enormous
selection of children's activities and special events for visitors.
Washington Irving described the enchantment of Westchester
in his short stories, one of which, "The Legend of Sleepy
Hollow," comes alive each year through the efforts of Historic
Hudson Valley—the headless horseman roams at Halloween.
On historic Route 9 in Westchester, visitors will be awed by
the Gothic castle, Lyndhurst, home of railroad tycoon Jay
Gould, and a working restoration of a Dutch mill at Philipsburg

261

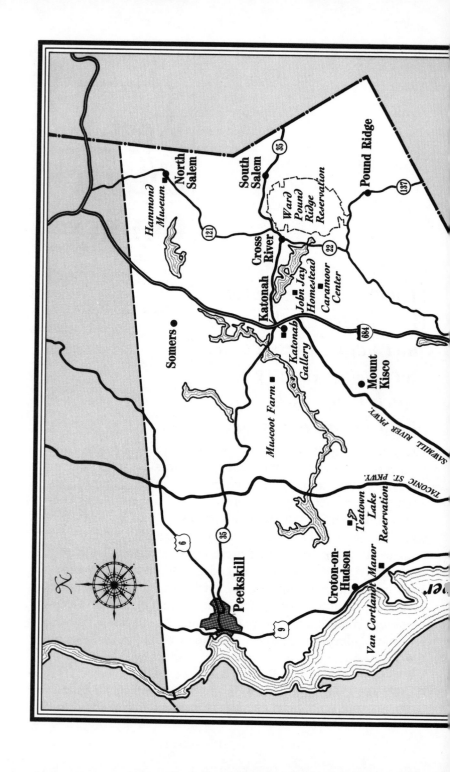

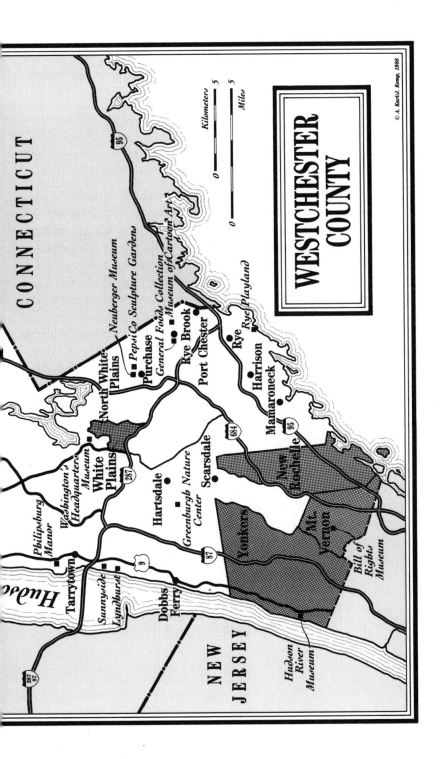

© A. Karl/L. Kemp, 1988

WESTCHESTER COUNTY

Kilometers 5
Miles

CONNECTICUT

95

Neuberger Museum
PepsiCo Sculpture Gardens
General Foods Collection
Museum of Cartoon Art
North White Plains
Purchase
Rye Brook
Port Chester
Rye
Rye Playland
Harrison
Mamaroneck
95
684
Scarsdale
New Rochelle
287
White Plains
Washington's Headquarters Museum
Hartsdale
Greenburgh Nature Center
Mt. Vernon
Philipsburg Manor
9
Sunnyside
Lyndhurst
Tarrytown
287 87
Dobbs Ferry
87
Yonkers
Bill of Rights Museum
Hudson River Museum
Hudson
NEW JERSEY

Manor. From the Pinkster Festival in the spring to December's candlelight tours of historic homes, Westchester is fun to visit year–round.

Cross River

Ward Pound Ridge Reservation This nearly 5,000–acre park was established in the 1920s and today visitors can enjoy a variety of outdoor activities here, including hiking, skiing, picnicking and exploring nature trails. Stop first at the **Trailside Museum**, a rustic stone structure that houses exhibits of environmental and historic interest. Native American artifacts, a weather station, maps, and animal and plant displays are found at the museum; hiking and trail guides to the reservation are available here, too. Directly in back of the museum is the wildflower garden, in which more than 100 varieties of flowers native to the area bloom in spring. For walkers and hikers, look for the four self–guided nature trails or try any of the miles of more rigorous hikes throughout the park. (In winter, some of these trails are available to cross–country skiers as well.) The Waccabuc River flows through the park, and fishing is allowed, although you must have a valid New York State fishing license. Special events are held throughout the year at the park; they include maple sugaring demonstrations, bird walks, hikes and a fiddling festival. Children are always welcome at the nature programs.

> DIRECTIONS *Located at the junction of Routes 35 and 121; accessible also from the Hutchinson River Parkway.*
> INFORMATION *Open all year, from 9 A.M. to dusk; the museum is open Wed. through Sun., 9 A.M. to 5 P.M. There is a small park use charge.*
> FACILITIES *Hiking trails, gift shop, rest rooms.*

Croton, Croton-on-Hudson

Teatown Lake Reservation This 400-acre reservation for the study of nature has marked nature walks and hiking trails, a museum and outdoor exhibits. Wildflowers are abundant here in the spring, and you may want to spend some time exploring the different styles of fences, a few of which have been duplicated on the site. The museum offers live exhibits of some local animals and plants, as well as permanent displays that tell the natural history of the area.

DIRECTIONS *Located on Spring Valley Road. Take the Taconic Parkway to exit 134; then take Grant's Lane to Spring Valley Road.*

INFORMATION *Open year-round, 9 A.M. to dusk; closed Mon.*

FACILITIES *Museum, gift shop, walking trails, rest rooms.*

Van Cortlandt Manor Built in the seventeenth century, the manor was home to the Van Cortlandts, supporters of the new nation during the American Revolution. Lafayette and Washington visited them here, and the family owned the manor until this century, when it was acquired for restoration. Inside the house, you will see a blend of styles and periods, since many of the furnishings and decorative objects came directly from the Van Cortlandt family. One of the most impressive household pieces is the fowling gun, a huge firearm that was fired into a flock of birds, reducing hunting time considerably. Outside are well-kept eighteenth-century gardens and orchards, which line the "Long Walk," a brick path that leads to a nearby inn.

DIRECTIONS *Located off Route 9 in Croton-on-Hudson.*

INFORMATION *Open daily, 10 A.M. to 5 P.M.; closed Thanksgiving, Christmas and New Year's Day. Admission fee charged. Several special events are held during the year, including an eighteenth-century Autumn Market, and crafts days. Tel. (914) 631-8200 for schedule.*

FACILITIES *Gift shop, picnic tables, rest rooms.*

Katonah

Caramoor Built in the 1930s by lawyer and banker Walter Tower Rosen, this estate was meant to be used as a setting for Rosen's magnificent collection of fine art from Europe and the Orient. The house itself was created by combining entire rooms from European villas with an American "shell;" the result is a unique, magical building that offers an architectural tour of the world in a few hours. Rosen's bedroom, for example, was taken from an Alpine cottage; the music room, from an Italian palace; portions of the outdoor theater from the south of France. Throughout the house are hundreds of pieces of priceless needlework, porcelain, furniture and art which date from the Middle Ages and China's Golden Age. Tours are offered, and lectures are given by art historians who illustrate their talks with examples from the collections. In addition to the house, don't miss the exquisite gardens at Caramoor, where fine statuary is set among plantings of evergreens and flowers. Caramoor is also the site of a world-renowned music festival, which is presented each summer in the Venetian Theater. This outdoor showcase was built around fifteenth-century Venetian columns; operas and concerts take center stage on warm evenings, while smaller chamber concerts are often held in the Spanish Courtyard.

> *DIRECTIONS From I-684, take exit 6. Go west on Route 35 to the stoplight, then make a right onto Route 22. Continue for three miles to Girdle Ridge Road.*
>
> *INFORMATION Open June through September—Thurs. through Sat., 11 A.M. to 4 P.M.; all other times by appointment only. Tel. (914) 232-5035 for concert schedules. Admission fee charged. Wheelchair accessible.*
>
> *FACILITIES Picnic area, rest rooms.*

John Jay Homestead This farmhouse was home to five generations of the Jay family. Probably the most famous family member was John Jay, who served as the President of the Continental Congress, and was the first Chief Justice of the

Supreme Court. The homestead has been restored, but still reflects the changes made by the various generations who lived there—from the construction of the simple eighteenth-century farmhouse to the addition of an elaborate portrait gallery added in this century. Special events held at the house include concerts, craft shows and a popular ox pull, in which these powerful creatures demonstrate their use on the farm.

DIRECTIONS Located on Route 22, three miles north of Bedford Village.

INFORMATION Open Memorial Day to late October—Wed. through Sat., 10 A.M. to 5 P.M. (noon to 5 P.M. after Labor Day), and Sun., 1 to 5 P.M. Tel. (914) 232-5651 for special events information. Admission fee charged.

FACILITIES Rest rooms.

Katonah Gallery A lively museum of the arts, several exhibits are mounted here each year, along with shows and lectures by local artists. Past exhibits have included "Sophisticated Ladies," which examined the creations of fashion designers, and "A Video Primer."

DIRECTIONS Located at 28 Bedford Road in Katonah.

INFORMATION Open Tues. through Fri., 2 to 5 P.M.; Sat., 10 A.M. to 5 P.M.; and Sun., 1 to 5 P.M. Tel. (914) 232-9555 for exhibit schedule. Admission is free.

FACILITIES Gallery, gift shop, rest rooms.

Mount Vernon

Bill of Rights Museum and St. Paul's Church Few people realize that the eighteenth-century libel trial of John Peter Zenger led directly to the establishment of the Bill of Rights in 1791; fewer still know that this all took place in Mount Vernon, and that an unusual museum preserves the story. Begin your visit with a tour of St. Paul's Church, which was founded in 1665 (the present building dates from 1763.) The church has a highly carved bishop's chair from 1639, as well as one of the oldest working church organs in the country. You will also see the Freedom Bell, sister to Philadelphia's Liberty Bell, which was cast at the same time in the same London foundry. At one time the church was used as a courthouse during the week, and lawyers such as Aaron Burr presented their cases here. The Bill of Rights Museum is located in the former carriage house and has exhibits that recall young America's drive to guarantee essential freedoms. Displays here include historic diagrams of Zenger at his trial; a working printing press; as well as books, papers and prints that tell the history of the Bill of Rights.

DIRECTIONS Located on South Columbus Avenue in Mount Vernon.

INFORMATION Open all year, except for Thanksgiving, Christmas, New Year's Day and Saturdays prior to Monday federal holidays—Tues. through Fri., 9 A.M. to 5 P.M.; Sat., noon to 4 P.M. Free guided tours of the church, cemetery and grounds available during the week if you call ahead; on Sat., tours are offered at 12:30, 1:30 and 2:30 P.M. The museum is self-guiding and handicapped accessible.

FACILITIES Gift shop, rest rooms.

North Salem

Hammond Museum and Oriental Stroll Gardens For lovers of Oriental philosophy and design, these gardens are a chance to step back into the Edo period of Japanese history. Created by Natalie Hays Hammond in memory of her parents, the gardens are actually fifteen small landscapes, including waterfall, Zen, azalea and fruit gardens. Each garden is lovely and also has a symbolic meaning; in the reflecting pool, for example, five water lilies are beautiful on their own, while also representing humanity, justice, courtesy, wisdom and fidelity. There is also a small museum here, which offers a mix of art, antiques and collectibles, but it is the gardens that must not be missed.

DIRECTIONS Located on Deveau Road in North Salem.
INFORMATION Open May through October—Wed. through Sun.,
11 A.M. to 5 P.M. Tel. (914) 669-5033. Comfortable walking
shoes advised.
FACILITIES Small restaurant, rest rooms.

North Salem Vineyard This small, privately owned vineyard produces three wines, and welcomes guests to tour its facilities and sample (and buy) the products. There is a charming picnic area here as well.
DIRECTIONS Take exit 7A off the Saw Mill River Parkway to
I-684 and get off at exit 8. Turn right on Hardscrabble Road,
continue 2¼ miles east and look for the sign on the right.
INFORMATION Open Sat. and Sun., 1 to 5 P.M. No admission
fee. Tel. (914) 669-5518 or (212) 534-7222.
FACILITIES Picnic area, rest rooms.

North White Plains

Washington's Headquarters Museum Self-guided tours of this small farmhouse museum are offered, and you can visit the rooms where Washington planned the strategy for the Battle of White Plains. On display here are unusual items such as one of the great general's boots, which appears very large until you discover that insulation was tucked inside to keep his feet warm. There's a rifle pellet still embedded in a piece of furniture, a remnant of the Revolutionary War, an early washing machine that was "child and stick" powered, and uneven floors that have been lifted by the roots of a 300-year-old sycamore tree. An old-fashioned, fun museum, it hasn't been completely redone but is worth the stop.
DIRECTIONS Located on Virginia Road.
INFORMATION Open Wed. through Fri., 10 A.M. to 3 P.M.; Sat.
and Sun., 11 A.M. to 4 P.M. Tel. (914) 949-1236. Admission
is free.
FACILITIES None.

Peekskill

Peekskill's Biggest Each September, Peekskill becomes the site of an unusual culinary event: to attempt to create the biggest food. The biggest brownie and popcorn ball and the longest apple strudel have all been prepared at the festival, which benefits a local health facility. Some of the foods have made it into *The Guinness Book of World Records*, and after the preparation and measuring, the treats are sold to the public—in small pieces, of course!

INFORMATION The site and date change. Tel. (914) 739-8105 for information.

Purchase

Neuberger Museum Although the focus here is on twentieth-century American and European art, their changing exhibits may also include ancient Greek art, African sculpture and Chinese ceramics. Visitors to the museum will also want to stroll around the SUNY campus, which has some intriguing outdoor sculptures and art installations.

DIRECTIONS Located on the SUNY Purchase campus on Anderson Hill Road.

INFORMATION Open all year, although hours change. Tel. (914) 253-5133. Admission is free.

FACILITIES Rest rooms.

PepsiCo Sculpture Gardens Located at the world headquarters of PepsiCo, Inc., the sculpture gardens are home to more than two dozen works by some of the greatest artists of this century. Conceived as an outdoor gallery of architecture, sculpture and nature, the gardens contain works by artists such as Rodin, Giacometti, Nevelson, Moore and Noguchi. Carefully landscaped with trees, ponds, reflecting pools and fountains, the gardens and paths change with the seasons, creating new ways to enjoy the art, the styles of which range from realist to abstract.

DIRECTIONS Located at PepsiCo Headquarters on Anderson Hill Road.
INFORMATION Open every day, dawn to dusk. Admission is free. Handicapped accessible.
FACILITIES None.

Rye

Rye Playland A true, old-fashioned amusement park, Playland in Rye is an architectural gem. Built in 1928, it was the first amusement park constructed according to a complete plan where recreational, family fun was the focus. Fortunately, the park's family atmosphere and Art Deco style are still here to be enjoyed. Set on the beaches of Long Island Sound, Playland offers a famous boardwalk, where the cool ocean breezes beckon. Also at the park: a swimming pool, gardens, a saltwater boating pond, areas to hike and fish, and of course, the amusement area. Nearly fifty rides swing and sway here, from the 82-foot-high Dragon Coaster to the Whirlwind Coaster and old-fashioned bumper cars. The showpiece of the park, however, is the carousel. Built in the 1930s, it's filled with flower-bedecked horses and, of course, proper carousel music. Although the rides close down for the winter, the Playland Ice Casino offers indoor skating facilities and ice shows.

DIRECTIONS Located off I-95, on Playland Parkway in Rye.
INFORMATION Open from mid-May until Labor Day; the Ice Casino, from October to March. Admission fee charged. For special events and fireworks schedules, call (914) 921-0373.
FACILITIES Picnic areas, snack stands, boat rentals, changing rooms, rest rooms.

Rye Brook

Museum of Cartoon Art If you were in love with Terry and the Pirates or looked every day for the latest in styles on Brenda Starr, then a stop at this unusual museum will certainly bring back memories. The history of cartoons is told here, along with hundreds of drawings, sculptures and textiles that capture the figures and the fun of this art—a papier-mâché Dagwood Bumstead taking a bath; Beetle Bailey trying to outwit Sarge in an original panel. Cartoon characters are even woven into the rug. There are also scalding political commentaries from Pulitzer Prize winners and special screenings of famous cartoon movies and television shows. The staff here can answer any questions you may have about the cartoon world.

DIRECTIONS *Located on Comly Avenue off King Street, in Rye Brook.*

INFORMATION *Open all year—Tues. through Fri., 10 A.M. to 4 P.M.; Sun., 1 to 5 P.M. Tel. (914) 939-0234.*

FACILITIES *Gift shop, rest rooms.*

General Foods Collection This corporate headquarters includes a food museum, and the tour is fascinating. General Foods offers by-appointment-only tours of its entire modern offices, but the real fun starts when you get to the museum. Displays show implements that relate to the preparation and serving of foods, and some of the items are more than 2,000 years old. A recent display was based on American folk art and food, and included such delightful items as a quilt with a teacup design and a tavern sign advertising good food and drink.

DIRECTIONS *Located at 800 Westchester Avenue in Rye Brook.*

INFORMATION *Tours must be arranged ahead of time. Tel. (914) 335-9111. Admission is free.*

FACILITIES *Rest rooms.*

Scarsdale

Greenburgh Nature Center Situated on thirty-two acres, this innovative nature center offers visitors a chance to explore several environments, including woodlands, a vineyard, orchards and cultivated gardens. There are more than thirty different tree species in the preserve, along with wildflowers, ferns and a host of songbirds. At the museum itself, there are animal exhibits and descriptive displays that explain some of the area's natural history. You can also pick up maps here to use on the self-guided nature walks. Many special events are held at the nature center, from concerts on the lawn to art exhibits in the center's lovely manor house.

DIRECTIONS Located on Dromore Road, off Central Avenue in Scarsdale.

INFORMATION Grounds open every day from 10 A.M. to dusk; the museum is open daily, from 10 A.M. to 5 P.M., except Fridays and holidays. Tel. (914) 723-3470. Admission is free.

FACILITIES Trails, gift shop, picnic area, rest rooms.

Somers

Historic Elephant Hotel Probably the only hotel in the country that was built in memory of an elephant. Recalling the birth of the American circus in the eighteenth century, the Elephant Hotel was erected by showman Hachaliah Bailey, who imported the first elephant to America in 1796. Called "Old Bet," the elephant journeyed with Bailey up and down the eastern seaboard as part of a traveling menagerie, until she was shot by a suspicious farmer in Maine. Today, the hotel houses a museum full of circus memorabilia, posters, photographs and a miniature big top.

DIRECTIONS Located at the junction of Routes 100 and 202 in Somers.

INFORMATION Open Fri., 2 to 4 P.M., or by appointment. Tel. (914) 277-4977.

FACILITIES Gift shop, rest rooms.

Muscoot Farm A showplace, this 700-acre farm is now run by the county. Built in 1885 by a pharmacist, Muscoot's farmhouse and outbuildings were once, and fortunately still are, the heart of a well-run, progressive agricultural enterprise. Today the main house is used for public meetings and special events like cooking demonstrations, while the farm itself is a great place to tour. The huge dairy barn was a model of construction for the time, with its hay chutes and natural insulation. Out in the carriage shed, exhibits show what it was like to depend upon horses to get from the farm to the town. The duck pond still fills with ducklings in the spring, and the herb and vegetable gardens are stocked with some old-time varieties and forgotten spices. Children will love to meet the farm animals up close, and the horses, sheep and cows are good natured. Special programs may feature a blacksmith or beekeeper demonstrating his trade, or maybe even a hayride. For walkers and nature lovers, Muscoot also has a series of trails that wind through the property, along which animals, ferns, wildflowers and an amazing number of birds make their homes; there are ponds, wetlands and meadows to explore as well.

DIRECTIONS Located on Route 100, along the Croton Reservoir.
INFORMATION Open May to October—Wed. through Sun., 10 A.M. to 4 P.M. Donation requested for admission. Guided tour offered; dress for an outdoor visit. Tel. (914) 232-7118 for special events schedule.
FACILITIES Picnic area, rest rooms (wheelchair accessible).

Tarrytown

Goebel Collectors' Club Hummell figurines are loved the world over: rosy-cheeked boys and girls dressed in German lederhosen or aprons. They were brought to life in the early part of this century in the art of Berta Hummell, a nun from the Siessen convent in Germany. Known at the convent as Sister Maria Innocentia, she enjoyed drawing scenes from her childhood. One day her sketches were spotted by Franz Goebel, a porcelain manufacturer, who decided that the charming children would appeal to his customers. Sister Maria and her convent sisters agreed to the commercial venture, and the famous M.I. Hummell figurines were born. Today, modern Hummell devotees can see a unique exhibit consisting of hundreds of figurines, plates, sketches (some by Sister Maria herself) and more at the Goebel Collectors' Club. This elegant brick building also houses works by other Goebel designers. And because this is a club as well as a museum, you can find the finest and the latest in porcelain settings for your table. In the theater here, a half hour film explains the techniques used in the making of fine porcelain, and throughout the year, various artists make guest appearances.

DIRECTIONS Located at 105 White Plains Road, right off exit 9 of the N.Y. Thruway.

INFORMATION Open year-round—Mon. through Fri., 10 A.M. to 4:30 P.M.; Sat., 11 A.M. to 4 P.M.; closed holidays. Admission is free. A film and self-guided tour featured. Tel. (914) 332-0300.

FACILITIES Rest rooms.

Lyndhurst The words "Gothic Revival" may bring to mind castles, turrets and crenellations, but it won't prepare a visitor for the wealth and magnificence of Lyndhurst. Built in 1838 for William Paulding, a former New York City mayor, the house and grounds were enlarged by the Merritt family. Lyndhurst was later owned by the notoriously wealthy Jay Gould. Much of the furniture, paintings and decorative accessories are original to the mansion, which was owned by the Goulds until 1961, when it was given to the National Trust. The rooms are sumptuous, and many are decorated in "faux" materials—a substance made to resemble something else. Ironically, in the case of marble, it often cost more to imitate it with wood and paint than it would have if real marble had been used. Outside you can walk around the rose gardens, visit the children's playhouse or take a nature hike among the dozens of different trees that were planted on the property. Special events here include antiques shows, a children's day and concerts.

DIRECTIONS Located on Route 9, just south of the N.Y. Thruway.

INFORMATION Open March through October—Tues. through Sun., 10 A.M. to 4:15 P.M.; November and December—Sat. and Sun., 10 A.M. to 3:30 P.M. Closed Thanksgiving and Christmas. For information about special events, call (914) 631-0046.

Admission fee charged. Guided tour of the house and self-guided tour of the grounds.
FACILITIES Picnic area, gift shop, rest rooms.

Old Dutch Church One of the oldest churches in the Hudson Valley region, this stout stone building was erected in the late seventeenth century and is still used for services. Surrounding the building is the churchyard, where you'll find many fascinating old Dutch and English gravestones. There is also a large memorial to one of the early ministers, as well as the grave of Washington Irving, which is itself a National Historic Landmark.

DIRECTIONS Located on Route 9, near Philipsburg Manor.
INFORMATION For church hours and guided tours of the cemetery, call (914) 631-1123, or write to the Friends of the Old Dutch Burying Ground, 35 South Broadway, Tarrytown, 10591.
FACILITIES None.

Philipsburg Manor Once the center of a 90,000-acre estate, Philipsburg Manor was founded by a Dutch immigrant, Frederick Philipse, in the late seventeenth century. The manor was the center of a bustling commercial empire, which included milling and trading concerns. For almost a century, the Philipses were respected colonists; then the family fled to England during the Revolutionary War, and their land holdings were broken up. Today, tours of the manor begin with a short film that traces its history. Then visitors cross the wooden footbridge that spans the Pocantico River and walk to the main site. At the two-story stone house and office building, the rooms have been restored to their seventeenth-century simplicity. The house was not the main residence of the family, so it was not furnished lavishly; but there are several bedrooms, a kitchen and the counting office to explore. The next stop is the mill, still run by waterpower, still grinding meal for the kitchen. (You can purchase the flour in the gift shop.) Here the miller explains the intricacies of a millwright's job, how grain becomes flour and how waterpower works, all the while working the noisy, dusty machinery. Then it's outside again to the barn and outbuildings, where costumed workers go about the business of running a small farm.

DIRECTIONS *Located on Route 9 in North Tarrytown.*

INFORMATION *Open all year—daily, 10 A.M. to 5 P.M.; closed New Year's Day, Thanksgiving and Christmas. A schedule of special events can be obtained by calling (914) 631-8200.*

FACILITIES *Picnic area, gift shop, rest rooms.*

Sunnyside Washington Irving once referred to his home as being "as full of angles and corners as an old cocked hat." The charming, wisteria-draped home of the author of "The Legend of Sleepy Hollow" and "Rip Van Winkle," is indeed an original. Irving purchased the small estate in 1835 and soon began to remodel it, adding weathervanes, gables, and even an oriental-style tower. Many of the original furnishings are still there, including Irving's desk and many of his books. Every year, Sunnyside is lovingly decorated for the Christmas season, reflecting Irving's pleasure at seeing his home bustling with family members and guests. The grounds are as carefully attended as they were in Irving's time; visitors can wander over paths that cross the estate, to the pond called the "Little Mediterranean," where swans still glide, and where there is a charming picnic area.

DIRECTIONS *Located on Route 9 (Broadway), at the Tarrytown-Irvington line.*

INFORMATION *Open all year—daily, 10 A.M. to 5 P.M., except Thanksgiving, Christmas and New Year's Day. Admission fee charged. There is a guided tour of the house, and special candle-light tours in winter; call (914) 631-8200 for schedule. Outside of Sunnyside on Route 9, watch for a marker indicating where Ichabod Crane was chased by the headless horseman in "The Legend of Sleepy Hollow."*

FACILITIES *Gift shop, picnic area, rest rooms.*

Yonkers

Hudson River Museum When financier John Bond Trevor built a nineteenth-century mansion called Glenview on a rise overlooking the Hudson River, he may not have envisioned it becoming a museum that focused on art and culture. But when the house was auctioned off, the city of Yonkers purchased it, and several rooms have since been made into exhibit and museum areas. Artwork, furniture, household goods and clothing of the last 100 years share space with modern paintings and sculptures in the galleries; special events like concerts and children's days are scheduled each year.

DIRECTIONS Located on Warburton Avenue; watch for signs.
INFORMATION Tours are available, but it is recommended that you call ahead for exhibit schedules and hours. Admission fee charged. Tel. (914) 963-4550.
FACILITIES Café, gift shop, rest rooms.

Activities

ANTIQUES

At **The Yellow Monkey Antiques** in Cross River, (914) 763-5848, look for lots of fine European furniture, as well as a wide selection of small collectible items, from kitchenware to sewing accessories. If you are in Valhalla, stop in at **Linda Horn Antiques**, 233 Lakeview Avenue, (914) 997-7122, where the showrooms contain very fine nineteenth-century furniture and decorative accessories. Bedford is also a stop for fine furniture: **Bedford Green Antiques**, (914) 234-9273. For an unusual shop, especially if you are interested in antiques, you may want to make an appointment with **Timothy Trace Antiquarian Books**, 144 Red Mill Road, Peekskill, (914) 528-4074, which specializes in books—both antique and new—about antiques, collectibles, needlework and textiles. Two towns that have a plentiful selection of antiques shops are Pound

Ridge (one treat is the **Gallery of Sporting Art**, (914) 764-5905) and Mamaroneck. Westchester also hosts some very large antiques shows throughout the year; check the local papers for listings. Look in particular for the Westchester Antiques Show in November; it attracts outstanding dealers and some record prices have been set at sales there.

FARM STANDS AND PICK-YOUR-OWN FARMS

Even though Westchester is more built up than many other Hudson River counties, farm stands still provide fresh local produce during the summer and fall harvest seasons. At **Haight Orchards**, Hardscrabble Road, Croton Falls, (914) 277-3507 (open daily, April to October), you'll find lots of orchard fruits like apples, peaches, plums and nectarines, along with sweets like honey and maple syrup. On weekends in the fall you might get a chance to sample fresh cider and doughnuts. Also in Croton Falls is **Outhouse Orchards**, Hardscrabble Road, (914) 277-3188 (open year-round), where you can pick your own apples on weekends, and take a farm tour. **Wilkens Fruit Farm**, 1313 White Hill Road off Mohansic Avenue, Yorktown Heights, (914) 245-5111 (open August 1 through December 31), offers pick-your-own peaches and apples on the weekends, a hay ride to the orchards and a well-stocked roadside stand. In December, they have cut-your-own Christmas trees. **Westchester Greenhouses**, 701 Dobbs Ferry Road, White Plains, (914) 592-4610 (open April through December), has a stand with fruits, vegetables, honey, maple syrup and cider, among other products. They have tours of the farm during the season; call ahead.

OUTDOOR RECREATION

Although Westchester has undergone a great deal of development in the past few years, there are many beautiful parks and outdoor facilities throughout the county. If bicycling is your sport, plan to take part in the **Bicycle Sundays** (May through September, except holiday weekends, 10 A.M. to 2 P.M.), when the Bronx River Parkway is closed to vehicular traffic. Or take a ride along the following scenic roads: Routes 6 and 202, Route 9D and the Bear Mountain–Beacon Highway. Hikers and walkers might like to stop at the **Mianus River Gorge**, Mianus River Road, Bedford, (914) 234-3455, for their Saturday guided hikes. Another long walk follows the **Old Croton Aqueduct**, via Route 129, to the Croton Dam Plaza. While the full walk is 30 miles, both hikers and bicyclers can follow as much or as little of the trail as they want; stop at the plaza spillway, which was considered an engineering marvel in its day. At the **Marshlands Conservancy**, on Route 1 in Rye, trails take the visitors through fields and woods, and along the seashore; a small museum has several exhibits and a selection of guides to the trails. The **Franklin Roosevelt State Park**, Route 202 and the Taconic Parkway, has hiking trails, fishing and a pool that is accessible to the handicapped. Bird-watchers should stop at the **Westmoreland Sanctuary**, Chestnut Ridge Road, Mount Kisco, a 625-acre nature preserve with three lakes and fifteen miles of trails open to the public every day from sunrise to sunset. A museum (open Mon. through Sat., 9 A.M. to 5 P.M.; Sun., 10:30 A.M. to 5 P.M.) contains exhibits of Westchester's flora and fauna. **The Ramsey Hunt Sanctuary**, North Salem Road, Cross River, consists of 173 wooden acres with several miles of hiking trails. One trail goes through a red maple swamp via a series of wood plank bridges and walkways. Plant lovers will be dazzled by the **Brooklyn Botanic Garden Research Center**, Kitchawan Road in Ossining, which besides its trails offers an unusual plant shop. In the winter, cross-country skiing is allowed at many of the area's parks and golf courses, including **Dunwoodie Golf Course**, Yonkers Avenue in Yonkers; **Saxon Woods**, Mamaroneck Avenue in White Plains; and **Sprain Lake Golf Course**, Grassy Sprains Road in Yonkers.

Those who want to go to the beach during the summer months can enjoy **Playland Beach** in Rye, Memorial Day through Labor Day from 9 A.M. to 5 P.M., (914) 921-0370; **Croton Point Beach** in Croton-on-Hudson, July 4 through Labor Day (weekends and holidays only), 10 A.M. to 7:30 P.M.,

(914) 271-3293; **Glen Island Beach** in New Rochelle, Memorial Day through Labor Day, 10 A.M. to 7:30 P.M., (914)
632-9500; and **Blue Mountain Reservation Beach** in Peekskill on Lounsbury Pond (chlorinated lake), Memorial Day
through Labor Day (closed Mondays), 10 A.M. to 7:30 P.M.,
(914) 737-2194.

SHOPPING

In Westchester, shopping can be as enjoyable as the purchases
themselves. The county's dozens of boutiques, shopping malls
and specialty stores cater to discriminating buyers. And since
many of the villages and towns are chockful of interesting
places to see, you may want to plan your shopping excursions
around a visit to a nearby historic site or art gallery. One mall
that is extra special and worth mentioning is the **Galleria
Mall** in White Plains, where top stores like Neiman-Marcus
dazzle shoppers with their selections. The mall itself is enclosed, making it pleasant even in the coolest weather. Also
here are several attractive restaurants. Another notable mall is
The Yellow Monkey Village on Route 35 in Cross River. The
shops are located in old-fashioned, early American buildings
and offer a wide range of new merchandise. Central Avenue,
which runs through White Plains, Hartsdale and Scarsdale, is
lined with dozens of small malls, discount stores and shops. A
leisurely drive through this part of Westchester is bound to be
a treat for avid shoppers. Department stores such as Bloom-
ingdale's, Macy's, Saks and Neiman-Marcus can be found
on Post Road, off I-287.

Where to Eat

*Auberge Argenteuil (42 Healy Ave., Hartsdale, (914) 948-
0597)* Set in a building that was a speakeasy in the 1920s, this
restaurant is hidden high up in a wooded area overlooking
Central Avenue. Specialties include lobster bisque, chicken
with tarragon or raspberry vinegar and veal with wild mush-

rooms. For dessert, the ice cream "bombe" is especially good. Not recommended for children.

OPEN *Lunch—Mon. through Fri, noon to 2:30 P.M.; dinner— Mon. through Sat., 6 to 9:30 P.M., until 10:30 P.M. on Sat., and Sun. from 1 to 8 P.M.*

Auberge Maxime *(Route 116, North Salem, (914) 669-5450)* Enjoy classical French cuisine with a nouvelle touch in this lovely country inn. Wall sconces, heavy draperies, comfortable chairs and beautifully appointed tables grace the dining room. The six-course prix fixe dinner includes specialties such as duck prepared with pear, green peppercorns, fresh ginger, plum or other sauces, as well as hot and cold soufflés. Children are welcome.

OPEN *Lunch—daily, noon to 3 P.M.; dinner—daily, 6 to 10 P.M. Closed Wed.*

La Camelia *(234 North Bedford Rd., Mt. Kisco, (914) 666-2466)* One of the best Spanish restaurants you will find anywhere, La Camelia is located in a 140-year-old landmark building. Grilled shrimp in garlic and lobster sauce is an appetizer specialty. Entrées include paella Valenciana for two with saffroned rice and excellent tapas. There is an extensive wine list, and the desserts are as exciting as the rest of the meal. Children are welcome; half portions served.

OPEN *Lunch—Tues. through Fri., noon to 3 P.M.; dinner— Tues. through Sat., 6 to 9 P.M., until 10:30 on Sat., and Sun. from 1 to 9 P.M.*

Cantina *(Saw Mill River Parkway, Ardsley, (914) 693-6565)* A beautiful, 100-year-old stone building is the site for this "restaurant in the park," which overlooks Woodlands Lake. Mexican food and fresh fish are the specialties here, and outdoor dining is featured in the warmer months. Children are welcome.

OPEN *Daily, 11:30 A.M. to 10:30 P.M., until midnight on Fri. and Sat.*

Chart House Restaurant *(High St., Dobbs Ferry, (914) 693-4130/4131)* This contemporary restaurant has a magnificent view of the Palisades, the Tappan Zee Bridge and the New York skyline. Specialties include prime rib, thick steaks and an enormous selection of seafood dishes. Their mud pie is renowned throughout the area. Children are welcome; special menu provided.

OPEN *Dinner—Mon. through Sat., 5 to 10 P.M., until 11 on Fri. and midnight on Sat.; Sunday brunch—11 A.M. to 2 P.M.; Sunday dinner—4 to 10 P.M.*

Le Chateau Restaurant *(Route 35 at Junction of 123, South Salem, (914) 533-6631)* This French restaurant with old-world charm is situated on 32 wooded acres and offers magnificent sunset views and lavishly decorated dining rooms. House specialties include wild mushroom soup, salmon in parchment, baby quail in raspberry sauce. An assortment of mousses set in crème anglaise are served for dessert. Children are welcome.

OPEN *Lunch—Tues. through Fri., noon to 2 P.M.; dinner— Tues. through Sat., 6 to 9 P.M.; and Sun. from 2 to 9 P.M.*

Chez Nous *(23 North Main St., Port Chester, (914) 939-7220)* A graceful, charming French atmosphere highlights this restaurant's high ceilings and dark-wood interior. House specialties are mussel chowder, coquilles St. Jacques and grilled breast of duck. Children are welcome.

OPEN *Lunch—Tues. to Fri., 11:30 A.M. to 2:30 P.M.; dinner— Tues. through Sun., 6:30 to 9:30 P.M.*

Il Cigno *(1505 Weaver St., Scarsdale, (914) 472-8484)* Specializing in northern Italian cuisine, this lovely restaurant has been owned and run by the DePietro family for many years. Featured here are grilled wild mushrooms, duck ravioli, fresh fennel and endive salad and filet mignon with walnuts and gorgonzola. Not recommended for children.

OPEN *Dinner—Mon. through Sat., 6 to 10 P.M., until 11 P.M. Fri. and Sat., and Sun. from 4 to 9 P.M.*

Emily Shaw's Inn *(Route 137, Pound Ridge, (914) 764-5779)*
Over the last 40 years, four American presidents have dined at
Emily Shaw's. The original building dates back to 1833. Specialties include prime ribs, rack of lamb, roast duckling and
fresh seafood. Children are welcome.

> OPEN *Lunch—Tues. through Sat., noon to 2:30 P.M.; dinner—
> Tues. through Sat., 6 to 9:30 P.M., until 10:30 P.M. Fri. and
> Sat.; Sun. from noon to 8:30 P.M.*

Horsefeathers *(94 North Broadway [Route 9], Tarrytown, (914)
631-6606)* One of the first and finest "grazing" restaurants in
Westchester, Horsefeathers has dark paneled walls and an antique bar. The menu features great hamburgers and steaks,
barbecued baby back ribs, overstuffed sandwiches and super-
thick New England clam chowder. The atmosphere is casual
and comfortable. Children are welcome.

> OPEN *Mon. through Sat., 11:30 A.M. to 11 P.M., until mid-
> night on Fri. and Sat. Full menu served at all times. Closed Sun.*

India House Restaurant *(199 Albany Post Rd. [Route 9A],
Montrose, (914) 736-0005)* Lots of greenery surrounds this attractive restaurant. Decorated to resemble a colorful handmade
tent, the dining rooms are covered with antique Indian tapestries. Tandoori (clay oven) dishes are the specialty here, featuring lamb, chicken or shrimp. The vegetarian entrées are also
excellent and can be prepared mild or hot and spicy, according
to taste. Children are welcome; no special menu.

> OPEN *Lunch—Mon. through Sun., 11:30 A.M. to 2:30 P.M.;
> dinner—Mon. through Sun., 5 to 10:30 P.M. Closed Tues.*

Jillyflowers *(309 Halstead Ave., Harrison, (914) 835-1898)*
Enjoy innovative French cuisine amid candlelight, exposed
brick walls, antiques and baskets of flowers. Some specialties
are grilled swordfish, roast duck in cranberry red wine sauce
and Maryland crabmeat ravioli. For dessert, try the macadamia
mousse. Children over 13 years old permitted.

> OPEN *Lunch—Mon. through Fri., noon to 2:30 P.M; dinner—
> Mon. through Sat., 6 to 10 P.M.*

Livano's *(200 Central Ave., White Plains, (914) 428-2400)* With skylights throughout and two 20-foot palm trees in the center of the restaurant, Livano's features contemporary cuisine. Both seafood and pasta are specialties here, and the menu is extensive. Children are welcome.

> OPEN *Lunch—Mon. through Sat., 11:30 A.M. to 4 P.M.; dinner—Mon. through Sat., 5 to 10 P.M., until 11 P.M. on Fri. and Sat.*

Long Pond Inn *(Long Pond Rd., Mahopac, (914) 628-0072)* This cozy, renovated log cabin is situated on a beautiful crystal clear lake and features outdoor dining on the deck in the summer. American cooking is the specialty here, and the menu changes with the seasons. Appetizers might include scallops and cider in puff pastry or a wild mushroom pierogi. For an entrée, choose from dishes such as grilled baby pheasant seasoned with sage butter and served with roasted vegetables. Desserts are equally creative and contemporary. Not recommended for children.

> OPEN *Dinner—Wed. through Sat., 6 to 9:30 P.M., until 10:30 P.M. Fri. and Sat., and Sun. from 5 to 9 P.M. Closed in February.*

Mallard's at Arrowwood *(Anderson Hill Rd., Rye Brook, (914) 939-5500)* Brass fixtures, wildlife paintings and soft lights combine here to create an atmosphere of understated elegance. American, English and nouvelle cuisines are featured, with appetizers such as lobster and scallop ravioli with red pepper and thyme sauce. The specialty is duck, served in a variety of ways. Desserts include a delectable white chocolate mousse. Children are welcome.

> OPEN *Lunch—Tues. through Fri., noon to 2:30 P.M.; dinner— Tues. through Sat., 6 to 9:30 P.M., until 10:30 P.M. Fri. and Sat.*

Maxime's *(Old Tomahawk St., Granite Springs, (914) 248-7200)* Features fine French cuisine served in an elegant country setting. Try their six-course, prix fixe dinner on Saturday nights; entrées might include specialties like foie gras, scallop timbale, veal chop and their famous chocolate terrine. Not recommended for children.

OPEN *Lunch—Wed. through Sun., noon to 4 P.M.; dinner— Wed. through Sun., 6 to 10:30 P.M.*

La Panetiere Restaurant *(530 Milton Rd., Rye, (914) 967-8140)* The building dates back to the 1800s and the Provençal interior features exposed beams, stucco walls and a huge grandfather clock. Appetizer specialties include warm oysters with leeks, duck terrine with truffles and pistachios, and fresh foie gras; for entrées, squab, venison and Dover sole filled with puree of artichokes. Six-course, prix fixe menu. Children are welcome.

OPEN *Lunch—Tues. through Fri., noon to 2:30 P.M.; dinner— Tues. through Sat., 6 to 9:30 P.M.; Sun. from 1 to 8:30 P.M.*

Le Pastis Restaurant *(6 Quarropas St., White Plains, (914) 949-2311)* A delightful bistro atmosphere can be found at this restaurant, which features French and Belgian cuisine. Some specialties include steamed mussels Belgian style, homemade pheasant pâté, bouillabaisse, steak au poivre, canard à l'orange and a variety of veal dishes. Children are welcome.

OPEN *Lunch—Mon. through Fri., noon to 2:30 P.M.; dinner— Mon. through Sat., 5 to 11 P.M., until midnight on Sat. Closed Sun.*

Paul Ma's China Kitchen *(2020 Crompond Rd. [Saw Mill River Rd.–Route 35], Yorktown Heights, (914) 962-7996/7999)* Paul Ma has created many of the specialty dishes based on his "hometown" favorites; they include chicken imperial, sea delicacy in nest and pan-fried flounder. Children are welcome.

OPEN *Lunch—Tues. through Sat., 11 A.M. to 3 P.M.; dinner— Tues. through Sun., 5 to 9 P.M.*

La Petite Affaire *(2 Union St. [Route 9], Briarcliff Manor, (914) 941-5556)* With all the charm and atmosphere of a French country inn, this restaurant features a working fireplace, elaborate flower arrangements and crisp linens on all tables. The food is exceptional, and there are seasonal specialties. In winter, choose from venison, pheasant or quail. Marvelous pastries are served for dessert. Children are welcome.

OPEN *Lunch—Tues. through Fri., noon to 2:30 P.M.; dinner—Tues. through Sat., 6 to 9:30 P.M., until 10:30 P.M. on Fri. and Sat., and Sun. from 5 to 9 P.M.*

Quarropas *(478 Mamaroneck Ave., White Plains, (914) 684-0414)* Quarropas, which means "White Swamp," is the original Indian name for White Plains. The dining room here is decorated with a unique collection of antique American packing-crate labels and food ads. Specialties include appetizers such as homemade ravioli filled with shrimp, crab and escarole or savory goat cheese and walnut strudel, and entrées such as grilled baby rack of lamb with apple pear mustard. All desserts are baked on the premises. Children are welcome.

OPEN *Lunch—Tues. through Fri., 11:30 A.M. to 2:30 P.M.; dinner—Tues. through Sun., 5:30 to 10 P.M.; Sunday brunch—11:30 A.M. to 3 P.M.*

Sassafras Restaurant *(1241 Mamaroneck Ave., White Plains, (914) 761-3660)* A country garden restaurant, this place is filled with trees, stained-glass windows, exposed brick walls, gaslights and scores of hanging plants. Some of the specialties are roast duckling, shrimp scampi, beef Wellington (on weekends only) and fresh fish prepared Cajun style. Children are welcome; no special menu or high chairs.

OPEN *Lunch—Mon. through Sat., 11:45 A.M. to 4 P.M.; dinner—Mon. through Thurs., 6 to 10 P.M. and Fri. and Sat., 5:30 to 11 P.M.; Sunday brunch—noon to 4 P.M., and dinner from 4 to 10 P.M.*

Ship's Galley *(5 Village Green [Route 9A], Ardsley, (914) 693-4878)* This family-owned and -operated restaurant specializes in fresh seafood dishes, including trout, red snapper, salmon, bouillabaisse and zuppa di pesce. The pasta is homemade, and steak and chicken are offered for guests who prefer meat or fowl to fish. Children are welcome; half portions available.

OPEN Lunch—Tues. through Fri., noon to 3 P.M.; dinner—
Mon. through Sun., 5 to 10 P.M., until 11 P.M. on Fri. and Sat.

Sorrento Restaurant (307 Railroad Ave., Peekskill, (914)
737-2624) This Peekskill landmark has been managed by the
same family for over 40 years. An antipasto bar is included
with all dinners; house specialties include steak pizziola, chicken
scampi, lobster parmigiana and pizza. Children are welcome;
special menu provided.

OPEN Lunch—daily, 11:30 A.M. to 3 P.M.; dinner—daily, 3
P.M. to midnight, until 2 A.M. on Fri. and Sat. Closed Tues.

Other Places to Dine in Westchester

Abhilash India Cuisine (30 Division St., New Rochelle, (914)
235-8390)

American Bistro Restaurant (606 Fenimore Rd., Mamaroneck,
(914) 698-0009)

Angsavanee Ristorante (163 North Main St., Portchester, (914)
939-9645)

Azuma Sushi Restaurant (219 E. Hartsdale Ave., Hartsdale,
(914) 725-0660)

Bengal Tiger Restaurant (140 East Post Rd., White Plains,
(914) 948-5191)

Benny's Irvington Diner (6 South Broadway, Irvington, (914)
591-9811)

Bistro 22 (Route 22, Bedford, (914) 234-7333)

The Box Tree (Routes 22 and 116, Purdys, (914) 277-3677)

Buffet de la Gare *(155 Southside Ave., Hastings, (914) 478-1671)*

Cafe Bazar *(53 Old Route 22, Armonk, (914) 273-1877)*

Cafe Keenan *(199 Main St., Ossining, (914) 941-2662)*

The Cheese Bazaar *(1202 West Post Rd., Mamaroneck, (914) 834-4540)*

China Lion *(1160 Boston Post Rd., Mamaroneck, (914) 381-2320)*

La Cote D'Argent *(2047 Boston Post Rd., Larchmont, (914) 834-2310)*

Covington Restaurant *(465 Main St., Armonk, (914) 273-5700)*

La Cremaillere *(Banksville, (914) 234-9647)*

Dario Restaurant *(754 White Plains Rd., Scarsdale, (914) 723-3002)*

Epstein's Kosher Delicatessen & Restaurant *(2369 Central Park Ave., Yonkers, (914) 793-3131)*

Epstein's Kosher Restaurant *(387 Central Ave., Hartsdale, (914) 428-5320)*

Ginza of Tokyo Scarsdale *(694 Central Park Ave., Scarsdale, (914) 472-8888)*

Glen Island Casino *(Glen Island, New Rochelle, (914) 635-6500)*

Golden Wok *(2250 Central Park Ave., Yonkers, (914) 779-8438)*

Gregory's Restaurant *(324 Central Ave., White Plains, (914) 684-8855)*

Le Gueridon *(53 Old Route 22, Armonk, (914) 273-1644)*

Hartsdale Garden *(285 N. Central Ave., Hartsdale, (914) 683-1611)*

Hunan Village Restaurant *(1828 Central Park Ave., Yonkers, (914) 779-2272)*

Hunan Wok *(415 N. Central Park Ave., Hartsdale, (914) 684-6505)*

The Jamaican *(2700 Central Park Ave., Yonkers, (914) 723-7950)*

Jason's *(478 White Plains Rd., Eastchester, (914) 961-9711)*

The Jockey Club *(99 Court St., White Plains, (914) 946-9315)*

The Korner Kitchen *(Cross River, (914) 763-8345)*

Larchmont Tavern *(104 Chatsworth Ave., Larchmont, (914) 834-9821)*

Marty's Mug & Munch *(875 Saw Mill River Rd., Ardsley, (914) 693-5140)*

La Mer *(331 Tarrytown Rd., Elmsford, (914) 592-5370)*

Meson Castellano *(135 East Post Rd., White Plains, (914) 428-8445)*

Michelangelo Restaurant *(208 Underhill Ave., White Plains, (914) 428-0022)*

Mr. Chan Restaurant *(55 Tarrytown Rd., White Plains, (914) 946-2220)*

Mona Trattoria Bolognese *(Route 22, Croton Falls, (914) 277-4580)*

Monteverde *(Bear Mountain Rd., Peekskill, (914) 739-5000)*

The Pagoda Restaurant *(701 White Plains Rd., Eastchester, (914) 472-1600)*

Peregrine's Restaurant *(50 South Buckhout St., Irvington, (914) 591-7208)*

Renee's Eatery *(1096 Wilmot Rd., Scarsdale, (914) 472-0035)*

La Riserva *(2382 Boston Post Rd., Larchmont, (914) 834-5584)*

Santa Fe Restaurant *(5 Main St., Tarrytown, (914) 332-4452)*

Sergio's *(20 N. Central Ave., Hartsdale, (914) 949-1234)*

Le Shack D'Alsace *(68 Gedney Way, White Plains, (914) 428-1264)*

Sweetwaters Restaurant *(577 North Broadway, White Plains, (914) 328-8918)*

Szechuan Empire Chinese Restaurant *(1335 North Ave., New Rochelle, (914) 235-6450)*

Takesushi Japanese Restaurant *(291 Central Ave., White Plains, (914) 948-6651)*

Tappan Hill Restaurant *(Tappan Hill, (914) 631-3030)*

Tony's La Stazione *(15 Saw Mill River Rd., Elmsford, (914) 592-5980)*

Travelers Rest *(Route 100, Millwood, (914) 941-7744)*

Umberto's *(2 Purchase St., Rye, (914) 967-1909)*

Valentino's Restaurant *(132 Bronx River Rd., Yonkers, (914) 776-6731)*

The Wampus Inn *(Route 128, (914) 273-6220)*

The following ice cream parlors are particularly worth stopping at for a refreshing snack if you are in the neighborhood.

Chocolates Plus *(104 S. Ridge St. [Rye Ridge Shopping Center], Rye Brook, (914) 937-0101)*

Neilsen Ice Cream Company *(173 Westchester Ave., Port Chester, (914) 939-2360. Also, 874 Scarsdale Ave., Scarsdale (914) 723-4925)*

Razzleberrys *(875 Saw Mill River Rd, Ardsley, (914) 693-7381. Also, 109 Katonah Ave., Katonah, (914) 232-7060)*

Sweet Cravings *(65 North Central Ave., Hartsdale, (914) 949-2060)*

Where to Stay

Arrowwood *(Anderson Hill Rd., Rye Brook, 10573, (914) 939-5500)* This full-facility resort is located on 114 wooded acres. There is a nine-hole golf course, indoor-outdoor pool, tennis, racquetball, squash, Universal gym and sauna. The Atrium Dining room, a multilevel restaurant that overlooks the grounds and gardens, offers one of the area's most sumptuous Sunday brunches; even if you do not stay here, the food makes it worth a stop. There is a pub for more casual dining, and Mallard's (see page 285) is also located here. Weekend packages are available during the spring and summer, and they are excellent value for the money. Open all year; 276 rooms. Children are welcome.

Crabtree's Kittle House *(Route 117, Mt. Kisco, (914) 666-8044)* This 200-year-old Colonial-style building has been an inn since the 1930s when Henry Fonda and Talullah Bankhead stayed here. One of the few inns in Westchester County, the

Kittle House is moderately priced. A complimentary Continental breakfast is served. Children are welcome. Open all year. Twelve rooms, all with private bathrooms, cable TV and telephones.

Holiday Inn-Crowne Plaza *(66 Hale Ave., White Plains, 10604, (914) 682-0050)*

La Reserve Hotel *(5 Barker Ave., White Plains, 10604, (914) 761-7700)*

The Rye Town Hilton Inn *(Westchester Ave., Port Chester, 10573, (914) 939-6300)*

The Stouffer Westchester Hotel *(80 West Red Oak Lane, White Plains, 10604, (914) 694-5400)* This hotel stands on the site of the turn-of-the-century estate called Red Oaks, which was owned by noted architect John Merven Carrere, co-designer of the New York Public Library. There are two fine restaurants here: The Woodlands, specializing in Continental cuisine, and the Oyster Bar, featuring seafood. Both offer a marvelous Sunday brunch every week from 10:30 A.M. to 2:30 P.M. In addition to the expected facilities like tennis, indoor pool and exercise room with whirlpool, this hotel features an illuminated jogging trail. Open all year; 364 rooms, including suites. Children are welcome.

The Tarrytown Hilton *(455 South Broadway, Tarrytown, 10591, (914) 631-5700)*

Westchester Marriott *(670 White Plains Rd., Tarrytown, 10591, (914) 631-2200)*

The White Plains Hotel *(South Broadway and Lyons Place, White Plains, 10604, (914) 761-5858)*

Authors' Note

We are already planning a new edition of *The Hudson Valley and Catskill Mountains* and would be grateful if you would tell us about your experiences in the area. Have you discovered any places we should know about? How have you liked the places we have recommended? Please send your comments to Joanne Michaels and Mary Barile, P.O. Box 425, Woodstock, NY 12498. Thanks!

Index

accommodations
  in Albany, 180–181
  in Columbia County, 204–205
  in Delaware County, 140–143
  in Dutchess County, 239–243
  in Greene County, 164–166
  in Orange County, 48–49
  in Putnam County, 258–259
  in Rockland County, 20
  in Sullivan County, 72–74
  in Ulster County, 115–121
  in Westchester County,
    292–293
airplane museum, 221–222
airplane tours, 153–154, 195
Albany, 167–181
  accommodations in, 180–181

architectural sites in, 173–174,
    175–176
arts and crafts shops in, 176–177
art shows in, 176–177
festivals in, 176
historical sites in, 173–176
museums in, 170, 174–175,
    176–177
restaurants in, 178–180
tours of, 177
Albany Institute of History and Art,
    170
American Museum of Fire Fighting,
    189–190
Annandale-on-Hudson, 210–211
antiques
  in Columbia County, 195–197

antiques *(continued)*
  in Dutchess County, 225–226
  in Greene County, 154–155
  in Sullivan County, 61–62
  in Ulster County, 97–98
  in Westchester County, 278–279
Apollo Plaza, 57
Apple Pond Farming Center, 54
architectural sites
  in Albany, 173–174, 175–176
  in Columbia County, 188–189,
    192–193, 194–195
  in Delaware County, 127–128,
    132
  in Dutchess County, 210–212,
    213–216, 218–219, 222–223
  in Greene County, 150–151
  in Orange County, 24–25, 30
  in Putnam County, 252–253
  in Rockland County, 8, 13–14
  in Ulster County, 81–82, 84–86,
    90–93
  in Westchester County, 265–267,
    275–277
Arkville, 126–127
art museums
  in Albany, 170
  in Columbia County, 192–193
  in Delaware County, 127
  in Orange County, 30–31
  in Westchester County, 267,
    268–269, 270, 271–272,
    274–275, 278
arts and crafts shops
  in Albany, 176–177
  in Dutchess County, 218, 224,
    226–227
  in Orange County, 33
  in Rockland County, 9
  in Ulster County, 96–97
  in Westchester County,
    267
art shows
  in Albany, 176–177
  in Delaware County, 130
  in Dutchess County, 227
  in Orange County, 33
  in Sullivan County, 62–63
ART Tours, 96

auctions in Delaware County,
    132–134
Auto Memories Museum, 126
automobile museums, 126

ballooning, 38
Balmville Tree, 31
Bard College, 210
beaches, 280–281
Beacon, 211–212
Bear Mountain, 4–6
Bear Mountain State Park, 4–5
Belleayre Mountain October
    Festival, 84
Bevier House, 90
bicycling
  in Dutchess County, 227–228
  in Westchester County, 279–280
Bill of Rights Museum, 267–268
bird-watching, 253
Jacob Blauvelt House, 7
boat cruises
  in Dutchess County, 228
  in Orange County, 38
  in Putnam County, 253–254
  in Ulster County, 99
Boscobel, 252–253
Madame Brett Homestead, 211–212
Brick House, 30
Broadway Theatre, 57
Bronck Museum, 150–151
John Burroughs Memorial Field,
    129–130
Julia Butterfield Memorial Library,
    249
Byrdcliffe Arts Colony, 96–97

Callicoon Center, 54
Campbell Hall, 24–25
Canal Towne Emporium, 60
canoeing
  in Delaware County, 134
  in Sullivan County, 63–64
Capitol Building, New York State,
    170–171
Caramoor, 266
Carmel, 248–249
Mary Flagler Cary Arboretum,
    216–217

Catskill, 148–150
Catskill Fly Fishing Center, 60
Catskill Game Farm, 151–152
Catskill Reptile Institute, 148
Chatham, 186–188
Cherry Hill, 173
Christmas festival, Dutch, 221
Christmas tree farms, 64–66
churches, 88, 267–268, 276
Church Street Station, 126
cider mills, 59
circus museum, 273
Clarence Fahnestock State Park,
  248–249
Clermont, 188–189
Cold Spring, 249–250
Columbia County, 183–205
  accommodations in, 204–205
  antiques in, 195–197
  architectural sites in, 188–189,
    192–193, 194–195
  fairs in, 186–188
  farm stands in, 198–199
  festivals in, 192
  hiking in, 199
  historical sites in, 188–189,
    194–195
  museums in, 187–188, 189–190,
    192–193
  restaurants in, 201–204
  scenic views in, 199–200
  skiing in, 200
  theaters in, 200–201
  tours in, 191–192, 195
concerts, 97
Congers, 6
Constitution Island, 36
Constitution Marsh Wildlife Preserve, 253
Cornwall-on-Hudson, 25
Coxsackie, 150–151
Cross River, 264
Croton, 265
Croton-on-Hudson, 265
Cuddebackville, 26
culinary festivals, 270
Culinary Institute of America, 213

decorative museums, 174

Delaware and Hudson Canal Park,
  26
Delaware and Hudson Historical
  Society Museum, 83
Delaware County, 123–143
  accommodations in, 140–143
  amusement parks in, 126
  architectural sites in, 127–128, 132
  art shows in, 130
  auctions in, 132–134
  canoeing in, 134
  fairs in, 131
  fishing in, 134–135
  hiking in, 135–136
  historical sites in, 127–128, 132
  mills in, 128–129
  museums in, 126, 128–129
  restaurants in, 139–140
  scenic views in, 136–137
  skiing in, 137–139
  trains in, 126–127
Delaware County Historical Association, 127–128
Delaware-Ulster Rail Ride (DURR),
  126–127
Delhi, 127–128
DeWint House National Shrine, 13
dinosaurs, 190–191
Dutch Christmas festival, 221
Dutchess County, 207–243
  accommodations in, 239–243
  antiques in, 225–226
  architectural sites in, 210–212,
    213–216, 218–219, 222–223
  arts and crafts shop in, 218, 224,
    226–227
  art shows in, 227
  bicycling in, 227–228
  boat cruises in, 228
  fairs in, 219–220
  farms in, 228–230, 243
  festivals in, 221, 227
  gardens in, 216–217
  hiking in, 230–231
  historical sites in, 210–212,
    213–215, 218–219, 222–223
  museums in, 212, 220–221,
    221–222
  nature centers in, 216–217

Dutchess County (*continued*)
  nature parks in, 223–224
  restaurants in, 234–239
  scenic views in, 231–232
  skiing in, 232–233
  theaters in, 233
  tours in, 217–218, 227–228, 228
  vineyards in, 233–234
  zoo in, 217

East Meredith, 128–129
Ellenville, 80–81
Empire State Plaza, 171–172
equestrian museums, 26–28
Erpf Catskill Cultural Center, 127
Executive Mansion, 173

factory outlets
  in Orange County, 39
  in Sullivan County, 57
fairs
  in Columbia County, 186–188
  in Delaware County, 131
  in Dutchess County, 219–220
  in Orange County, 28
farms, farm stands
  Christmas tree, 64–66
  in Columbia County, 198–199
  in Dutchess County, 228–230,
    243
  game, 151–152
  in Greene County, 151–152,
    155–156
  honey, 82–83
  in Orange County, 39–41
  in Putnam County, 254
  in Rockland County, 7–8, 14–15
  in Sullivan County, 54–55, 64–66
  in Ulster County, 82–83, 100–101
  in Westchester County, 273–274,
    279
festivals
  in Albany, 176
  art, 227
  in Columbia County, 192
  culinary, 270
  Dutch Christmas, 221
  in Dutchess County, 221, 227
  in Greene County, 152

  mum, 93–94
  October, 84
  in Orange County, 33–34
  Renaissance, 33–34
  shad, 192
  theater, 152
  tulip, 176
  in Ulster County, 84, 87, 93–94
  in Westchester County, 270
fire-fighting museum, 189–190
fishing
  in Delaware County, 134–135
  in Greene County, 156–157
  in Rockland County, 15
  in Sullivan County, 66–68
  in Ulster County, 101–102
Fishkill, 212
Alice and Hamilton Fish Library,
  251
fly-fishing museum, 60
food museum, 272
Fort Delaware Museum of Colonial
  History, 58
Foundry School Museum of the
  Putnam Historical Society,
  249

game farms, 151–152
gardens
  in Dutchess County, 216–217
  in Westchester County, 268–269,
    270–271
Gardiner, 81–83
Garrison, 250–252
Garrison-on-Hudson, 252–253
General Foods Collection, 272
Germantown, 188–189
Goebel Collectors' Club, 274–275
Goshen, 26–28
Graymoor, 251
Greenburgh Nature Center, 272–273
Greene County, 145–166
  accommodations in, 164–166
  amusement parks in, 151
  antiques in, 154–155
  architectural sites in, 150–151
  farms in, 151–152, 155–156
  festivals in, 152
  fishing in, 156–157

Greene County *(continued)*
  hiking in, 157–158
  museums in, 148, 150–151, 153
  restaurants in, 161–164
  scenic views in, 158–159
  skiing in, 159–161
  tours in, 149–150, 153–154

Hall of Fame of the Trotter, 26–27
Hammond Museum, 268–269
Hanford Mills Museum, 128–129
Harriman State Park, 4
High Falls, 83–84
High Falls Grist Mill, 83–84
Highmount, 84
High Tor Vineyards, 7
hiking
  in Columbia County, 199
  in Delaware County, 135–136
  in Dutchess County, 230–231
  in Greene County, 157–158
  in Orange County, 41
  in Rockland County, 15–16
  in Ulster County, 102–103
  in Westchester County, 280
Hill-Hold, 24–25
historical museums
  in Albany, 174
  in Dutchess County, 212
  in Greene County, 150–151, 153
  in Orange County, 29, 31–32, 37
  in Putnam County, 249
  in Sullivan County, 58–59
  in Ulster County, 83
  in Westchester County, 267–268, 269
historical sites
  in Albany, 173–176
  in Columbia County, 188–189, 194–195
  in Delaware County, 127–128, 132
  in Dutchess County, 210–212, 213–215, 218–219, 222–223
  in Orange County, 24–25, 26, 27–28, 29, 30, 31–32, 34–36, 36, 43
  in Putnam County, 252–253
  in Rockland County, 7, 10, 12–13

  in Sullivan County, 55, 56, 58–59
  in Ulster County, 81, 84–86, 86–87, 88–93
  in Westchester County, 265–268, 273, 275–277
Historical Society of Newburgh Bay and the Highlands, 31
Historical Society of Rockland County, 7
Historic Elephant Hotel, 273
holism, 222
honey farms, 82–83
Hook Mountain State Park, 10
Edward Hopper House, 10
horse racing, 58
Hudson, 189–193
  tours of, 191–192
Hudson River Maritime Center, 86–87
Hudson River Museum, 278
Hudson River Shad Festival, 192
Huguenot Street's Stone Houses, 91–92
Hurley Patentee Manor, 84–85
Hurley Stone Houses, 85–86
Hyde Park, 213–216

Ice Caves Mountain, 80–81
ice-skating, 41
Innisfree Gardens, 216
Interarts Festival, 152
Iona Island, 5–6

John Jay Homestead, 266–267

Katonah, 266
Katonah Gallery, 267
Kennedy-Dells County Park, 7–8
Kenoza Lake, 55
Kinderhook, 194–195
Kingston, 86–89, 98
Kingston Urban Cultural Park Visitors' Center, 87–88
Knox Headquarters, 34–35

Lawrenceville, 151–152
libraries, in Putnam County, 249, 251
Lindenwald, 194–195

Little Wings Wildlife Sanctuary, 81–82
Locust Lawn, 81
Lost Treasure of Rip Van Winkle, 148–149
Lyndhurst, 275–276

Manitoga, Man with Nature Center, 251–252
Marbletown, 90
Marlboro, 90–91
Maverick Concerts, 97
Middletown, 28
Millbrook, 216–217
Mill House, 90–91
mill museums, 128–129
mills
  cider, 59
  in Delaware County, 128–129
  in Sullivan County, 59
  in Ulster County, 82, 83–84
Mills Mansion, 222–223
Minisink Battleground, 56–57
Minisink Ford, 56–57
Mohonk Mountain House, 92–93
Monroe, 29
Montfort Reptile Institute, 220–221
Montgomery, 30
Montgomery Place, 210–211
Monticello, 57–58
Monticello Raceway, 58
Mountainville, 30
Mount Lebanon Shaker Village, 187
Mount Vernon, 267–268
Mum Festival, 93–94
Muscoot Farm, 273–274
Museum of Cartoon Art, 271–272
Museum of the Historical Society of Early American Decoration (HSEAD), 174
Museum of the Hudson Highlands, 25
museums
  airplane, 221–222
  in Albany, 170, 174–175, 176–177
  art, 30–31, 127, 170, 192–193, 267, 268–269, 270, 271–272, 274–275, 278
  automobile, 126

circus, 273
  in Columbia County, 187–188, 189–190, 192–193
  decorative, 174
  in Delaware County, 126, 128–129
  in Dutchess County, 212, 220–221, 221–222
  equestrian, 26–28
  fire-fighting, 189–190
  fly-fishing, 60
  food, 272
  in Greene County, 148, 150–151, 153
  historical, 29, 31–32, 37, 58–59, 83, 150–151, 153, 174–175, 212, 249, 267–268, 269
  ice-skating, 41
  mill, 128–129
  nature, 4–5, 264, 280
  in Orange County, 25, 26–27, 29, 30–31, 31–32, 33, 37, 41
  in Putnam County, 249
  reptile, 148, 220–221
  in Rockland County, 4, 6
  Shaker, 187–188
  in Sullivan County, 58–59, 60
  trolley, 89
  in Ulster County, 83, 89
  in Westchester County, 264, 267–269, 269, 270, 271–273, 274–275, 278, 280
Museum Village, 29

Narrowsburg, 58–59
nature centers
  in Dutchess County, 216–217
  in Putnam County, 251–252, 253
  in Westchester County, 272–273
nature museums, 4–5, 264, 280
  in Orange County, 25
  in Rockland County, 6
nature preserve, in Westchester County, 264–265
Neuberger Museum, 270
Newburgh, 31–32
New City, 7–8
New Paltz, 91–93
New Windsor Cantonment, 35–36

New York Renaissance Festival, 33–34
North Branch Cider Mill, 59
North Salem, 268–269
North Salem Vineyard, 269
North White Plains, 269
Nyack, 8–10

observatories, 94–95
October festivals, 84
Olana, 192–193
Old Chatham, 186–188
Old Dutch Christmas, 221
Old Dutch Church, 88, 276
Old Rhinebeck Aerodrome, 221–222
Omega Institute, 222
Opus 40, 94
Orange County, 21–49
  accommodations in, 48–49
  architectural sites in, 24–25, 30
  arts and crafts shops in, 33, 37
  art shows in, 33
  ballooning in, 38
  boat cruises in, 38
  factory outlet in, 39
  fairs in, 28
  farms in, 39–41
  festivals in, 33–34
  hiking in, 41
  historical sites in, 24–25, 26, 27–28, 29, 30, 31–32, 34–36, 36, 43
  ice-skating in, 41
  museums in, 25, 26–27, 29, 30–31, 31–32, 33, 37, 41
  nature museums and parks in, 25
  restaurants in, 43–48
  scenic views in, 42
  skiing in, 42
  tours in, 29, 38
  vineyards in, 42–43
Oriental Stroll Gardens, 268–269
Overlook Observatory, 94–95

Palenville, 152
parks, amusement
  in Delaware County, 126
  in Greene County, 151
  in Westchester County, 271

parks, historical, in Ulster County, 87–88
parks, nature
  in Dutchess County, 223–224
  in Orange County, 25
  in Rockland County, 5, 11
  in Ulster County, 80–81, 81–82
  in Westchester County, 264–265
parks, recreational
  in Putnam County, 248–249
  in Rockland County, 4–5, 6, 10
  in Westchester County, 280
Peekskill's Biggest, 270
PepsiCo Sculpture Gardens, 270–271
Philipsburg Manor, 276–277
Piermont, 11
Piermont Marsh, 11
Pinksterfest, 176
Poughkeepsie, 217–219
Zadock Pratt Museum, 153
Pratt's Rocks, 153
Prattsville, 153
Purchase, 270–271
Putnam County, 245–259
  accommodations in, 258–259
  architectural sites in, 252–253
  bird-watching in, 253
  boat cruises in, 253–254
  farms in, 254
  historical sites in, 252–253
  libraries in, 249, 251
  museums in, 249
  nature centers in, 251–252, 253
  recreational parks in, 248–249
  restaurants in, 254–257
  scenic views in, 254
  skiing in, 254
  tours in, 249–250, 253–254
  wildlife preserves in, 253

Quarryman's Museum, 94

racing, horse, 58
rafting, 63–64
rappeling, 103
Renaissance festivals, 33–34
reptile museums, 148, 220–221
restaurants
  in Albany, 178–180

restaurants (*continued*)
  in Columbia County, 201–204
  in Delaware County, 139–140
  in Dutchess County, 234–239
  in Greene County, 161–164
  in Orange County, 43–48
  in Putnam County, 254–257
  in Rockland County, 16–20
  in Sullivan County, 70–72
  in Ulster County, 109–115
  in Westchester County, 281–292
Rhinebeck, 219–22
Rockland County, 1–20
  accommodations in, 20
  architectural sites in, 8, 13–14
  arts and crafts shops in, 9
  farms in, 7–8, 14–15
  fishing in, 15
  hiking in, 15–16
  historical sites in, 7, 10, 12–13
  museums in, 4, 6
  nature museum in, 6
  nature parks in, 5, 11
  recreational parks in, 4–5, 6, 10
  restaurants in, 16–20
  tours in, 8–9, 13–14
  vineyards in, 7
Rockland Lake State Park, 6
Roebling's Suspension Bridge, 57
Rondout Landing, 86–87
Franklin Delano Roosevelt Home
  and Library, 213–214
Roscoe, 60
Roxbury, 129–130
Roxbury Arts Group (RAG), 130
Rye Brook, 271–272
Rye Playland, 271

St. Paul's Church, 267–268
Sam's Point, 80–81
Saugerties, 93–95, 98
Scarsdale, 272–273
scenic drives
  in Columbia County, 199–200
  in Delaware County, 136–137
  in Dutchess County, 231–232
  in Greene County, 158–159
  in Orange County, 42
  in Putnam County, 254

  in Sullivan County, 68–69
  in Ulster County, 103–104
Schuyler Mansion, 175–176
sculpture museums, 270
Senate House, New York State, 88–89
shad festival, 192
Shaker Museum, 187–188
skiing
  in Columbia County, 200
  in Delaware County, 137–139
  in Dutchess County, 232–233
  in Greene County, 159–161
  in Orange County, 42
  in Putnam County, 254
  in Sullivan County, 69–70
  in Ulster County, 104–106
  in Westchester County, 280
Snyder House, 91
soaring, 60–61
Somers, 273–274
Staatsburg, 222–223
Stone Arch Bridge Historical Park,
  55
Stony Kill Environmental Education Center, 223–224
Stony Point, 12
Stony Point Battlefield, 12
Storm King Art Center, 30–31
Sugar Loaf Crafts Village, 33
Sullivan County, 51–75
  accommodations in, 72–74
  antiques in, 61–62
  art shows in, 62–63
  canoeing in, 63–64
  factory outlet in, 57
  farms in, 54–55, 64–66
  fishing in, 66–68
  historical sites in, 55, 56, 58–59
  horse racing in, 58
  mills in, 59
  museums in, 58–59, 60
  rafting in, 63–64
  restaurants in, 70–72
  scenic views in, 68–69
  skiing in, 69–70
Sunnyside, 277

Tallman Mountain State Park, 11
Tappan, 13–14

Tarrytown, 274–277
Teatown Lake Reservation, 265
Terwilliger House, 81–82
theater festivals, 152
theaters
  in Columbia County, 200–201
  in Dutchess County, 233
tours
  airplane, 153–154, 195
  of Albany, 177
  bicycle, 227–228
  of Catskill, 149–150
  of Cold Spring, 249–250
  in Columbia County, 191–192,
    195
  in Dutchess County, 227–228,
    228
  in Greene County, 153–154
  of Hudson, 191–192
  of Nyack, 8–9
  in Orange County, 29, 38
  of Poughkeepsie, 217–218
  in Putnam County, 253–254
  in Rockland County, 13–14
  of Tappan, 13–14
  in Ulster County, 96, 97, 99
  of Woodstock, 96, 97
trains, in Delaware County,
  126–127
Trevor Teaching Zoo, 217
Trolley Museum, 89
tubing, 106–107
Tulip Festival, 176
Tuthilltown Grist Mill, 82
Tuxedo, 33–34

Ulster County, 77–121
  accommodations in, 115–121
  antiques in, 97–98
  architectural sites in, 81–82,
    84–86, 90–93
  arts and crafts shops in, 96–97
  boat cruises in, 99
  farms in, 82–83
  farm stands in, 100–101
  festivals in, 84, 87, 93–94
  fishing in, 101–102
  hiking in, 102–103
  historical parks in, 87–88

historical sites in, 81, 84–86,
  86–87, 88–93
mills in, 82, 83–84
museums in, 83, 89
nature parks in, 80–81, 81–82
rappeling, 103
restaurants in, 109–115
scenic views in, 103–104
skiing in, 104–106
tours in, 96, 97, 99
tubing in, 106–107
vineyards in, 107–108
United States Military Academy,
  36–38

Vail's Gate, 34–36
Val-Kill, 214–215
Van Cortlandt Manor, 265
Vanderbilt Estate, 215
James Vanderpoel House, 194
Van Wyck Homestead Museum,
  212
Vassar College, 218
vineyards
  in Dutchess County, 233–234
  in Orange County, 42–43
  in Rockland County, 7
  in Ulster County, 107–108
  in Westchester County, 269

Walton, 131
Wappingers Falls, 223–224
Ward Pound Ridge Reservation,
  264
Warner House, 36
Washington's Headquarters, 31–32
Washington's Headquarters Museum, 269
Wavecrest, 215–216
Webatuck Craft Village, 224
Weed Walks, 97
Westchester County, 261–293
  accommodations in, 292–293
  amusement park in, 271
  antiques in, 278–279
  architectural sites in, 265–267
  arts and crafts shops in, 267
  bicycling in, 279–280
  farms in, 273–274, 279

Westchester County (*continued*)
  festivals in, 270
  gardens in, 268–269, 270–271
  hiking in, 280
  historical sites in, 265–268, 273, 275–277
  museums in, 264, 267–269, 269, 270, 271–273, 274–275, 278, 280
  nature centers in, 272–273
  nature parks in, 264–265
  nature preserves in, 264–265
  outdoor recreation in, 279–280
  recreational parks in, 280
  restaurants in, 281–292
  shopping in, 281
  skiing in, 280
  vineyard in, 269

West Kortright Centre, 132
West Point, 36–38
Widmark Honey Farm, 82–83
wildlife preserves
  in Putnam County, 253
wineries, *see* vineyards
Wingdale, 224
Woodstock, 95–97
  tours of, 96, 97
Wurtsboro, 60
Wurtsboro Airport, 60–61

Yonkers, 278
Young-Morse Historic Site, 218–219

Zoom Flume, 151
zoos, 4
  in Dutchess County, 217